The Story of Victory Noll

Victory Noll, Huntington, Indiana — Motherhouse of Our Lady of Victory Missionary Sisters. *This air view was taken in the late fifties, before the Archbishop Noll Memorial Chapel and Holy Family Building were erected.*

The Story of

VICTORY
NOLL

by Sister Elizabeth Ann Clifford, O.L.V.M.

©1981 by Our Lady of Victory Missionary Sisters, Huntington, Indiana

Our Lady of Victory Missionary Sisters
Victory Noll, P.O. Box 109
Huntington, Indiana 46750

PRINTED IN THE UNITED STATES OF AMERICA

Printed by Keefer Printing Company, Inc.
Fort Wayne, Indiana U.S.A.

TO

Our Lady of Victory

Our Patroness and Our Mother

CONTENTS

ILLUSTRATIONS — in the first 8-page photo section

John Joseph Sigstein in 1898
Father Sigstein in 1932 and Father George Pierson
William Frey and Father Michael F. D. Collins
The Mission on Dearborn Street, Chicago, in 1907
Catechists Benes and Doyle with Will Frey and children at Shoemaker,
    out-mission from Watrous, N.M., 1923
Archbishop Daeger of Santa Fe with Will Frey in 1922
The Catechists' convent at Ocate, N.M., in 1923
Getting stuck in an arroyo in New Mexico, 1924
Father Sigstein and Father Blaufuss, June 1925
Peter O'Donnell and his wife Julia, of Long Beach, California
Dedication Day at Victory Noll, July 5, 1925
Catechists Helen Srill and Edna Like with some of the families at
    Chaperito, New Mexico, in 1925
Victory Mount, Las Vegas, New Mexico
Catechists Sullivan and Leven serving families at the soup kitchen in
    Las Vegas, N.M.
Catechists Vigil and Richardson with graduates of CCD Institute, San
    Ysidro, N.M., in 1933
Sister Adelle Heintz with children at Limonera Camp

ILLUSTRATIONS — in the second 8-page photo section

Catechist Catherine Olberding, first Superior General
First General Council elected in 1938
Bishop Noll at his desk at Victory Noll in 1944
Mother Cecilia Schmitt, Superior General, 1950-1962
Sister Florentine Lohr, President, 1962-1971
Sister Gertrude Sullivan, President, 1971-1977
Sister Jeanette Halbach, President, 1977 —
General Assembly in 1971
Postulants and novices in 1953
Sister Mary Helen Rogers and friends
Sister Carmen Montoya and sewing class in East Los Angeles
Sister John Francis Radler, administrator of Clinic in Tucson, AZ
Sister Mary Camillus Spisak, R.N., 1961
Sisters Carolyn Ortega and Mary Edna Butler in Oruro, Bolivia
Sister Margaret Ann Harrison distributes Holy Communion
Sister Otilia Mendoza in San Antonio, Texas
Chapel overview of General Assembly in 1971
Father Sigstein shortly before his death in 1963

FOREWORD

To contribute a Foreword to a book is always a privilege, but it is especially so when the book is a history of one's own Congregation. In 1973 the General Council asked Sister Elizabeth Ann Clifford to undertake the work of writing a documented history of our Congregation. We believed that the time was right for our history to be put down in book form. We were celebrating fifty years as a religious community; our beloved Founder had recently died; our first Sisters had also gone to heaven, but many of our pioneer Sisters were still living. We knew it was important to preserve the memories they had of the actual happenings of our beginning. We wanted the history to be authentic, to recount as accurately as possible the events and the spirit of our Congregation.

Sister Elizabeth Ann was the perfect person to write the history. She had worked closely with Father Sigstein in editing *The Missionary Catechist* and in other areas of public relations. She knew Father well not only as our Founder, but also as priest and person — a man of vision, of prayer, of "holy boldness." She knew his weaknesses and his strengths. She knew our pioneer Sisters and she herself experienced mission life in Utah, California, Texas, and Missouri. But even more important, Sister Elizabeth Ann is a woman of integrity and would write a truthful history, not glossing over the sorrows, the foibles, the mistakes we have made; but also not fearing to write honestly of our joys and successes. Sister Elizabeth Ann has done her work well. On behalf of the Victory Noll Sisters I want to say thank you!

I am pleased and proud and excited to say *this is our history, our heritage.* It is a history of strong, spirited women, daring to be different from what was expected of women religious, convinced that what they were doing was right and was needed, firm in their dedication to proclaim the Good News even in the most difficult or unlikely circumstances, and happy in their life with the poor. Our first Sisters were pioneers not only in their ministry, but also in the lifestyle that ministry necessitated. They were willing to be criticized and even ostracized for being different. But they persevered and were blessed.

This is our heritage, a heritage that compels us to risk the challenge of the unknown future, to continue to be pioneers. Where this call will lead us we do not know — perhaps to blaze new trails for women and religious life. Ours is a heritage of faith, shared vision, and dedication, all for the sake of the Kingdom. In this spirit we continue the struggle.

Sister Jeanette Halbach, O.L.V.M.

President, Victory Noll Sisters

May 24, 1980
Feast of Our Lady of Victory

PREFACE

In the past decade a number of religious have published histories of their institutes. Vatican II asked us to return to the Gospel, the source of all Christian life, and to the original spirit of our founders, being ever mindful of the changed conditions of our times. By researching their roots religious institutes make real this admonition of the Council given in Article 2 of the *Decree on the Appropriate Renewal of Religious Life.*

I have talked to Sisters who were given the task of writing the chronicles of their communities. For some of them their assignment was made more difficult because important documents had not been kept; others, because many records were in a language other than English. I was more fortunate. First of all, ours is an American Congregation and is not so old as many other institutes, having been founded in 1922.

Moreover, our Founder, the Rev. John J. Sigstein, had a sense of history. He kept *everything.* He insisted on our making copies of letters, conferences, even interviews he had when he thought these were significant. All this typing, making carbons, was sometimes irksome to the Sisters who worked with Father Sigstein. To make it more annoying he was constantly revising rules, Constitutions, prayers, conferences.

Today we are grateful for these records, even the minutiae. Our Founder's revisions show how he updated as conditions changed. All this material makes the Victory Noll Archives invaluable and a primary source for the historian. Besides, it was my privilege to have worked closely with Father Sigstein during the early days of our Congregation. I lived much of the history I have written.

Rather than list names of everyone who has been helpful, let me just say I am deeply grateful to my Sisters for the encouragement and support they have given me in writing our history. I hope that the book will help all of us to appreciate our heritage and deepen our commitment to Jesus through Mary.

INTRODUCTION

"Meet modern needs with modern means."

This was the ideal with which the Rev. John Sigstein, Founder of the Society of Missionary Catechists of Our Blessed Lady of Victory, (now known as Our Lady of Victory Missionary Sisters) challenged his Catechists.

Nearly every Congregation of men or women came into being to meet a particular need in the Church. Founders were in tune with the "signs of the times." Father Sigstein was no exception. And though the Sisters might take different approaches today to meet modern needs, the ideal remains.

The Victory Noll apostolate can still be described as three-fold: religious education, social service and health care — all on a non-institutional basis. Religious education, the catechetical apostolate, was from the beginning always primary. The very title "Catechist" rather than Sister, a title used during the first twenty-five years of the community's existence, indicated this. Caring for the material needs of the poor naturally followed.

"They can't be real Sisters," people would say of the Catechists. "Their hair shows, they don't have a rosary hanging from their belts, they use their family name, they go around visiting homes when other Sisters are in school. They even drive cars!"

These were some of the criticisms that the Sisters met with in the early days of their existence. Though some parents tried to dissuade their daughters from joining a community that departed so much from tradition (or at least from their idea of what Sisters were like), there were others who encouraged their daughters and looked upon the Catechists as filling an actual need in the Church.

Criticisms and objections that the Sisters met with in the 1930s and the following two decades — that they could not be real religious because of certain externals that were innovative — sound quaint and trivial now; but remember, this was still long before Vatican II.[1] Until very recently, most people thought of women religious as teachers in parochial schools or nurses in Catholic hospitals.

In the early sixties when the American edition of Cardinal Suenens' *The Nun in the World* appeared, this stereotyped image of a Sister began to change.[2] From the time they were founded in 1922, the Victory Noll Sisters had been, in a sense, "nuns in the world"; but for many persons they were a novelty, if not almost a scandal. How often they had to explain patiently that they were professed Sisters, not postulants. "But you *look* like postulants!"

In the course of time various attempts were made to change the image of the Catechists and bring it into line with the more conventional picture of women religious. Father Sigstein resisted these attempts and refused to listen when some thought the Catechists should lengthen their uniform (for years it was never referred to as a "habit") and cover their hair completely with the traditional head piece.

The things that involved externals were only minor matters. The Founder's biggest concern was that while the Society was still only a diocesan community, the members might be pressured into teaching in parochial schools, into conducting institutions.[3] One bishop almost insisted on this. Rather than capitulate to him, Father Sigstein was ready to withdraw the Catechists from the diocese. Their work was in religious education and in caring for the "souls and bodies of the poor wherever found."[4]

Though this is a history of the Congregation of Our Lady of Victory Missionary Sisters and not a biography of its Founder, the Rev. John Joseph Sigstein of Chicago, the priest was so intimately bound up with the community during its first decades that it is necessary to understand the man before it is possible to understand his life work.

However, to appreciate the values and goals of Father Sigstein and the Congregation he founded, everything must be judged in terms other than that of the contemporary Church and society, a time vastly different from the religious culture of the twenties and the three decades that followed.

Father Sigstein's vision, great as it was, could not alone have brought the Congregation to full fruition in its early years. More than this was necessary.

It was the late Bishop of Fort Wayne, the Most Rev. John Francis Noll, who helped Father Sigstein achieve the end for which he founded the Society of Missionary Catechists.[5] The Founder acknowledged this when he wrote, on the tenth anniversary of the episcopal consecration of Bishop Noll: "Victory Noll stands a priceless memorial of the charity of a bishop who looked beyond the confines of his own diocese, and like the Divine Shepherd, saw and loved those other sheep besides his own who were to be brought into the sheepfold."[6]

This was the ideal held up to bishops by the Fathers of the Second Vatican Council. "As a member of the episcopal college and a legitimate successor of the Apostles, each bishop is obliged by Christ's decree and command to be solicitous for the whole Church. This solicitude, though it is not exercised by an act of jurisdiction, contributes immensely to the welfare of the universal Church."[7]

Both John Joseph Sigstein and John Francis Noll shared responsibility in the founding and growth of the Victory Noll Sisters, each in his own way. Each had a decisive role in the history of Our Lady of Victory Missionary Sisters.

Notes to Introduction

1. The Twenty-First Ecumenical Council of the Church, Vatican II, opened October 11, 1962, and closed December 8, 1964. The sixteen texts promulgated during this time had far-reaching effects on the life of the Church, setting in motion reforms in liturgy, religious life, priestly formation, and in other areas that touched intimately the life of every Catholic.

2. Leon Joseph Cardinal Suenens, Archbishop of Malines-Brussels, *The Nun in the World: New Dimensions in the Modern Apostolate,* (Westminster, Md.: The Newman Press, 1962)

3. Before pontifical approval, a religious congregation has first the status of a diocesan institute with closer ties to the local bishop.

4. Original Constitution, Society of Missionary Catechists of Our Blessed Lady of Victory, 1922.

5. John Francis Noll, fifth Bishop of Fort Wayne, was born January 25, 1875. He was ordained a priest June 4, 1898, and consecrated bishop June 30, 1925. Pope Pius XII made him an assistant to the papal throne March 14, 1941, and archbishop *ad personam* September 2, 1953. Archbishop Noll died July 31, 1956; he is buried in the cemetery at Victory Noll. At the time of his appointment as bishop, the Diocese of Fort Wayne comprised the northern half of Indiana. Subsequently the Dioceses of Lafayette (1944) and Gary (1957) were created. In recognition of the importance of South Bend, the diocese was designated as Fort Wayne-South Bend.

6. *The Missionary Catechist,* Huntington, Indiana, June 1935, p. 11.

7. Vatican Council II, Dogmatic Constitution on the Church *Lumen Gentium,* tr. in W.M. Abbott (ed.), *The Documents of Vatican II* (New York, 1966) p. 45.

1

Founder

JOHN SIGSTEIN'S WHOLE LIFE was, in a sense, a paradox. Constantly in ill health, he lived to his eighty-eighth year. "Look at me," he would say; "nearly all my close friends are dead and I am still here. God's ways are surely not our ways."

He insisted on a deep spiritual life for the Catechists, not only during their period of preparation for mission work, but throughout their lives. He referred to himself as the Spiritual Director of the Society and wanted the Sisters to consult him and follow his direction in all matters. And yet he placed them in out-of-the-way missions where Mass could be offered only once or twice a month at most — places where other Sisters would not go because they would be deprived of the sacraments over a long period of time.

Though Father Sigstein insisted on, even demanded absolute obedience to superiors — which, ultimately, always meant himself — he encouraged initiative and even saw to it that the Catechists conduct what we would today call para-liturgies in those mission places that were seldom visited by a priest. The Sisters read Scripture and actually "preached" the Word of God to these spiritually starved people gathered around a pot-bellied stove in their poor little mission chapels in New Mexico.

Throughout his long life John Sigstein had the reputation for almost never being on time for anything, for putting off till tomorrow what should be done today. At the same time he demanded punctuality from the Sisters; he insisted on their keeping to a strict schedule. He was constantly changing and adjusting schedules; his own (which he never kept) and those he made for the Catechists. He often seemed to act impulsively, thinking nothing of sending Catechists to

1

New Mexico or California on very, very short notice. On the other hand, he deliberated endlessly before attacking a problem that needed immediate attention.

Father Sigstein was deeply devoted to his own mother and to his friends, but he asked the Sisters to practice absolute detachment from family and friends. John made friends easily, friends who, with few exceptions, were devoted to him throughout his long life. No matter how exasperated they might be because of his procrastination in answering letters and keeping appointments, they were always ready to excuse him. This magnetism, this special charism, was a part of him to the very end of his life.

The priest was always planning some type of organization. Some of these came to fruition and then were taken over by others, causing pain to him who had given so much to establish them. Other plans never went beyond the initial stage, though Father spent much time and effort in trying to make the project a reality.

Even in his old age, shortly before he returned to Victory Noll in 1960, John Sigstein collected funds and was given tentative encouragement from ecclestical authorities to organize a group of women religious who would look after poor people in their homes. This would not be a duplication of the work of the Dominican Sisters of the Sick Poor. The aged whom Father had in mind were not incapacitated but rather were elderly persons who wanted to stay in their own little homes as long as possible but who needed to be visited and to be helped with transportation problems, shopping, visits to doctor, dentist, etc. When Father learned that an established congregation of religious had definite plans to do this work, he turned over to them the funds he had collected.

Of all the works that John Sigstein planned or partly carried out, only his beloved "Society" was to continue. And then it seemed that even this was taken away from him. In a sense it was, for after the first canonical elections in 1938, Father Sigstein left Victory Noll, and the government of the Congregation was now out of his hands. But never, never did Father view this as an injustice. He could have remained as Spiritual Director of the Society, but this was not in his nature to do. He had to be all, to govern the Congregation as he had been doing since its foundation, or he had to remove himself from it. He chose the latter, for he knew he could not function otherwise.

John Joseph Sigstein, Founder of Our Lady of Victory Missionary Sisters, was born in Chicago, Illinois, October 29, 1875, the only son of John and Mary Massoth Sigstein. He had three sisters, two of whom died in infancy. The third, the youngest of the family, married, but died when she was twenty-five years old.

Mary Massoth was from Alsace-Lorraine and John used to say that in many ways he was like her, combining characteristics both French and German. At any rate, it seemed that his mother was a greater influence in his life than his father who died in 1906.

John was deeply devoted to his mother and appreciated the sacrifices she made so that he could study for the priesthood. Mrs. Sigstein cooked for the priests at St. Vincent's, their parish church, and also did some nursing in homes. After his ordination John cared for his mother, taking her with him when he left Chicago. Mary Sigstein died at Victory Noll, Huntington, Indiana, the Motherhouse of Our Lady of Victory Missionary Sisters, January 9, 1931.

Throughout his life John revered the Vincentian priests who staffed both his parish church and St. Vincent's College, forerunner of DePaul University of Chicago. His association with the sons of St. Vincent de Paul might account for his great love for the saint, though it would be easy to guess that this devotion was a natural to John who, from the time of his boyhood, had such great compassion for the poor and down-trodden. Later, in founding the Society of Missionary Catechists, John found a counterpart, an ally, as it were, in the canny seventeenth century priest who circumvented Church authorities and departed from the only acceptable (at that time) image of women religious. This was something Francis de Sales and others had not succeeded in doing.[1]

John Sigstein's early education was in his home parish. After leaving high school he attended St. Vincent's College but before taking his degree, left school to work as a bookkeeper for a drug company. During this time his health broke and he went out to Manitou Springs, Colorado, where he spent a year. This was in 1898. An old picture shows him selling mineral water from a horse-drawn vehicle.

It was the late Father William J. Howlett, then parish priest at Colorado City, who explained that John "would not be idle so he got a burro and a cart and worked up a good route of customers for mineral water. He would go to the springs and fill his bottles with soda or iron water and carry it to his customers of which I was glad to be one. In this way he lightened expenses for himself and his mother who was with him. That winter was a cold one but not even a snowstorm made John miss any of his appointments with his patrons."[2]

John's friendship with William Howlett continued through the years. At that time the priest was working on his biography of Joseph Machebeuf, first Bishop of Denver. Though the book was published only privately (in 1908), it proved a valuable source for Willa Cather when she wrote *Death Comes for the Archbishop*. Paul Horgan also acknowledged his indebtedness to Howlett's book in his monumental *Lamy of Sante Fe*.[3].

When John Sigstein returned to Chicago he resumed his college studies and, with his friend, George Pierson, became very active in the Society of St. Vincent de Paul.

Every morning John and George served the early Mass celebrated by the pastor and director of the college, Father Bernard Gock. George left home to begin studies for the priesthood, but during summer vacation the two friends continued to serve Mass together. It was during the summer months that they no-

3

ticed a young man, about twenty years old, who not only came to Mass but received Holy Communion every morning. This was something unusual in those pre-Piux X days. John and George had been going to Communion three or four times a week until Father Gock told them they could receive every day.

Something about this newcomer attracted the two servers. They introduced themselves to him and learned that he was Martin Francis Dominic Collins from Duquesne, Illinois. (His new friends always called him Francis.) He had come into the city and was working in a coffin factory.

"Do you have any time off?" John asked.

"Well," Francis answered rather hesitantly, "I have Sundays."

"Would you like to join the St. Vincent de Paul Society? We have a fine branch here and I think you'd like it very much."

Francis waited a bit; then he said, "Well, I'll tell you. I *used* to have Sundays to myself and I'd go around to visit different churches. One Sunday I went down to St. Peter's and all along Clark Street, Dearborn, and Van Buren I saw a lot of men sitting outside along the curb. Some of them were drunk and some half-drunk. Others were sober. They all looked like they were Irishmen.

"I found out that all were Catholics but were not practicing their faith. These Irishmen work on the track elevation, elevating the tracks coming into the city. They live in box cars outfitted with bunks, cafeteria and all. I learned that they work for three or four weeks and then the railroad pays them. They come in and go to the saloons and spend nearly all their money on drink. They stay in cheap lodging houses where they pay ten cents a night for a bed on Saturday and Sunday nights. When they get drunk, they are often robbed. You know how that goes.

"Don't get the idea that these fellows are fooling around with women," he hurried to add. "The lodging houses are cleaner that way than good hotels. No women are allowed to stay there. These men are not bad; they just have a weakness for drink. They haven't anything else to do on weekends. I've been going to the lodging houses on weekends and I always find some of the poor men sick and almost dead. I get them to the county hospital, get a priest for them and they go to confession. I got a lot — some lots — at Calvary Cemetery for them so they can be buried decently."

"Oh," John said, "that's a wonderful work. Come up and tell the St. Vincent de Paul men about it."

Whenever John Sigstein recounted the story, he would add, "It was a wonderful talk, a real tear-jerker. The Irish have that gift and Francis could put it across. But he did it from his heart because it was natural for him."

George and John joined Francis in trying to rehabilitate these poor men. Shortly afterward the three of them attended a meeting of the whole St. Vincent de Paul Council of the city. Francis Collins gave an eloquent talk which so deeply moved the men that they appointed the three zealous friends to what

4

they called the Lodging House Committee. They suggested renting a place to house the poor men or at least bring them there for wholesome entertainment and an opportunity to receive the sacrament of penance.

The project was to be supported by the St. Vincent de Paul Society. However, there was no source of income except the poor boxes in the church and their own contributions. This was too sporadic, so John Sigstein went to Charles Mair, son-in-law of Mr. McLaughlin of the Manor House Coffee Company and told him the story. The upshot of the visit was that Mr. Mair financed the project which became known as Our Blessed Lady of Victory Lodging House Mission.[4]

In the beginning the three "apostles" used to visit the lodging houses on weekends and take the men to St. Peter's for confession — those who wanted to receive the sacrament. On Sunday they went with them to Mass and Holy Communion.

This arrangement did not prove satisfactory, however. The men were scattered about for lodging and it was hard to keep track of them. Francis knew of a woman who had rented an empty store where she had catechetical instructions for a small group of little Syrian children. When Francis told her about the work they were trying to do for the men, she suggested that they use the store and she would find another place for her apostolate.

The location was ideal — on Dearborn Street, not far from either St. Peter's or St. Mary's. The former was the old church so well known to travelers (it was close to the Dearborn Station) and referred to as "Old St. Peter's." It was only long afterward (1953) that the church was razed and the new one built in the heart of the Loop.

John and Francis fitted out the store to serve their needs. They had a reading room, a small room where the men could talk privately to a priest, an area for a kitchen and dining room, and a large room that served for entertainments.

Throughout his life John Sigstein seemed to have a special predilection for "home talent shows." In his parish work as a priest he organized dramatic clubs for young people. Perhaps this was the era of do-it-yourself-shows, for it was a less sophisticated time than our own with its TV, stereo, and passive entertainment. In later years Father Sigstein expected the Catechists to whip up a "show" sometimes on very short notice to celebrate a special occasion, feast day, homecoming of someone in the community, anniversary, etc.

The Wednesday night "variety shows" at the Mission were the drawing card for the men. For this, John enlisted some of the young women from his parish. Priests — usually Jesuits, Franciscans, Carmelites, or Paulists — were present. After the entertainment one of the Fathers would address the captive audience and then invite the men to go to confession. Many availed themselves of the opportunity.

On Sunday morning John and Francis, and George Pierson when he was

5

home from the seminary, would march with the men to Old St. Mary's Church where they would receive Holy Communion together. On certain occasions they would be joined by other St. Vincent de Paul men (Father always mentioned particularly policemen and firemen) who did not hesitate to identify themselves with the poor men and march down the street to Mass with them. Eventually the number of men in the procession reached three hundred. Then the women — perhaps the ones who had no talent for performing — served breakfast to the men at the Mission.

The first entertainment almost ended in disaster. Francis had the men make benches. Someone donated a piano, but no one thought of trying it before the obliging young women arrived on the scene. Alas, more than one bench collapsed under the weight of the unsuspecting audience, and the piano turned out to be one that had seen better days. Some of the keys went down but refused to come up. Others would not sound at all, much to the embarrassment of the talented musicians.

The late Paulist priest James M. Gillis, once referred to this work in a syndicated column he wrote for NC News Service called *Sursum Corda,* with the subtitle, "What's Right With the World." He called it a "club for hoboes to whom we would preach, sneaking in a sermon in the midst of a vaudeville show. The sermon was a preliminary to the pledge and to confession. It was always the same story — booze."[5]

Eventually the men who took the pledge and joined the Temperance Society made their home at the Mission. It was Charles Mair who made it possible to expand the operation and provide a larger building in which to house the men. It was in the same district, on Dearborn Street. This meant much more work for John and Francis, especially for Francis during the school year, for in 1902 John entered Kenrick Seminary in St. Louis to study for the priesthood.

It was at this time that they were joined by another apostolic layman, William Frey. Unlike the other three, Will never became a priest, but he played an important part in the early days of the Society of Missionary Catechists. Will was a native Chicagoan, a very simple man with little formal education, but with a dry sense of humor. Before he joined the Mission team he lived in a dreary tenement on the West Side of Chicago.

These four men — John Sigstein, George Pierson, Martin Francis Collins, and Will Frey — who worked together and became fast friends, had in common a deep compassion and love for the poor and downtrodden. Otherwise they could hardly have been more unlike except for their faith and piety and their great devotion to the Mother of God.

Though George Pierson was several years older than John Sigstein, the two were great friends, almost inseparable. George was ordained several years before John although both were late vocations. Father Pierson died in the flu epidemic of 1919. Father Sigstein loved him dearly and lamented his early death. He kept a large framed picture of his friend on the wall of his dining room in his apartment at Victory Noll and kept in touch with the Pierson family all his life.

John used to refer to Martin Francis Collins as an extraordinary character, an unforgettable character. His method of dealing with the men at the Mission was completely different from John's. In his zeal Francis often became impatient when the men showed a reluctance to quit drinking. He sometimes even "collared" them, Father would say. On the other hand, he himself used a sentimental approach, appealing to the memory of a man's "poor old mother in Ireland."

Evidently Francis was somewhat of a male chauvinist. "He had no way with women," Father Sigstein would say, "but merely tolerated them." Though he was grateful for their contribution — providing the entertainment and preparing the Communion breakfasts that involved more and more work as the months passed — he often "put his foot in his mouth" and it was up to John to smooth the waters and see to it that the offended ones were mollified.

John often referred to himself as a trouble shooter. He had to patch up the difficulties not just with the women, but with the men. He thought, and probably rightly, that Francis was sometimes too hard on them. He expected too much of them. John would tell him, "Don't do that. These poor men are not bad; don't be so hard on them."

Sometimes Francis would call them down so severely that they would walk out. Then John would go after them and say, "Come back here. Come back, Mike." He would put his arm around the fellow and say, "Collins is excited now. Please don't pay any attention. He'll be all right. He'll probably give you ten dollars the next time he sees you."

The role of trouble shooter or reconciler, Father Sigstein always added when recounting these events, was good training for him, good training in dealing with all kinds of people.

Francis, for all his rough ways, loved these poor men and gave himself completely to them. The building that became home to the men who had taken the pledge, was a large four-story place. Collins lived there and took care of it. John described him as being able to do housework, cook a meal, do anything. "He was a great one. He was wonderful. I never saw anybody like him."

Charles Mair paid the monthly rent on the building and the St. Vincent de Paul men helped with its upkeep. Though the Communion breakfasts got larger and larger, the money for them was always provided by generous people who saw what a great work was being done. One friend, a police sergeant named Hogan, would stop in on Saturday and give Francis Collins ten or twenty dollars and say, "Go and buy a fish." In those days one could buy a whole slab of bacon for a few dollars.

But often after Hogan was gone, some poor fellow would come along with a hard luck story and say, "Oh, Mr. Collins, I'll be put out on my face if I don't pay my rent."

"How much is it?" Collins would ask. And he would give the money to the man, forgetting all about the breakfast. Before morning, however, he would have the money. One of the men would sometimes say, "Mr. Collins, I've got a job now. I got paid. I'm going to give you some money." It would be just enough to pay for the breakfast supplies.

In every need Francis Collins appealed to Our Blessed Mother with the most implicit trust that she would hear him. And she did. Many were the stories Father Sigstein would tell, stories that sound almost miraculous but were every day occurrences at the Mission. "Never, never have I known anyone who loved Our Blessed Mother so dearly," Father Sigstein would say. He claimed that it was to him that he himself owed his deep love for Mary. Francis never called his friend John, but used his middle name Joseph because it was St. Joseph who looked after Our Blessed Mother with such loving care. With Francis, St. Joseph naturally came first after Mary.

The two friends referred to the Mother of God as Our Blessed Mother, Our Sweet Mother, seldom if ever using names like Our Lady, Mary, etc. And she was to them a Mother in every sense of the word. It was a love, a heritage that Father Sigstein would pass on to the members of his Society. His whole life was marked by his great devotion to Our Blessed Mother.

The story of Our Lady of Victory Mission would not be complete without mentioning another aspect of it, a most important aspect. And that is the weekly Sunday School conducted for the children of the neighborhood. The Chicago diocesan paper, *The New World,*[6] dated April 11, 1908, carried a most interesting, a touching, even brilliant account of this work. It might be suspected that the writer, Charlotte Lodge, could have been one of the corps of men and women who gave themselves to this apostolate. If she did not actually teach religion to the children or perhaps help march them in a body to St. Mary's Church for Mass, she certainly was a very astute reporter.

Any CCD instructor who reads the account today will easily identify with these dedicated men and women of over seventy years ago. Children have not changed so much in all that time. These were children of the poor, children whose parents were, for the most part, immigrants. The reporter describes the bedlam, almost a stampede when they arrive and surround their teachers. But there is discipline, and the Mission Sunday School comes to order at ten-thirty, after the return from Mass. Sometimes it takes more than one stroke of the bell, "for they are a wild lot, and frequently while rushing to their proper places make much noise, and do a great deal of subdued talking. At such times the bell stroke sounds again, louder than before, and these untamed youngsters read the sharp, sudden warning of the bell and respond . . . At the Mission one does not meet a collection of bread and butter, submissive, clean-faced angels, but a mass of rumple-haired, bright-eyed, fiercely alert small humanity."

The reporter futher observes that "dealing with the jetsam of child humanity from the ghetto requires much more resource and patience than is usually

8

necessary in the handling of the conventional Sunday School class." The class hour is followed by what the children refer to as their "vocal lesson" a singing session for the older ones. This is not obligatory but "it is evidently one of the happiest times, for there is never a vacant chair."

Mr. Collins is extolled as the leader who "hides his worries behind his kindly and ever-ready smile."

Among his worries was the added expense that this phase of the work of Our Lady of Victory Mission entailed. There was constant need for used clothing and for funds to provide prizes (medals, statuettes, pictures) for the children, and for their recreational outings.

A means of publicity was the *Journal of Our Lady of Victory Mission*. According to the masthead it was "published monthly at Our Lady of Victory Mission, 406 Dearborn Street, Chicago, Illinois." One volume of the magazine is extant, the first volume, published in 1907. Whether this was also the last volume is not clear, but it might well have been.

Most of the articles were true life stories of the men who came to the Mission to find shelter and entertainment but whose lives were changed.

The cover was always the same: a drawing of Our Lady of Victory flanked by two knights, one carrying a banner with the words *Omnia pro Jesu et Maria,* "All for Jesus and Mary." Later Father Sigstein changed this motto to "All for Jesus *through* Mary," and it became the motto of the Society of Missionary Catechists. On the cover also were the words which described the special work of the Mission: Total Abstinence, Frequent Communion, Temperance.

It would be tempting to recount more and more stories of Our Blessed Lady of Victory Lodging House Mission days, but we will confine ourselves to descriptions of the St. Patrick's Day celebration and the May Crowning ceremony. Both of these, written in John Sigstein's own hand, are typical of him and typical of the minute details he insisted upon in ceremonies and celebrations in which later the Catechists would take part.

In the May procession, for example, the men walking on the left side were to hold their candles in their left hand; the men on the right side, with their right hand. This would sound very familiar to the Catechists during Father's time when they walked in procession every twenty-fifth of the month praying the rosary and singing the Litany of Loretto. These devotions were begun in 1925 to honor the Incarnation of Our Lord and the Annunciation of Our Blessed Mother, for an increase of vocations, a monthly devotion that continues to be held at Victory Noll today.

There were special celebrations at the Dearborn Street Mission for special days: Christmas, Easter, the great feasts of Mary, St. Joseph's feast, and St. Patrick's. Nothing was left to chance. John Sigstein spelled out every direction. For example, for St. Patrick's Day the first thing was to "get out dodgers printed in green ink. Have framed picture of St. Patrick on easel on platform, draped with the flag of Ireland and surrounded with shamrocks. Have Mission decorated with green flags and arrange program: Irish airs, Irish songs, jigs, instrumental music. Have 'St. Patrick's Day' sung, also 'Kathleen Mavourneen,' and the 'Wearing of the Green.' Have lecture on St. Patrick by priest. Distribute shamrocks to those who take the pledge and join the club. After conclusion of program, enrollment in scapular, pledge, and confession."

The regular monthly Communion Sundays were planned down to the most minute detail: "Appoint coffee waiter, potato waiter, ham (or bacon) and eggs, and cake waiter, each one to attend to his own duty only . . . March back from church in the same order we went. Arrived at Mission, say to each man as he comes in, 'God bless you,' from the heart, and give each one a good hearty shake of the hand." Directives for serving are given, then: "Say grace before and thanksgiving after breakfast. Joke with the men and see that each one has plenty to eat. Sit down with the waiters after all the others are finished. Dishes to be then taken up, but washed next day."[7]

When John left for St. Louis to begin his studies for the priesthood at Kenrick Seminary, Francis carried on at the Mission with Will Frey to help him. During the summer vacations John would take over. Their thoughtful benefactor, Mr. Mair, sent Francis away for a rest, usually to Colorado. One year he sent him to Old Mexico.

The summer "vacations" almost wore out the always frail John Sigstein. Besides the daily work with the men, he spent a lot of time fixing up the place. Francis never noticed the repair jobs, the need for a new coat of paint; or if he were aware of the necessary repairs, he never found time to take care of them.

At one time Francis Collins had begun studies for the priesthood, but had to discontinue them because of his poverty. After Father Sigstein's ordination in 1909 Francis resumed his studies. It is known that it was his friend John who helped him financially though he never admitted it. It was also Father Sigstein who got him into Kenrick.

Somewhere along the way Francis' impetuosity and his zeal for helping others created an incident that caused him to be asked to leave the seminary. Later, when the whole story was revealed, it became clear that it was a misunderstanding on the part of someone in authority, but naturally it hurt Francis deeply and caused him much suffering. He went back to his work of helping others, this time Navy men in the Brooklyn shipyards, for this was in the days of the First World War. Years later he was adopted, at the intercession of John Sigstein, by Bishop Christopher Byrne of Galveston.[8] After ordination he became pastor of Our Lady of Victory Church, Sour Lake, Texas, and sent Marie Bodin to Chicago to become a Missionary Catechist. Marie was the third candidate for Father Sigstein's band.

Martin Francis Collins died suddenly June 17, 1936, all alone in a hotel room in Houston. He was fifty-nine, having been a priest sixteen years. According to his request, his body was sent to Chicago for burial. John went from Huntington to Chicago for the funeral, but his grief was so great that he could not bring himself to take part in the services. Robert McCann, who took Father to Chicago, reported that they drove round and round the church before John even went in.

But what happened to Our Lady of Victory Lodging House Mission and the work John and Francis had built up so carefully and with so much personal sacrifice? Some months after his ordination (he was curate at the time at St. Pius' Church in Chicago) Father Sigstein went to Archbishop Quigley and asked if he might give his life to the Lodging House Mission work. The Archbishop said he might, but he would make him assistant at St. Patrick's (in the same district) and he could work from there.

John knew that his first loyalty would be to the parish. Moreover, he knew that the pastor was not in sympathy with the work and he was afraid the arrangement would not be satisfactory. He talked it over with his spiritual director, the famous Jesuit, Father Charles Coppens, educator and author of numerous works in philosophy and theology. (It was Father Coppens who had given him permission to talk to the Archbishop. All his life John consulted a spiritual director.)[9]

Father Coppens was well aware of how much work was involved and told John not to accept under these circumstances. Shortly afterward the pastor of Old St. Mary's went to the Archbishop and claimed the Mission because it was in his parish. Quigley acceded to the request.

John Sigstein and Francis Collins saw the Mission not as a parish work, but as a work that belonged to the Society of St. Vincent de Paul. Otherwise it would simply be something "added on" to other parish ministries. It was too much to expect a pastor or his assistants to continue the Mission work as it had been established.

Though the decision of Archbishop Quigley almost broke the hearts of the two "Founders," they withdrew. Their forebodings of what would happen proved correct. After a year or two the whole thing collapsed. When speaking of what happened, Father Sigstein would always add, "Of course it was God's holy will and I know now that if it had been otherwise, my life would have been different. The Society would not have come into being."

Notes to Chapter I

1. In the seventeenth century it was unheard of for nuns to leave their enclosure and go out into the streets. Although St. Francis de Sales (d. 1622) intended his Visitation Sisters to minister to the sick poor in their homes, he was thwarted in his plans by ecclesiastical authorities, and the Sisters were confined to their convents. St. Vincent de Paul (d. 1660) had his Daughters of Charity take vows only from year to year and thus avoid their being called religious. In this way they were able to visit the poor in their homes. See e.g., Louise M. Stacpoole-Kenny, *Francis de Sales* (London, 1924); also Lady Alice Lovat, *Life of Louise de Marillac* (New York, 1916).

2. Letter of October 22, 1930, to Catechist Richardson, and now in the Victory Noll Archives. William Howlett, a native of New York State, was ordained in 1876 for the Diocese of Denver. He was pastor of a small country parish between Manitou and Colorado Springs when John Sigstein first met him. In 1913 Father Howlett became chaplain of the Motherhouse of the Sisters of Loretto at Nerinx, Kentucky. He died there in 1936.

3. Howlett's *Life of Bishop Machebeuf,* first published by the author in Pueblo in 1908, was published again in 1954 by the Register College of Journalism, Denver, Colorado. Bishop Machebeuf died in Denver July 10, 1889.

4. It was Charles Mair and his wife, the former Florence McLaughlin, who were instrumental in bringing the Little Company of Mary, a religious community, to the United States in 1893.

5. The piece appeared in a number of Catholic papers. The copy in the Victory Noll Archives is from *The Messenger Edition of Our Sunday Visitor,* the official newspaper of the Diocese of Covington at that time, February 14, 1954.

6. The name was changed to *The Chicago Catholic* in September 1977.

7. The story of the Lodging House Mission is from the extant volume of the *Journal of Our Lady of Victory Mission* and from Father Sigstein's own notes in the Victory Noll Archives. Further details and direct quotes are from a taped conversation made by Sister Margaret Ann Harrison at Father Sigstein's apartment in Chicago June 28, 1959.

8. Bishop Byrne, a native of St. Louis, was the fifth Bishop of Galveston, having been appointed July 18, 1918. He died in 1950. The Diocese is now known as Galveston-Houston.

9. Charles Coppens was born in Belgium in 1835. He entered the Society of Jesus in his own country in 1853 but came to the United States and completed his novitiate at Florissant, Missouri. He was ordained priest in St. Patrick's Cathedral, New York City, in 1865. Father Coppens died at St. Ignatius College, Chicago, December 14, 1920. See *Holy Family Parish, Chicago, Priests and People* (Chicago, 1923).

2

Missions

Today we would refer to John Sigstein's vocation as being a delayed one. Though his classmates were, for the most part, men younger than he, they were his lifelong friends. Three of them especially were very close to him and gave generously of their time, moral support, and what money they had, in the early days of the Society of Missionary Catechists. These were Anthony Blaufuss of the Diocese of Leavenworth;[1] Dan Hurley from St. Patrick's parish in Chicago but ordained for St. Louis; and Jim Douglas, St. Louis. Of these three, Anthony came first.[2]

Though John liked to refer to Anthony Blaufuss as Co-Founder of the Society, the priest disclaimed the title. He would say that his role, rather, was that of "cheer-leader, one who stood on the side lines and encouraged Father in the work of organization."[3] But his role was much more than that. Anthony was deeply interested in the work of the Society and was always ready to help his friend John in any capacity he could, stopping short of joining him in directing the work of the Catechists, much as John would have liked this arrangement.

John knew he could call on his three priest friends for help when he needed it and he did; though ultimately the worries, the decisions, the setbacks, the problems were his to be met alone. Father Anthony was the only one who survived him, and then for only a few months.

After his ordination on June 5, 1909, Father Sigstein was appointed associate to the pastor of St. Pius Church, Chicago. Here he distinguished himself for his work with young people. When visiting the families in the parish, he learned that parents were much concerned about their young sons — eighteen and older — who drank too much, were neglecting Mass and the other sacraments, and had nothing constructive to do in their leisure time.

There was a large auditorium at St. Pius' and Father wanted to equip it as a gym and fix up club rooms for the young men. When he asked permission of the pastor, the older priest refused, said the boys were bums and nothing would help them.

A few weeks later John tried a second time, after praying fervently to Our Blessed Mother to let him do something for the young men. But again the pastor said no. He said he had given them club rooms once before, but nothing came of it. They just used them as a place to hang out. John asked whether a priest had been with them and the pastor said no.

Then it dawned on Father Sigstein that the pastor was reluctant to spend any money, so he took his problem to his old friend of Lodging House days, Charles Mair, and between them they decided that $700 would do the job. Mr. Mair would pay the bill. A third time he went to the pastor (he was always persistent) and this time he told him he had the money. The pastor said he could go ahead, but he was still skeptical of results.

Father's plan was to enlist the help of a few of the outstanding young men and make the club so attractive that others would want to join. That is just what happened. It was a success from the start. The club rooms were open every night from five o'clock to ten and the young assistant made himself available to the young men each evening. This gave him the opportunity to know the boys personally and help them with their problems.

So successful was the venture that the pastor, somewhat sheepishly, asked his curate to do something for the young women of the parish.

"I don't want to put more work on you," he said hesitantly, "but the sodality consists of just a few old maids and is dead."

John protested that he had his hands full with the boys, but the pastor pushed his point.

Father Sigstein called together a few of the young women and explained his plan for a sodality. It consisted not just of receiving corporate Communion and having a monthly meeting, but included activities apostolic, cultural, and recreational. As outlined, it was surprisingly like the sodality as Father Daniel A. Lord planned it years later. Father said he got most of his ideas from the Y.M.C.A. and Y.W.C.A.

The pastor provided club rooms this time and the sodality was a success from the start. Both clubs sponsored parish dances and soon six young women were engaged to six young men. Many girls went to the convent also. Before that, four women had gone and had returned home.

One of the first activities proposed was a musical. John thought this might be the simplest plan for a starter. He always loved music and appreciated it. He

14

had a good singing voice but his professional training went no further than that of the average seminarian of his day. He knew he would need help with his glee club so he went to Lyon and Healy, *the* music store in Chicago, to ask whether they could recommend a woman to coach the young women in singing.

John never did anything, not even the least thing, without giving some time to prayer for guidance. In this case we might say that luck was with him on his visit to the music store. *He* would say, when recounting the story, that Our Blessed Mother sent him there exactly at the right time and heard his prayer in a wonderful way.

While Father Sigstein was waiting to see someone at the store and discuss his problem, he struck up conversation with a young woman who was examining sheet music. When she learned of Father's project, she told him she was a voice teacher and offered to help him. She not only gave her time and talent to the "St. Cecilia's Guild," but remained a friend of John's. Years later, this same woman, Helen Hartke, came to Victory Noll to teach singing to the Catechists.

Besides his club work Father was a full time assistant and took care of practically all the sick calls, day and night. As a result his health broke. This was to happen over and over during his long life. Always organizing, always making plans, not content with what he considered halfway measures, John Sigstein pushed himself to the limit. He could give advice to others, but he never seemed to learn from his own experience. His always frail body could not keep up with his active mind and the result was nervous exhaustion. He simply collapsed.

John had a good friend in the chancery in Chicago, the Rev. Edward F. Hoban, a friend from Lodging House Mission days. Father Hoban had been ordained in 1903. Later he was to become Chancellor of the Archdiocese, Auxiliary Bishop of Chicago and then Bishop of Rockford. In 1942 he was made Coadjutor to Bishop Schrembs of Cleveland and succeeded to that see in 1945. Like so many others, he remained Father Sigstein's friend to the end of his life and on many occasions went out of his way to help him.[4]

Msgr. Hoban knew of Father's breakdown in health and arranged for him to go to a small country parish in Iowa. He felt that Father would benefit from the country air. The Archdiocese of Dubuque needed priests for country places and had appealed to Chicago for help. "Mother Sigstein," as everyone called her, went along with her son to keep house for him.

When he told of this episode in his life, Father would recall that there were two Archbishops of Dubuque by the same name, Keane, and both had the initials J.J. John J. had the reputation of being very kind and gentle and was referred to as "Sugar Keane." His successor, James J., evidently of the opposite disposition, was called "Hickory Keane." Father's own association with him was not close but neither was it unpleasant in any way. He laughingly conceded that his description of the two men was somewhat simplistic and perhaps legendary in part.[5]

John's first appointment was in a small parish near the Minnesota border, New Albin. He replaced the pastor for a couple of months when he went home to Ireland.

Then he moved to Roseville. Perhaps it was fortunate that he knew little about the recent history of the parish except a rumor that it was "difficult." It was made up for the most part of German and Bohemian farmers. The pastor was leaving for another place and Father Sigstein's stay would be temporary. Exactly how long it would be before another pastor was appointed was not known, but it did not take John long to realize that all was not well. There were two "factions," a result of continuation of the trustee troubles that plagued the Church in the United States during the latter part of the nineteenth century and early part of the twentieth.[6]

The outgoing pastor introduced Father to the parish and when something was said about a salary (the pastor suggesting that they pay him one in advance), John said, "No, my mother and I can get along on what we have."

He had prayed hard for prudence when he was given the inkling that Roseville had a reputation for being a difficult place. By refusing a salary, he saved himself from a lot of trouble. The poor ex-pastor left without a salary for himself.

Instead of the two trustees each parish was supposed to have, this parish had four, each "faction" having elected two. No one would pay an assessment that was being asked for a diocesan project. Father immediately began a parish visitation to try to get the families to meet their obligation. Using all his powers of persuasion, he managed to get about $300 of the $500 assessed, much to the surprise of the Archbishop.

The winter was bitterly cold and John had to go from farm to farm in a horse-drawn sleigh. He was frequently invited to dinner but always refused. He would say he wanted to go home and be with his mother, that it would not be right to have her eat alone. This was true, but also he knew that if he ate at one home, he would have trouble with others.

Mother Sigstein suffered a slight heart attack and when the doctor came to see her, he said that she would recover quickly but that Father should get out of Roseville if he did not want to be a nervous wreck!

When John wrote this to Msgr. Hoban, he arranged for him to take a six months' leave of absence and sent him to a sanitorium where he stayed for a short time and then went to the Southwest. This was in 1914 and was to be a real turning point in John Sigstein's life and in the history of the Society of Missionary Catechists of Our Blessed Lady of Victory.

Father Sigstein went first to Canon City, Colorado, at the invitation of Father Robert Hennessey, an old friend and schoolmate at St. Vincent's College. From there he went to Colorado Springs, where he had spent a year before the turn of the century.

But it was New Mexico that especially attracted him. He had long been interested in its history and specifically in the history of the Church in New Mexico. Italian Jesuits were working in the Archdiocese of Santa Fe and Father had heard especially of Father Mandulari, a zealous missionary from Naples. He knew that he could tell him what missions, what places to see.

Father Mandulari received John cordially and suggested that he visit Isleta, the Pueblo Indian village near Albuquerque. There he met a Miss Watson, a government teacher. She was very kind to him, showed him around, and invited him to stay and meet the Archbishop of Santa Fe whom they expected early that same afternoon.

A little later a short, stocky, heavy-set man wearing a Roman collar came up the road. Father Sigstein was surprised to be introduced to him and discover he was the Archbishop, a plain, simple man. This was Jean Baptiste Pitaval. He had been appointed Auxiliary to Archbishop Peter Bourgade in 1900 and had succeeded him as Archbishop of Santa Fe in 1909. Pitaval resigned in 1918 because of ill health, and died in his native France ten years later. His successor was the Franciscan, Albert T. Daeger, the simple friar whom many continued to call Padre Alberto, and who befriended John Sigstein and the Catechists throughout his life, up to his untimely death in 1932.

Archbishop Pitaval invited Father Sigstein to have lunch with him. John was delighted to have the opportunity to learn at first hand about the missions in New Mexico. There were at the time two or three parochial schools for 120,000 Catholics. The people were extremely poor. Even if they could build parochial schools, they could not maintain them. They were not even able to support their pastors.

"In many of these little places the pastor gets a stipend of twenty-five cents for a baptism," the Archbishop said.

While they were talking, an old, old priest joined them. The Archbishop introduced him to Father as having been his own pastor back in France.

"What kind of mission have *you*, Father?" John inquired.

"Oh," the priest answered, "I have a very poor mission. My church is falling to pieces. It is built of adobe. When it rains during Mass I have to have one of the parishioners hold an umbrella over the altar. I cannot afford to have a new roof put on."

"And how are you fixed for vestments?"

"I have some of the old vestments that the Spanish friars brought here three hundred years ago."

John Sigstein had long been interested in the foreign missions. He was a life member of the Society for the Propagation of the Faith and read in their publication about the work of catechists in foreign lands and how much the missionaries depended on them. Without catechists they could do little.

As the Archbishop and the old missionary talked, Father Sigstein recalled the articles he had read. If the catechists are so successful in foreign missions, he thought to himself, why can't they be successful here? This is what the priests need, helpers to catechize children and adults, care for little mission churches, act as sacristans, organists, choir directors, train acolytes, visit the people and help them with their problems.

Thoughts such as these were going round and round in John's mind as he listened to the conversation. Yes, the priests in New Mexico could use catechists. They needed them just as much as in the foreign missions. In fact, these men were worse off here because they were so extremely poor. Most of the foreign missionaries were members of religious orders who saw to it that their men were supported. The priests in New Mexico had nowhere to turn. The Archbishop said he had tried to interest parishes in the East in his poor missions but had not been very successful.

When Father Sigstein's leave of absence was over and he returned home, Msgr. Hoban saw to it that he was given a less demanding assignment than that of parish priest. He was appointed chaplain for the Religious of the Sacred Heart and the students at their Academy in Lake Forest, Illinois, just outside Chicago. His health had improved greatly and he came back determined to do something constructive to help the poor missions in the Southwest and elsewhere. His mind, as usual, was planning, planning as he made notes of persons whom he could call on for help.

On November 1, 1915, he formally organized the Society of Missionary Helpers of Our Blessed Lady of Victory, a group of women, both married and single, who would sew for the missions and sponsor benefits to raise funds for missionaries. He hoped to include men also in the Society but it was only later that men became active. Of course the women called on their husbands and other men to help, and Father Sigstein received donations from business men, not to mention the vestments and altar vessels given him by men who owned the big religious goods stores. But it seems that men were not actually members of the Society in the same way the women were until much later.[7]

The parishes of St. Vincent, St. Sebastian, and Holy Family (all in Chicago) were the first to take interest in this work. Father Sigstein was careful, however, to emphasize its *private* character. He was not trying to duplicate the efforts of the Society for the Propagation of the Faith. Nor did it have any connection with other diocesan organizations. It was simply a means of helping poor missionaries and more importantly, giving zealous Catholics the opportunity to exercise charity in a very practical manner. In all his talks to members and to prospective members Father would point out the great spiritual advantages for those who engaged in this work.

Though he was careful to avoid running into interference on a higher level, John Sigstein knew that unless the Society was given some publicity, it would never grow. Besides, it was not part of his nature to do anything except on a grand scale.

Each year the Society sponsored at least one "affair" which included an exhibit of church goods gathered together by women or made by them, a talk by a missionary and, of course, one by Father himself in which he reported on the progress of the work and thanked the members for all they had done. In these talks he never failed to spend most of the time on the great spiritual benefits to the members.

The Society was growing. It numbered 160 women in 1918. A year later the number had increased to 250 members, active and associate. Recruits were drawn from among the large numbers of people who attended these exhibits. According to the printed programs, besides the talks and the exhibit, there were included some surprisingly good musical numbers.

The programs were replete with advertisements and a list of patrons and patronesses. There were ads from the church goods companies who no doubt paid to let it be known that they had donated a number of sacred vessels, altar furnishings, etc. And there were ads from "dry cleaners who cleaned and/or dyed the vestments you see on display." Another firm advertised (and probably paid to do it) that they had lacquered the metal goods, candlesticks, etc. Evidently these had been donated by various churches in Chicago that had replaced their own altar furnishings and given the old ones to Father Sigstein for the missions. One program carried the notation "Harp courtesy of Wurlitzer Company."

Many of the missionaries who talked at these affairs sponsored by the Society of Missionary Helpers were from North and South Dakota. The Bishop of Bismarck, the Most Rev. Vincent Wehrle, O.S.B., spoke on a number of occasions.[8] Father Sigstein's connection with him went back at least to 1916 when he began to provide for the poor missions in his diocese. On more than one occasion Bishop Wehrle and other missionaries enjoyed John Sigstein's hospitality whenever they passed through Chicago.

Right from the beginning of the Society Father Sigstein provided in a special way for the spiritual needs of the members by arranging for a retreat for them over Labor Day weekend. This was held at the Academy of Our Lady on the South Side of Chicago. The School Sisters of Notre Dame, to whom Longwood Academy as it was also known, belonged, graciously gave hospitality to the mission group. The members sent out letters inviting young women to join them on this retreat, and this served naturally to recruit new members.

At these Labor Day retreats John Sigstein was always present and himself described the needs of missionaries and their poor missions. Whenever possible he had the missionaries also tell their stories. On at least one retreat weekend (in 1919) Bishop Wehrle addressed the women.

Father Sigstein always had an instinctive "feel" for the kind of story that held the interest of an audience and moved them to help the cause he was promoting. Some missionaries were especially adept at reaching their hearers. Naturally Father called on them for these occasions. John used to say of one of them, Father Rosewinkel, S.J., that he could make people "see through a stone wall."[9] Some of the stories the missionaries told, John copied out for his own use when he himself described the work the Missionary Helpers were doing. One of his favorites concerned a newly ordained Benedictine. This is how Father Sigstein told the story:

> Missionary priests have to offer up the Sacrifice of the Mass under the greatest difficulty. A friend of mine, a young Benedictine priest, was sent by his superior to open up a new mission in what was formerly the great pine country of northern Wisconsin. In one of the places where he went to offer Mass he did not see even a table or box which could serve for an altar. Imagine his surprise when two of the parishioners brought him two loaded kegs of dynamite, placed a board across them and told him this would serve as his altar. He was uncomfortable enough when he saw this, but was more uncomfortable still when they got a couple of old bottles and put the candles in them and lighted them. He told me that during the time he was offering up the Holy Sacrifice of the Mass he expected any minute to go up to heaven quicker than by any other route.[10]

Though figures are sometimes cold and tell only half the story, they are also impressive. A report to Msgr. Hoban summarized the contribution of the Society of Missionary Helpers from November 1, 1915, to April 20, 1921. According to this report the Society had supplied needy missions with 1,000 sets of vestments, 3,500 pieces of altar linens, 430 chalices, ciboria, and ostensoria, besides a number of smaller items. They sent to the missionaries thousands of dollars for Mass stipends, and built and furnished a chapel at Raub, North Dakota.

Not mentioned but equally impressive must have been the hours of work involved in collecting, sorting, refurbishing, and packing the articles, to say nothing of the freight charges.

From a letter Bishop Wehrle wrote to Father Sigstein October 27, 1919, it was evident that John himself donated funds to build at least one mission church. The Bishop tells Father to send the check to Father Paul Letter, Elbowoods, North Dakota, and informs him that he will dedicate the chapel in December or, if the weather is too cold, in the spring of 1920. He hopes Father will attend the dedication. It can be seriously doubted that John accepted the invitation, for his pattern was always to keep himself out of the picture as much as possible.

The Society of Missionary Helpers continued to increase in members and to give valuable assistance to missionary priests by sending them much needed vestments, linens, ritual books, and church furnishings; not to mention Mass stipends on which they depended for their day to day living expenses.

At the beginning of the year 1922 when the Society of Missionary Catechists was actually beginning to take shape, Father Sigstein was making plans for still another organization which he referred to as an auxiliary to the Society of Missionary Catechists. This auxiliary would be known as the Associate Catechists of Mary and its object would be to raise funds for burses to support the Catechists in the mission field.

In a letter to his friend Anthony Blaufuss, John outlined his plan for the Associates. They would be lay persons (he underlined these words), men and women organized in groups of ten or twelve under the direction of a promoter. Each group or band would work to build up a particular burse and to keep in personal touch with the Catechist to whom the burse was assigned. Anthony agreed that this was a splendid idea and offered right away to try to organize a band in his parish.

A month later John was telling his friend that because he had been ill (it was flu this time) he had not as yet been able to carry out his plan for the Associate Catechists of Mary. It was still very much on his mind, though, down to the last detail. They would have a constitution and the officers would be lay persons. He named them: Eula Lee, a woman who worked as a lay missionary in New Mexico in the early twenties, president; Will Frey, treasurer. Theodore Thoma, editor of *The Southwestern Catholic* at this time (later he became associate editor of *The Cincinnati Catholic Telegraph,* a position he held for many years), and Charles Eckert, cashier of the First National Bank of Santa Fe, were to be honorary vice-presidents. Although, as things developed, these persons did not assume responsibility in the Associate Catechists of Mary, each did have a part in the history of the Society of Missionary Catechists.

John urged Anthony to remember this intention in his daily Masses. "It will be a wonderful thing for us if it works out well, and I feel sure that with the grace of Our Lord and the help of Our Blessed Mother, it *will* work out successfully. Just think," he continued exuberantly, "all we need is 667 promoters and a donation of $150 from each band, and we have the magnificent sum of $100,000. This is enough to support sixteen Catechists."

Then, without even beginning another paragraph, he wrote of his plans for *The Missionary Catechist,* the monthly journal he had had in mind for several years. It would not only publicize the work of the Society but also be an excellent way to recruit Associate Catechists of Mary bands all over the country! Though the magazine did not begin until two years later, Father Sigstein touched on it in many letters to his friends, even engaging writers and planning format and illustrations that would hold the interest of subscribers.

The plan for the Associate Catechists *did* work. Not long after the first bands were organized, John Sigstein could report that two burses were already completed. Through the years the Associate Catechists worked tirelessly and magnanimously to build up burses. Though a few individuals founded burses, most of the funds that went into the others were made up of contributions of the "little people," those who have traditionally supported the Church and its works of charity throughout its long history. To these Associates, Our Lady of

Victory Missionary Sisters owe a tremendous debt of gratitude.

Because most of the members of ACM Bands, as they were called, were interested in "their" Catechist, and the needs of her particular mission, they were not content with raising money by promoting a card party or sponsoring another fund raising event; they sent clothing, religious goods, and other needed articles to the missions. It was almost inevitable, then, that the Associate Catechists and the Missionary Helpers would merge. This happened almost imperceptibly because members often belonged to both club groups, especially in Chicago where they originated.

Notes to Chapter II

1. The Diocese of Leavenworth, established in 1877, was changed to Kansas City in Kansas in 1947.

2. Anthony J. Blaufuss was born February 22, 1885. He was ten years younger than John Sigstein. Msgr. Blaufuss (he had been made a Domestic Prelate in 1954) died in Greeley, Kansas, on the feast of Our Lady of Mount Carmel, July 16, 1963. It was while he was making his accustomed daily holy hour before the Blessed Sacrament in his parish church of St. John Baptist that he suffered a heart attack and died immediately.

3. Anthony J. Blaufuss, "Thousands Arise to Bless Them," in *The Missionary Catechist,* June 1935, p.4.

4. Bishop Hoban died September 22, 1966.

5. John J. Keane was Archbishop of Dubuque from 1900 to 1911. He was succeeded by James J. Keane who died in 1929.

6. See "Trusteeism" in *New Catholic Encyclopedia,* Vol. 14, p. 323 ff

7. Though the name of this organization was almost identical to the name Father Sigstein gave to the institute he founded — Society of Missionary *Catechists* of Our Blessed Lady of Victory — it was not a forerunner of the congregation. It developed later, as will be seen, into the Associate Catechists of Mary, a lay group that helped the Missionary Catechists in a material way.

8. Vincent de Paul Wehrle was ordained priest at the Benedictine Abbey of Einsiedeln in Switzerland in 1882. After coming to the United States he served as a missionary in Arkansas and in Indiana before going in 1886 to what was then the Dakota Territory. He was made first Bishop of Bismarck in 1910. Worn out by his labors, he resigned his See in 1939. He died November 2, 1941.

9. Joseph R. Rosewinkel died November 9, 1922.

10. This talk, like most of the others quoted in this book, is in the Victory Noll Archives.

3

Julia and Marie

USY AS HE WAS with his duties as chaplain and his activities directing the work of the Missionary Helpers, John Sigstein never lost sight of his dream of providing catechists for the poor missions he had visited and read about, especially those in New Mexico. It weighed on him that many children of Catholic heritage were not receiving adequate religious instruction, some of them not even minimal instruction.

Most parishes in the Southwest had no Catholic schools. Missionaries were usually responsible for ten, twelve, or more "stations," many of them at considerable distance from the parish center. In these places Mass could be offered once a month at most. Sometimes it was only three or four times a year. It was impossible, under such circumstances, to provide religious instruction for the children.

Father Sigstein was convinced that only self-sacrificing, dedicated women, with the special vocation to spend their lives in the service of the poor, neglected children in the mission fields could succeed in such an apostolate as he envisioned. Plans and ideas were going round and round in his ever active mind.

In 1916 John was in touch with Father John Lyons, S.J., founder of the Catholic Instruction League, a kind of forerunner in the United States, of the Confraternity of Christian Doctrine.[1] The Confraternity was centuries old, dating back to the Council of Trent. The Code of Canon Law reads: "It is the duty of diocesan Ordinaries to see to it that Confraternities of the Blessed Sacrament and of Christian Doctrine be established in every parish." (Canon 711.2)[2] Father Sigstein found the Confraternity of Christian Doctrine active in only a few dioceses in the United States. Pittsburgh was one of them, and in 1917 he began correspondence with the Rev. T.F.O'Shea, diocesan director at the time. Later (in 1923) he wrote to Father O'Shea's successor, the Rev. E.A.Lawless, and arranged to have two Missionary Catechists visit him for information.

During the latter part of the twenties and into the fifties, the Confraternity of Christian Doctrine in the United States was closely associated with the Rural Life Bureau of the National Catholic Welfare Conference. This is understandable since religious vacation schools were being promoted in rural areas owing in great part to the vision and efforts of the late Most Rev. Edwin V. O'Hara, Bishop of Great Falls, Montana, and later of Kansas City, Missouri.[3]

In recent years most Catholics know what C.C.D. stands for. It is interesting, however, that the Second Vatican Council, four centuries after Trent, explicitly asked that the Confraternity be established. In the Decree on the Bishops' Pastoral Office, *Christus Dominus,* we read:

> Pastors should bring the faithful to a full knowledge of the mystery of salvation through a catechetical instruction which is adapted to each one's age. In imparting this instruction, they should seek not only the assistance of religious but also the cooperation of the laity, and should establish the Confraternity of Christian Doctrine. (Art. 30, No. 2)[4]

In 1912 Father Lyons had organized women to give catechetical instructions to the many children in Chicago who did not attend parochial schools. The work spread to other cities. It was especially active in Detroit where one of the principal leaders was Josephine Van Dyke Brownson, granddaughter of the famous convert, Orestes Brownson.[5]

It was evidently through Father Lyons that John Sigstein came to know David Smith and his wife who were lay catechists in Mississippi. In August 1915, with the blessing of the Most Rev. John E. Gunn, S.M., Bishop of Natchez-Jackson, Mr. and Mrs. Smith began their catechetical work in Magins, Mississippi.[6] Subsequently they worked in various places in the diocese: Wiggins, Pascagoula, Gulfport, among others. They had gone to Mississippi from Chicago where Mrs. Smith had been one of Father Lyons' early religion teachers.

The Smiths were originally from Sidney, Australia. They were unique in that they taught religion in the South as a husband and wife team. Mrs. Smith died in May 1927, and David carried on alone, into his eighty-eighth year. He visited Victory Noll in August 1927 and again in the summer of 1935. The Sisters remember him as a pleasant little man with a Van Dyke beard. In many ways he was avant-garde in his teaching methods. He used catechetical songs (many of them original), slides, dramatic presentations, etc. He always signed his letters "David J. Smith, Catechist."

Whether the Smiths actually worked in Australia with the Sisters of St. Joseph of the Sacred Heart, a catechetical community, is not clear, but in 1918 Mr. Smith was writing John Sigstein that he had been "working for over ten years to have them take up work in the U.S.A. and Canada. Archbishop Quigley is most anxious to have them. Msgr. Kelley has invited them . . . Archbishop Ceretti, while Apostolic Delegate in Australia, also urged them. He was a great friend of the order and said his daily Mass in their chapel when he was home. Two years ago at the General Chapter of the Sisters it was resolved to the great joy of Dr. Ceretti that as soon as conditions would warrant it, two Sisters would be sent to reconnoitre and advise the Mother General."[7]

In the same letter, David told Father Sigstein he was sending him a copy of the life of Mother Mary of the Cross, Foundress of this catechetical community. It must have made an impression on John. Later the book became regular fare for spiritual reading at Victory Noll and in the mission convents of the Missionary Catechists.

What especially appealed to Father Sigstein was the fact that these Australian Sisters had to forego daily Mass and many other spiritual benefits that were ordinarily the privilege of religious, in order to minister to the people whom they served. John knew well that this was a sacrifice a community which he envisioned would have to make if the work was to be effective.

Father himself had corresponded with these Australian Sisters and in 1918 asked them for a copy of their Constitutions. Nothing ever came of the efforts of Dave Smith and others to bring them to the United States. They continued to work in the bush country in Australia.

Years later (1951) there was another exchange between Victory Noll and a community of women religious "down under." This time it was the other way around. The Rev. John G. Wallis had founded the Home Missionary Sisters of Our Lady in Tasmania in 1944. He made a trip halfway across the world to Huntington, Indiana, to get new insights for his Missionary Sisters whose work was so much like that of the Victory Noll Congregation.[8]

Mr. Smith was convinced that the South needed lay missionaries to work among the poor, especially the migrants who had come down from northern states and moved from place to place. He envisioned "an order of catechists, especially of married people willing to give like the first Christians to the cause of Christ, to undergo a three-year course of preparation and then to go out Bohemian style into the scattered places and give light to the poor benighted ones who are kept in the dark by those who know not the doctrine of the Catholic Church."

Then he made an impassioned plea to Father Sigstein: "Here I have twenty acres with church and all that is essential, a very fair library; all this I am willing to give as well as the personal service of Mrs. Smith and myself if you would act as Founder of this Catechist Order. I feel sure the Holy Father Benedict XV would welcome such a move, for he calls the catechist his right hand."[9]

Father Sigstein admired what the Smiths were doing, but the ministry he had in mind was to be done by dedicated, single women and also by celibate men, for Father, from the beginning, hoped also to found an order of men cate-

25

chists. These would be priests and brothers who would do the same type of work the women did, but among boys and men. Though John Sigstein worked hard to bring about such an arrangement, it never got beyond the planning stage. Again and again he tried to persuade priests to join him to help him especially with the direction of the Missionary Catechists but, as will be seen, nothing ever came of it. Either the priests themselves were convinced that this was not the work to which God was calling them, or their bishops refused to release them.

Various dates have been given as the founding year of the Society of Missionary Catechists of Our Blessed Lady of Victory or, as it is known today, the Congregation of Our Lady of Victory Missionary Sisters. These dates range from 1917 to 1922. The Founder himself, John Sigstein, used different dates. Eventually he referred to 1922 as the real foundation year. This is also the date that the late Bishop Noll of Fort Wayne gave to the Sacred Congregation of Religious when he sent documents to Rome requesting pontifical status for the Congregation.

It was September 8, 1917, that Father Sigstein began his first draft of plans for establishing his Society of Catechists. He always chose a feast of Our Blessed Mother to begin anything especially significant in his life, so it was to be expected that when he actually committed to writing the project that was so dear to him, he should do it on the feast of the Nativity of Mary. Two months later, on Thanksgiving Day, his friend Bishop Wehrle of Bismarck visited him at the Academy of the Sacred Heart, Lake Forest, Illinois, and together they reviewed the plans for the Society.

John valued the opinion of the Benedictine Bishop who was himself a veteran missionary. When Bishop Wehrle returned home he wrote to thank Father for his hospitality and referred again to the proposed Society: "Your plan regarding a Missionary Band of Catechists is very dear to my heart. I hope God will bless this undertaking and give us the right Catholic young ladies, self-sacrificing and courageous and persevering."

Though Wehrle says "give *us* the right Catholic young ladies," he refers in subsequent correspondence to their working in the South and West. Perhaps at the time he had in mind that they would work in these parts of the country *besides* working in North Dakota in his own Diocese of Bismarck. In January 1919 Father Sigstein wrote his cousin, Father Baldus Biegel in Elwood, Indiana, that Bishop Wehrle was most anxious for the work to begin in his diocese at an early date.[10]

Other letters between Vincent Wehrle and John Sigstein indicate that the Bishop envisioned the catechetical work as being the forerunner of the parish school. And in a letter to a would-be applicant, the Bishop said that he thought the Missionary Catechists should teach school "for the very purpose of teaching catechism to the children."[11]

Meanwhile, true to form, Father Sigstein looked for not just moral support and the backing of Church authority, but — always most important for him in any undertaking — he sought prayerful, spiritual help. On the feast of the Immaculate Conception, December 8, 1917, he called on his friend and confidante, Mother Coletta, Abbess of the Poor Clare Colettines, at their convent on Laflin Street in Chicago. He unfolded his plans to her and she pledged a perpetual novena and prayers of the Poor Clares not only in Chicago but in Cleveland and Omaha. Mother Coletta and her Sisters remained staunch friends of Father Sigstein and his Society of Missionary Catechists, a friendship that did not end with Mother Coletta's death in 1942.

In September 1918 at the close of the annual Labor Day weekend retreat of the Missionary Helpers, Father Sigstein told Mother Aquinata, S.S.N.D., superior of Longwood Academy, of his plans for establishing the Society of Missionary Catechists. Mother Aquinata promised unstinted support, a support that was to be truly magnanimous. To this dedicated woman Father Sigstein and his Catechists were to be deeply indebted. If it had not been for Mother Aquinata's generosity, the beginnings of the Society would have entailed even more hardships than they actually did.

From 1922 to 1924 some members of the newly formed Society of Missionary Catechists resided at the Academy of Our Lady. Mother Aquinata not only gave them room and board but arranged instructions for them in subjects that would be useful in the missions. They attended Sister Lamberta's Spanish classes and were given music lessons by Sister Elpedia. Father reserved for himself their instruction and guidance in the spiritual life.

For their part the young women folded clothing in the laundry and washed dishes in the kitchen. At least for a time they slept in the little girls' dorm and helped the children dress in the morning. They also sat at table with them and assisted them in the dining room.

Mother Aquinata, perhaps more than anyone else at this time, realized the burdens Father Sigstein assumed in these early days of the Society. With Sister Leo she visited Victory Noll in 1929 and spoke of the heartaches and setbacks he experienced:

> The first days of the Society of Missionary Catechists were difficult ones. Many, many times Father Sigstein was almost a martyr because of persecutions and obstacles. It is too early to write these difficulties in your history. Now it would not be discreet to mention them. Often it seemed as though your good Spiritual Father must succumb beneath the burdens he carried. Many times I would say to him, "Never mind, Father; difficulties and obstacles are the stones out of which God's houses are built." The stones came. The difficulties and obstacles were the stones. Love of God and of Our Blessed Mother was the cement that held together this magnificent spiritual temple of which your beautiful home, Victory Noll, is the symbol. I might say that every stone typifies some difficulty that beset the founding of this Society. Everything worthwhile costs a great

deal. "How much did it cost?" is the usual question. The answer is given in terms of money. But when spiritual things are involved, the answer is not given in terms of money but in terms of sacrifice. And how much did it cost? It cost many, many prayers; it cost many, many headaches and heartaches and much labor. But see what has come of it! You have come from the north, east, south, and west to be the living stones in this temple, to do God's work and the work of Our Blessed Mother. Sister Leo and I are edified at all we see and we thank God that it has come to this . . . .[12]

Mother Aquinata made no mention of her part during this time, but neither Father Sigstein nor the first Catechists ever forgot her generosity and her interest.

It was in the year 1918 that John Sigstein was transferred from the chaplaincy at Lake Forest to St. Bernard's Hospital on Harvard Avenue in Englewood in Chicago's South Side. The hospital was then, as it is today, under the direction of the Religious Hospitallers of St. Joseph. In writing to Bishop Wehrle about this transfer Father Sigstein reported that "This is a great field for labor. We have about 150 beds here and they are occupied all the time . . . I am happy to say that the Sisters who are in charge of the hospital do a great deal of charity work."[13]

At the time of John's transfer the work was heavier than usual, for this was at the height of the serious flu epidemic that claimed so many lives in the United States and elsewhere in the world. One of the victims was John's dear friend, George Pierson, who died at St. Bernard's Hospital December 6, 1918.

In disclosing his plans for the Society of Missionary Catechists Father Sigstein emphasized over and over that the members must be generous, self-sacrificing, zealous young women because they would have to forego not only material things, but also many of the spiritual advantages that are taken for granted as a part of religious life.

From the time of his ordination to the priesthood John had many contacts with young women. They sought him out as confessor and spiritual director. Among them were many who were called to religious life. Recognizing that each person is fitted for a specific work and, in the case of a religious vocation, called to a particular congregation, John directed these young women to various communities according to their aptitudes. Most of them were attracted to established institutes that engaged in the teaching apostolate, nursing, caring for orphans, etc. From among these fine young women Father Sigstein was ever on the alert for the special qualities he believed necessary for the first recruits for his proposed Society of Missionary Catechists.

The first two who actually became members and began the work in New Mexico in 1922 were Julia Doyle and Marie Benes of Chicago. They met John Sigstein in 1915 when he was chaplain at Lake Forest, but each under very different circumstances. Julia was one of the first members of the Missionary Helpers, but Marie was never a member.

One day Father Sigstein, always eager to broaden his knowledge of missionaries and their work and needs, stopped at the Consolidated Clipping Service in Chicago. This was a service where various items from metropolitan newspapers and other media were clipped and filed according to specific categories. It was patronized by researchers, teachers, business executives, and others seeking articles containing information pertinent to their special interests. The clients paid a fee for the service.

On John Sigstein's first visit to the Clipping Service he was waited on by Julia Doyle, one of the many employees. He asked her to save for him articles on missionaries and mission work. On subsequent visits he always asked for Julia, for he was not only impressed with her courtesy and friendliness but he discovered that his interest in missions at home and abroad was one she shared with him. This was the beginning of a beautiful relationship, one that was to have far-reaching consequences.

At this time John was still chaplain at the Academy of the Sacred Heart and from time to time gave retreats there. Julia accepted his invitation to make a retreat, an experience she repeated as often as she could during the next few years.

Very little is known of Julia Doyle's early life. She was born September 10, 1875, in Zanesville, Ohio, and baptized in St. Thomas Aquinas Church there. When the family moved to Chicago is not clear, but Julia made her First Communion in the Cathedral of the Holy Name on May 31, 1888, and was confirmed the same day. Julia and other children in her neighborhood attended "Sunday School" conducted by young women who had been educated by the Religious of the Sacred Heart. She used to say that she always wanted to teach poor children as these generous women had taught her.

Julia was forty years old when she met Father Sigstein, just one month his senior. And there was a difference of twenty-two years between her and Marie Benes, her first companion in New Mexico!

Julia was not the kind who talked much about herself. Because she was very matter of fact, it was not so easy, on first acquaintance, to see her many sterling qualities. Those who were privileged to know her well, however, soon became aware of the depth of her character.

It is usually difficult to point out any outstanding virtue in those who practice real charity, for such persons are also generous, self-sacrificing, humble, etc. So it was with Julia Doyle. If we were to single out her special qualities, it would be her humility and simplicity.

Julia herself would be the first to disclaim this. She often lamented her *lack* of humility and of patience. Though she was extremely sharp and was quick to size up a situation, she was the last one to cast judgment, to criticize. Occasionally, when she did, she expressed her regret later. There were times when she had to make adverse judgments, but she softened them whenever she could.

Julia Doyle was blessed with a fine sense of humor, a quality that she shared with Marie Benes and that no doubt kept both of them from discouragement in their early mission experiences. Julia's wit was the dry kind. Father Sigstein used to describe her letters (and later the brief stories she wrote at his request for the community's mission magazine) as "pithy." It is an adjective not often used, one that the dictionary defines as being "concise and brief but full of substance, meaty." Such a word suited Julia's writing perfectly. In a few lines she could pack a world of meaning.

Although Julia Doyle and Marie Benes were so far apart in years, there was no generation gap between them. Each complemented the other. Marie's health was always frail and though Julia was solicitous for her and tried to spare her from much physical exertion, she did not over-protect her, though she was old enough to be her mother.

Marie Benes was born in 1897 in a suburb of Vienna, Austria. Her father was head gardener or "manager of gardens" as he was called, on the large estate of a wealthy family. In 1906 Marie's mother died and a year later her father decided to take his three little girls to America. Nearly all of his relatives had left Austria for the United States, and his only sister, who lived in Chicago, urged him to come there with his motherless girls. There were rumors of war even then and Mr. Benes felt that this would be the best time to make the move.

In Chicago he applied for a job in the public parks and thought he had been accepted. However, there was some misunderstanding. Mr. Benes' ability was recognized, but his citizenship was questioned, even though he had taken out his first papers as soon as possible.

It did not take long for him to find work elsewhere. He was employed by the Swift family in Lake Forest, one of the many gardeners needed to care for their extensive grounds. He was especially grateful for this position, because he could keep his little family together. During their first few months or so in the United States they had stayed with Mr. Benes' sister. She and her husband gave them warm hospitality, but they had a number of children of their own.

The Swifts were very kind to their new gardener and his three motherless little girls. The children attended a public school in Lake Forest but Miss McGrath, a tutor at Swift's, helped them with their English.

It was in 1915 that Marie Benes first had any contact with Father Sigstein. Father, who was chaplain at the Academy of the Sacred Heart, used to assist the pastor of St. Mary's Church, Lake Forest, on Sundays. He always celebrated the second Mass, the Mass the Swift children's tutor, Miss McGrath, attended. Marie and her two sisters accompanied her. The devotion with which Father offered Mass impressed them. Also, Marie found herself paying particular attention to his carefully prepared sermons.

It was to be quite some time after she began to assist at Father Sigstein's Mass, however, that Marie actually met him. One evening at dusk when she was on her way home, she realized she was being followed. Fearfully she hurried and ran up the steps of a little house she was passing. It was on the grounds of the Academy of the Sacred Heart. Imagine her surprise to have Father Sigstein open the door, the priest whose Mass she liked to attend on Sunday. John summoned one of the school workmen to see that she got home in safety.

Marie recalled later that even in her fright she found herself comparing the priest's humble surroundings with the palatial homes of the clergy that she remembered from her childhood in Europe. John lived in this little cottage with a huge St. Bernard dog. Whether his mother was with him at this time is not clear.

This was the beginning of Marie Benes' friendship with John Sigstein. Evidently she went to him now and then for direction, but it could not have been over a very long period, for soon afterward Father was transferred to St. Bernard's Hospital. Today it is comparatively easy to drive from Lake Forest to the South Side of Chicago, but in 1918 it was a long trip, a real journey; so it was not until a year or more later that Marie saw John Sigstein.

In her early adolescent years Marie Benes suffered an attack of rheumatic fever that left her with a weakened heart. She had hoped to become a nurse but because of her heart condition was not able to enter training. Instead, she accepted a position in a doctor's office, an experience that she was always grateful for and that served somewhat to satisfy her natural inclination toward a nursing career. When the doctor was called into service during World War I, Marie worked in different families caring for sick children. This experience was a remote preparation for her missionary work in New Mexico, and Marie always looked on it as providential though at the time she had no idea of what the future held for her.

Notes to Chapter III

1. John Lyons, S.J., established the Catholic Instruction League at Loyola University, Chicago, in 1912.
2. See "Confraternity of Christian Doctrine" in *New Catholic Encyclopedia,* Vol. 4, p. 155.
3. Edwin Vincent O'Hara was born in Lanesboro, Minnesota, September 6, 1881. He was accepted for the priesthood in the Archdiocese of Oregon City (later changed to Portland). Father O'Hara was instrumental in forming the Rural Life Bureau and was its first president. The first conference was held in St. Louis in 1923. In 1930 O'Hara was appointed Bishop of Great Falls, and in 1939 to the See of Kansas City in Missouri (changed in 1956 to Kansas City-St. Joseph). For the Victory Noll Sisters Bishop O'Hara is especially remembered for his work in organizing the Confraternity of Christian Doctrine in the United States. He convoked the first congress in Rochester, N.Y. in 1935. Bishop O'Hara died in Italy in 1956 on his way to the Assisi Conference on Liturgy.
4. *The Documents of Vatican II,* tr. in W.M. Abbott (ed.) p. 418.
5. See Chapter XVII.
6. Since 1977 called Diocese of Jackson.

7. Letter from David Smith to John J. Sigstein dated August 28, 1918. Victory Noll Archives.

8. Father Wallis visited Victory Noll again in 1971 and happily reported the progress of the community he had founded.

9. Letter from David Smith to John J. Sigstein dated December 6, 1917.

10. Father Biegel's real name was Balthasar but he was known as Baldus. He had a brother Peter, also a priest of the Diocese of Fort Wayne.

11. Letter of Bishop Wehrle to Sister Lidwina December 24, 1918.

12. Mother Aquinata's only visit to Victory Noll took place July 25-26, 1929. The talk she gave was copied by one of the Catechists and put into the Victory Noll Archives. Mother Aquinata died October 5, 1951.

13. Letter of Father Sigstein to Bishop Wehrle dated January 4, 1919.

John Joseph Sigstein in 1898;
twenty-three years old.

Father Sigstein in 1932.

Father George Pierson.

William Frey.

Father Michael F.D. Collins.

The Mission on Dearborn Street, Chicago, in 1907. John Sigstein kneeling, left; Francis Collins, right. Will Frey is in the back row on the right side, directly under the cross. The men pictured are not just those who resided at the Mission, but members of the Society of St. Vincent de Paul who helped support it.

Marie Benes (left), Julia Doyle, Will Frey with children at Shoemaker, an out-mission from Watrous, N.M., 1923. The man on the far right is the father of some of the children.

Archbishop Daeger of Santa Fe and Will Frey, 1922.

The Catechists' "convent" at Ocate, N.M., 1923, described as a one-time saloon.

Getting stuck in an arroyo and having to be pulled out by horse and wagon was a common occurrence in the early days in New Mexico; 1924.

Father Sigstein and Father Blaufuss at Victory Noll, June 1925. From left the Catechists are: Marie Benes, Sophie Renier, Caroline Meister, Marie Bodin. Inset: Catechist Julia Doyle.

Peter O'Donnell and his wife, Julia, of Long Beach, California, whose generosity made it possible for Bishop Noll and Our Sunday Visitor to build a motherhouse for the Catechists.

Part of the crowd that attended the Dedication Day at Victory Noll July 5, 1925. Bishop Noll and Father Sigstein are in the forefront.

Catechists Helen Srill (left) and Edna Like
with some of the families at Chaperito, N.M., 1925.

Victory Mount, Las Vegas, N.M., formerly the old Santa Fe RR Hospital.
Peter O'Donnell bought the property for the Catechists in 1926.

Catechist Sullivan (left) and Catechist Leven with some of the families who received food at the soup kitchen in Las Vegas, N.M., in the early thirties. The building, formerly the Christian Brothers' school, served as the Catechists' convent.

*Catechist Vigil (left) and Catechist Richardson with graduates
of their fifth CCD Institute, San Ysidro, N.M., 1933.*

*Familiar sight — accompanying children from their public school
to their CCD classes; Sister Adelle Heintz, Limonera Camp near
Santa Paula, California.*

4

Academy Of Our Lady

OHN SIGSTEIN WAS VERY CAREFUL to whom he revealed his plans for establishing the Society of Missionary Catechists of Our Blessed Lady of Victory. Some of his caution might have been because of his previous experience with his Lodging House work. It had been taken from him and he did not want to risk having it happen again. Possibly it was the natural reticence a person has to speak freely about an idea or plan that might not be understood. In any case, the persons whom he had taken into his confidence were few: Bishop Wehrle; Charles Coppens, S.J., his confessor and spiritual director; Edward F. Hoban, Chancellor of the Archdiocese; his friends, Anthony Blaufuss, George Pierson, Dan Hurley, and Martin Francis Collins (not yet a priest); Bruno Hagspiel, S.V.D., Techny, Illinois; and Mother Coletta and Mother Aquinata.[1]

It does not seem that Father actually spoke of his plans to Julia Doyle before 1918 and, as will be seen, it was not until August 1919, that he specifically mentioned them to Marie Benes. However, he was carefully observing the women who came to him for spiritual direction, especially those who felt drawn to religious life and in whom John Sigstein discerned such a call.

It was at the close of the Missionary Helpers' Labor Day Retreat in 1918 that John told Mother Aquinata what he had in mind. As we have seen, she encouraged him and told him she would help him in any way she could. It was after this same retreat that a young woman expressed the desire to be a member of the new Society. She had been coming to Father Sigstein for direction and he had told her something of his plans. He recognized the exceptional qualities of this young woman and told her that in a short time he would set up a course of instructions to prepare prospective members for their pioneer undertaking. He would invite other young women like herself to enroll in the course. As subsequent events show, this young woman did attend many of the instructions but she did not actually enter the Society.

Meanwhile Julia Doyle was very active as a member of Father Lyons' Catholic Instruction League. She and other women under his direction were teaching poor children in various locations in Chicago. Julia was active also in the Missionary Helpers Society. In fact, she was one of the original members. Her name appears as secretary and she is listed among the patrons and patronesses on the program of the exhibits and other fund raising projects.

In January 1919, Father Sigstein wrote to Bishop Wehrle that because of the flu epidemic he had not been able to begin the course of instructions for "the proposed members of our Society of Missionary Catechists. No gathering of any kind could be held here during this time . . . A number of devoted, zealous young women have signified their intention of taking this course of instructions. I shall begin with three or four and am certain that before long we shall have at least six members at the instructions."

Then he tells the Bishop that the Chancellor and the Jesuit Fathers who have examined the plans were very favorably impressed, and "my Spiritual Director urged me by all means to go on with the instructions which would serve as preliminary training in the life of Christian and Religious Perfection for those who would enter the Society as postulants, once the Society has been established."[2]

It was on the Feast of the Annunciation, March 25, 1919, that the long-planned instructions finally got under way. Four women met with Father Sigstein at St. Bernard's Hospital. Julia Doyle was there, also the young woman who wished to become a member of the Society but who did not persevere in her desire. There were two others, one of them being Lillian Pierson, sister of John's deceased priest friend. Apparently Lillian came because of her friendship with Father Sigstein. John might have hoped she would become a member of the Society, but she never did. The fourth young woman came from Elwood, Indiana, having learned of the instructions from her pastor, Father Sigstein's cousin, Baldus Biegel. She planned to travel to Chicago by train Saturday, stay over night, attend the instructions on Sunday afternoon and return home that evening. This entailed some inconvenience. Whether this was the reason or whether she changed her mind about becoming a member of the proposed Society, is not known; her name never appeared again. It might even be suspected that subsequent instructions were too sporadic for her to follow through on them. John Sigstein thought nothing of calling meetings (or calling off meetings) on very short notice, and the young woman might have been discouraged from making the effort to go to Chicago. Whatever the reason, her name does not appear on any record or in any letters after this first gathering in March 1919.

Marie Benes was not in the little group that attended the first instruction. Though she had spoken to Father Sigstein of a desire for religious life, she felt drawn to a nursing career. Perhaps this was why, in the beginning, Father did not think of her as a candidate for his Society. Instead, he arranged an interview for her with the novice mistress of a congregation engaged in hospital work. Marie's reaction, however, was that this was not the community for her.

With Helen Gaylord, a dear friend whom she had known for many years, Marie planned a vacation trip in the summer of 1919. Their first stop was in Wellsburg, West Virginia, where Helen's father, a physician, lived. Many of his patients were poor miners. He knew that Marie had done home nursing and that she was especially good with children, so he asked her if she would help with a sick child by showing the mother how to care for her. Besides having twins to look after, the mother had this year-old baby who had been born prematurely and had been ill from birth. Marie went to the home every day for three weeks and helped care for the undernourished little one.

"This experience," Marie said later, "was my first contact with the very poor and I saw how desperately they needed assistance. I made up my mind then and there that I would help them. I saw the heart-rending conditions among which these miners lived and I determined that work among the poor would be my work."

Before leaving Chicago for the East, Marie must have visited Father Sigstein and told him about her proposed trip. Or perhaps he learned of her whereabouts through her sister or one of her friends. At any rate, John now wrote her and told her of his plans for the Society of Missionary Catechists. This letter, dated August 21, 1919, is so important that we are reproducing it in its entirety. It describes not only the work of the Society as Father envisioned it, but reveals much of what he expected from the first candidates and summarizes the spiritual instructions he proposed to give them to prepare them for their future life.

Dear Marie

I was surprised to hear that you had left Wellsburg and that you are now in New York. I am very pleased to hear that you are so near to church and that you may visit our dear Lord in the Blessed Sacrament every day.

I am sure the novena which you made to Our Blessed Lady of Victory has been of the greatest help to you in making known to you your vocation to the religious life. I felt from the very beginning that you had such a vocation, and I felt too that Our Blessed Mother wishes you to sanctify your soul and to labor for the salvation of others in this most holy state of life.

I think it would be well for you to make another novena to Our Blessed Mother ending on the feast of her Nativity, September 8. In this novena ask her to please help you to know and do God's Holy Will and her good pleasure in reference to the kind of religious life you are to embrace. If you feel that you have a calling to labor as a religious among the sick, I have no doubt but what I could arrange matters for you to enter our religious community here in the hospital. If, however, you feel that you would like to consecrate your life in religion to the noble and holy work of teaching catechism to poor, neglected children in the scattered mission places of our country, I will write you all about the Society of Missionary Catechists we are forming here to take up this work in the poor missions of the far West and South where no other Sisters care to go.

In the poor missionary dioceses out in North and South Dakota, Idaho, Montana, and other far western states, and down in South Texas, Arizona, and New Mexico, thousands of Catholic children are losing their Faith because there is no one to give them instructions in the catechism. There are nearly 2,000,000 Catholic children who are not attending Catholic schools in this country. Someone must go to these children and save them to Holy Church by giving them instructions in Christian Doctrine.

The Society, which Bishop Wehrle of Bismarck, North Dakota, and myself are establishing, has for its end this one purpose — of sending capable, devout young women to these mission places where they will gather the children together and teach them the catechism. These Catechists will be formed into a Society which will no doubt become a religious community when the Holy See approves of this work. Should you feel called upon to take up this work, I will explain to you more fully our plans as soon as you return to Chicago.

You will understand from what I have written you here, that the highest, holiest, and noblest calling Our Blessed Mother could obtain for you, where you could do the most good, would be in a Society like this. So, I would ask you to pray that you may know God's Holy Will and the good pleasure of Our Blessed Mother in this regard.

In the near future I shall send you some typewritten instructions on the principles and practices of the Spiritual Life. Meanwhile, try to follow the plan I have given you and above all, remember to keep yourself always in the Presence of God. By walking in the Presence of Our Lord and Our Blessed Mother you will always be sure of doing God's Holy Will. God's Will, you know, is the rule of our life, and if you carry out the Divine Will faithfully, you will become in a very short time holy and pleasing to the Sacred Heart.

You say that you are not able to think of Our Lord and Our Blessed Mother very much during the time you are out with the children. You are not expected to have your mind continually fixed on Our Lord in prayer. All that you need to do is to make an Act of Pure Intention as often as you can during the day, particularly every time you change occupation. You will remember that I pointed out the necessity of making, the first thing in the morning, your Morning Offering to the Sacred Heart, and your intention of gaining all the indulgences you can daily. Now, the saints strongly urge us to renew these Acts of Pure Intention whenever we change our occupations so that according to this plan, whenever you go out with the children, offer all to Jesus through Mary. Whenever you return, renew this offering. When about your household duties, continually renew this offering of your intention. In this way you will follow the command of Our Divine Lord of "watching and praying always."

Trusting that this explanation will help you to gain many great graces and merits every day of your life, and hoping to hear from you very soon, I remain, dear Marie,

Your sincere friend in O.B.L.V.,

(signed) Rev. J.J. Sigstein

Marie Benes returned to Chicago in September and joined the group taking instructions from Father Sigstein. By now it numbered ten women, most of them teachers or office workers whom John had become acquainted with through the Society of Missionary Helpers or through retreats he had given.

The instructions continued at St. Bernard's but not always with the same women present. Some came and went. Not even the place of meeting was always the same. Sometimes it was in the dining room, sometimes in John's office, again in his bedroom. It was rather puzzling to the Sisters who did not know just why these lay women were coming to see their chaplain. It often happened that the meetings had to be put off for one reason or another.

On February 2, 1920, the feast of the Presentation of Jesus in the Temple, Julia Doyle and Marie Benes made their Act of Consecration to Jesus through Mary, but each in a different place: Julia in the Church of the Immaculate Conception and Marie at Holy Name Cathedral. This was the Consecration according to the True Devotion as taught by St. Louis Marie Grignion de Montfort, known today as the Montfortian Devotion. Father Sigstein himself had been living this Consecration since he had made it in 1910, a year after his ordination.

God the Father chose Mary to be the Mother of his Son who was to become man for the salvation of the world. The core of devotion to Mary as patterned after the True Devotion of Louis de Montfort consists in making an Act of Consecration which is a renewal of one's baptismal consecration to Christ and with him to the Father. The Consecration is made through Mary, the woman of faith and Mother of the Church, because she is the model of this covenantal baptismal commitment.[3]

This is the heritage, the legacy Father Sigstein wished to give his daughters. This Marian thrust was to be the spirit of the Congregation dedicated to the service of God's poor under the patronage of Our Lady of Victory. Father's instructions had been in preparation for this initial Consecration to Jesus through Mary. Julia and Marie were now ready to make it and expressed the wish to do so. Father had hoped to have the ceremony at St. Bernard's Hospital early in the morning but because the two women were working, it was impossible for them to go there, and so they made the Consecration in their parish churches.

Two months later Marie Benes had a recurrence of rheumatic fever. She was very ill and was confined to a hospital for three months. At first the doctors said she would not be able to do work of any kind for at least a year. Marie felt that this was the end of her dream to be a member of the proposed Society of Missionary Catechists. However, she began to improve — to the amazement of the doctors, her family, and friends. When Father Sigstein saw how well she was getting along, he decided that she could resume the instructions. In September she was back with the group.

John thought it would be well for Marie to take a business course, that it would be helpful later on if she were able to type. Marie had been thinking along these lines also and she planned to enroll in a business college. But before she did, Father Sigstein talked it over with Mother Aquinata at the Academy of Our Lady and she suggested that Marie board at Longwood and attend classes there. It would be easier for her. It turned out that it made things easier in every way. The instructions could continue there instead of at the hospital, and because Marie lived there it would be an "excuse" for the other women to meet at Longwood. So it was that in July 1921, Marie Benes took up residence at the Academy of Our Lady on 95th and Throop Streets.

The cover-up might seem strange, but John Sigstein insisted on secrecy during this whole time of preparation. The prospective candidates were permitted to confide only in a Jesuit, Father Spirig, who was stationed at Holy Family Church.[4] We know now that Father had approached Archbishop Mundelein (he had succeeded Archbishop Quigley in 1915), hoping to be released from duties in order to devote himself to the Society. He had been rebuffed and would be for some time. However, he was not actually forbidden to do any organizing so he continued as before. Perhaps the Archbishop thought it was something too nebulous to bother with or maybe he believed the whole thing would be dropped.[5]

Every Saturday afternoon the women came to the Academy for their instructions. The first hour was devoted to the study of the Spanish language. Mother Aquinata herself taught the first few weeks and then turned the class over to Sister Mary Lamberta. At two o'clock Father's spiritual instruction was scheduled. In pleasant weather this was held on the lovely grounds of the Academy. But many a Saturday no Father appeared. He often called at the last minute and said he could not make it. Sometimes it was because the patients at the hospital needed him. He had, as always, too many irons in the fire.

The third class was concerned with the teaching of religion to children.

Whether Sister Lamberta had this course also is not clear, but it is likely because she and Mother Aquinata were the two Sisters who were involved in the whole program.

The classes continued throughout the winter. The "subjects" or "probationers," as Father Sigstein referred to them, came and went. Some turned out to be a disappointment to Father and he himself advised them not to return. Others lost interest.

In spite of this, John was giving glowing accounts of things to Bishop Wehrle and others. He wrote of the splendid young women who signified their intention of joining the Society and were attending classes in preparation for their work in the mission field. This was always characteristic of Father Sigstein. He suffered many reverses and there were times when someone else would have given up completely. Yet he was able to paint a rosy picture that was probably a picture of the way he wished things were! Surely he did not mean to deceive. He was, in many ways, an optimist and was always convinced that better times were just around the corner.

This attitude seemed to be natural to him, but most likely it was a result of his conviction that what he was doing was God's Will and a work dear to Our Lord and his Blessed Mother. They would not abandon him, no matter how black the picture sometimes looked.

To his intimate priest friends, especially to Francis Collins, he gave a more realistic description of what was going on. Francis knew personally some of the women who were coming for instructions, and to him John could write freely about his problems. A serious disagreement had evidently arisen between two of the women. One "showed a proper Christian spirit of reconciliation." The other, much to John's surprise and disappointment, refused to be reconciled. Another "makes no determined effort for spiritual advancement, so, much as I regret it, I shall have to ask her to go her way." Still another is unable to come to any definite decision. "Two of the good probationers have been compelled to give up their studies and preparation for the time being. Both are on the verge of a complete nervous breakdown." As it turned out, none of these women persevered; only Julia and Marie.

John asks his friend Francis Collins to remember all these young women in his Masses. But in spite of the woes, he is at peace and tells Collins: "It has pleased our most dear Lord and our most Blessed Mother to send us other crosses as a proof of their love for the Society and its work. May they be forever praised and may the adorable Will of God be blessed for evermore!"[6]

And then in May of this same year (1922) there came to the Society the first out-of-town member, Marie Bodin of Sour Lake, Texas, a parishioner of Father Collins'.

Marie Bodin was born in Vacherie, Louisiana, November 22, 1891. Her family moved to Sour Lake in 1915. Because Marie was bi-lingual, speaking both English and French, it was easier for her to learn Spanish than it was for Julia

39

or Marie Benes. She quickly picked up the fundamentals in classes at the Academy and then Father Sigstein sent her to the Berlitz School of Languages in downtown Chicago.

Even though Marie Bodin was almost thirty-one years old at the time, it must have taken some courage for her to leave a very small town in Texas and go north to join a religious community whose future was rather nebulous, to say the least. The Sisters who knew her recall her special devotion to the rosary of Our Blessed Mother. She was one of the first of the pioneers to die and it is significant that her death took place on the feast of the Holy Rosary, October 7, 1939.

Notes to Chapter IV

1. Bruno Hagspiel, a Divine Word Missionary, was one of John Sigstein's lifelong friends. He died in 1961 at the age of seventy-five, having been a priest fifty-one years. Father Bruno was well known throughout the United States especially for his retreats to priests and religious. He was author of many books and pamphlets published by the Divine Word Missionaries.

2. Letter to Bishop Wehrle January 14, 1919. Victory Noll Archives.

3. See St. Louis Mary DeMontfort, *True Devotion to the Blessed Virgin Mary,* tr. Frederick William Faber, revised edition, (Montfort Fathers' Publications, Bay Shore, N.Y., 1950).

4. There were *three* Jesuits by the name of Spirig who had some connection with Holy Family Parish, Chicago: Alfred J. (d. 1947), John B. (d. 1923), and Robert F. (d. 1937). The Father Spirig referred to here was probably Robert who, for a number of years, was superior of St. Ignatius College, Chicago. See Thomas M. Mulkerins, S.J., *Holy Family Parish, Chicago, Priests and People* (Universal Press, Chicago, 1923).

5. George Mundelein, consecrated Auxiliary Bishop of Brooklyn 1909, was promoted to the See of Chicago December 9, 1915. Nine years later he was made a Cardinal. He died October 2, 1939.

6. Letter to Martin F. Collins June 6, 1922. Victory Noll Archives.

5

Providence

ESIDES RECRUITING MEMBERS and training them, Father Sigstein was occupied with many other things that were necessary for the founding of the Society. There was the all-important matter of funds. There was the equally important matter of finding a permanent location for a novitiate or training school. John knew that as time went on, it would not be possible nor practical for candidates to live at the Academy of Our Lady. This would be asking too much of the hospitable School Sisters of Notre Dame.

The decision would soon have to be made as to the best place for the location of the first mission center. And there would have to be some publicity if the Society were to grow. This was a delicate matter because of the situation in the Archdiocese of Chicago.

Though John Sigstein had early confided his plan to Bishop Wehrle of Bismarck and had sought his advice; though he even referred to the proposed community as "the Society Bishop Wehrle and I are founding," the Benedictine never looked upon himself as a co-founder. It was John Sigstein's work. He was completely in sympathy with it, but from his correspondence it is evident that he thought the Catechists would be more effective in the Southwest and in the Far West. Like so many other Bishops in the United States, Bishop Wehrle was a "Catholic school man." From the very beginning of their friendship it was understood that the Bishop would be given Catechists when they were available. However, in April 1919, Bishop Wehrle called on Father Sigstein at St. Bernard's Hospital and asked to have a band of Catechists sent out to take charge of a poor district in his Diocese of Bismarck. He wanted them to open a parochial school. John informed him that this could not be done. It was not the purpose of the Society to staff parochial schools.

In a letter to Father Sigstein dated October 27, 1919, Bishop Wehrle wrote:

I should think the best place for the work of the Catechists is Texas and New Mexico. There are large stretches of country with an entirely Catholic population and the school conditions so poor that in a great many places they do not have even public schools. In Washington I had a talk about this with the Archbishop of Santa Fe and also with the Jesuit Bishop in Texas. This moment I cannot think of his name and have no Directory with me to consult. Both say these people have the faith and are very willing. Both have the deepest conviction that religious instruction is all these people need to preserve them in the faith and to make really good Catholics of them.

I wish you would correspond with the Archbishop of Santa Fe. He is one of the nicest men and has apostolic zeal. In my diocese, for several reasons, the school laws of the state being the strongest of them, we can use such teachers during the time when public schools are in session, and only if they teach the full school curriculum during the time when the public schools are open. If you have two Catechists who can teach all branches of the public school program, I will see to it that they will have a school next fall.

The Jesuit whose name eluded Bishop Wehrle was Anthony J. Schuler who had been Bishop of El Paso since 1915. The meeting of the United States Bishops in Washington in the fall of 1919 was the first such meeting Archbishop Daeger attended. In May of that year he had succeeded Archbishop Pitaval who had resigned from the See of Santa Fe three months previously. At the meeting Archbishop Daeger made an impassioned plea for help for his extremely poor Archdiocese which included the entire state of New Mexico and part of Arizona besides. He needed funds and personnel. His simplicity, his personal poverty, and his winning personality made a tremendous impression on his fellow bishops. He spoke with conviction, having spent all his priestly life in New Mexico.

Father Sigstein lost no time in getting in touch with Archbishop Daeger. The Archbishop was already enthusiastic about the proposed Society of Missionary Catechists and was anxious to meet John and talk things over with him. The flu epidemic was at its height in the winter of 1919 and the earliest date the two men could arrange for a meeting was in February of the following year.

John had very little money for train fare, but Congressman John Rainey secured a pass for him to San Antonio, Texas, and return. He managed to pay the usual clergy rate for the rest of the trip. His first stop, February 20, 1920, was in San Antonio where he had an appointment with Bishop Drossaerts who listened with interest to Father Sigstein's plans and promised to sponsor the Society in his diocese. He was anxious to have a band of Catechists as soon as they were ready.

From San Antonio John went to El Paso where he called on Bishop Schuler.

He too wanted to secure the services of the Catechists for his very poor diocese. It was not until 1935, however, that the first convent in El Paso was opened. Bishop Drossaerts waited still longer — until 1944.[1]

On February 22 Father Sigstein reached Santa Fe where he was welcomed heartily by Archbishop Daeger. The two were kindred spirits. Together with his chancellor, Bernard Espelage, O.F.M., the Archbishop examined in detail the plans for the Society.[2] He asked for Catechists immediately, but John had to inform him that they were not yet ready, not yet sufficiently prepared. They did decide tentatively that Wagon Mound would be the best place to begin operations in New Mexico when the Society was actually established.

Michael Dumarest was pastor of Wagon Mound and its missions. He had heard about the proposed Society and knew what a boon it would be for his poor district. He would place the old public school building in Wagon Mound at the disposal of the Catechists. The Archbishop concurred with this plan and suggested that Father Sigstein visit Father Dumarest and discuss the matter with him. Accordingly, the following day John went by train to Las Vegas, New Mexico, where Dumarest met him in his Model T and drove him to Watrous and to Wagon Mound.

Father Dumarest had come to the Southwest from his native France in 1898. He had proved himself a zealous, self-sacrificing missionary and could offer John Sigstein valuable advice. He was already convinced of the worthwhile contribution the Catechists could make to the Church in New Mexico. He offered the Society a residence that had been the former home of the Jesuits, plus five acres of land in Tiptonville, a mile and a half from Watrous. John declined the offer. He was not interested in acquiring property. He made no immediate commitment but seemed to favor having the first band of Catechists go to Wagon Mound where they would work under Father Dumarest's direction.

On his way back to Chicago John Sigstein stopped at Lillis, Kansas, to visit his friend, Anthony Blaufuss. Together they went over the plans for the Society, refining and re-defining the character of the work as it would be carried out in New Mexico.

As early as June 1919, John Sigstein wrote to his cousin, Baldus Biegel, then pastor in Elwood, Indiana, about a "proposition relative to the future foundation of our Society of Missionary Catechists." He was referring to having the Society incorporated under the laws of the State of Indiana in order to "insure perpetuity of the work and its financial upkeep . . . so that, should anything happen to me, the work would go on just the same, for I believe that our good Mother will raise up the proper agents and means for carrying on this work so dear to her Immaculate Heart." He would like to have Father Baldus and his brother, Father Peter, to be officers of the Corporation.

Then John outlined again the plan for establishing burses, the interest of which would maintain the Catechists. At this time a completed burse was to be $5000. A year or two later Father set the goal at $6000. In his usual optimistic way, he gave his cousin a glowing account of pledges already made, of moneys alreay collected. A "charitably disposed woman of means" had promised to donate "the entire amount for the first burse as soon as she disposed of some property in Canada." (The promise was not fulfilled.) This burse would be named in honor of Our Lady of Victory. Toward the second burse, in honor of the Sacred Heart, Father had collected $300 and hoped to be able to obtain more during the summer. "So you see, a good beginning has been made."

Perhaps John thought of being incorporated in Indiana because his two priest cousins were in the Diocese of Fort Wayne. His mother's closest relatives lived in and around Crown Point. Father Sigstein must have mentioned this to his friend Bishop Wehrle also, for in May 1920, the Bishop wrote him that he would be glad to be a member of the Corporation.

After Father Sigstein's visit to New Mexico and arrangements with Archbishop Daeger there, it was obvious that the best plan for incorporation would be in that State. John began negotiations with this in mind. Finally on July 8, 1921, the first meeting of the newly formed Corporation of the Society of Missionary Catechists of Our Blessed Lady of Victory of America was held in Santa Fe. Present were: Most Rev. Albert T. Daeger, O.F.M., Honorary President; Rev. John J. Sigstein, President; Rev. Michael Dumarest, Vice President and Financial Secretary; Rev. Anthony J. Blaufuss, Recording Secretary; Rev. Daniel J. Hurley, Director. The purpose of the Corporation would be "the training and equipping of Catechists to be of service in the cause of religion in the sparsely settled districts of our country." The Society now had "power to receive and distribute bequests and donations according to its charter."

Previously Albert Daeger had arranged with John Sigstein to provide a "motherhouse" for the Society in Santa Fe. This was a humble little house near the Archbishop's own residence, close to the Cathedral of St. Francis of Assisi.

So it was that the Society of Missionary Catechists was now incorporated in New Mexico though it had only two prospective members in Chicago; that is, two women who gave every indication of persevering in their determination to become Catechists: Julia Doyle and Marie Benes. It was this same month, July 1921, that Marie took up residence at the Academy of Our Lady. Julia lived in her own apartment, worked every day, and attended the instructions at Longwood when they were held.

In 1920 Father Sigstein had arranged for his old friend Will Frey to go to New Mexico as the "advance guard" and his own "agent" of the Society there. Will lived for a time in Wagon Mound; later, in Santa Fe. Father had never given up the idea of a Mission Society of Priests and Brothers with Will as one of the initial members. Too, John worried about his friend's health. He was plagued with respiratory trouble and Father felt that the dry air of New Mexico would be beneficial for him.

With the establishment of a base for operations John Sigstein sent out letters and articles to publicize the Society of Missionary Catechists. He was careful, however, not to use his own name in any reference to the work. He outlined the purpose of the Society in a lengthy article which he sent to *Our Sunday Visitor* and other Catholic papers. Then he had reprints made with the title "Reprint of Article Published in *Our Sunday Visitor* and Other Leading Catholic Papers, September 18, 1921."

After reading the minute description of the work of the Catechists, the reader no doubt thought at least a dozen or more women were already engaged in their catechetical apostolate and that others were in training in the building provided for them by the Most Rev. Albert T. Daeger, Archbishop of Santa Fe. The article states: "It is here that the Catechists fit themselves by a special course of training to enter upon their truly apostolic labors for the salvation of thousands upon thousands of souls in the needy, scattered missions of New Mexico."

During this same month of September John Sigstein was writing to his old friend David Smith in Mississippi telling him that "the beginning is very simple and humble. We have only five subjects for our Society. We can scarcely take more to begin with but these five young women are of the highest type." Then he explains that "for the past two years they have been making a prayerful and painstaking preparation for their life work," and he describes the particular part of their training that they had just finished: "Red Cross work which will enable them to go into the homes of the poor and assist them in a temporal way as well as spiritually."

Their chief work, however, would be "to give the children a thorough training in their religious duties. This will mean more than simple catechetical instructions. For this reason the Catechists will specialize in this kind of work. They will never teach any secular branches."

The next part of his letter is an explanation of the burse plan to raise funds for the Society, for the Catechists were to receive no remuneration whatsoever from the poor among whom they would labor. John told David that he could not make any public appeal in Chicago for either funds or workers. "His Grace Archbishop Mundelein, although he has not disapproved of this work, would not care to have me make a public appeal in the Archdiocese. Therefore, in conjunction with the Archbishop of Santa Fe, we are directing practically all the work from our Mother House in Santa Fe. I trust you will not mention my name to anyone in connection with the work."

Then Father Sigstein suggests that "since you are so interested in this work, you may be able to do much good in its behalf." And he asks David to write a letter to Father Noll, Editor of *Our Sunday Visitor,* and "tell him you read the article in his paper and that it is your understanding that the Catechists will need the support of charitably disposed Catholics in the United States." Father added that such an article "would take well in *Our Sunday Visitor* especially if you give it a personal touch by recounting some of your missionary experiences as a catechist in Mississippi and West Virginia."

Whether Mr. Smith followed John's suggestion is not known, but meanwhile John F. Noll, Founder and Editor of *Our Sunday Visitor,* and pastor of St. Mary's Church, Huntington, was observing the beginning of the new Society and gave evidence of being interested in it. He visited Father Sigstein twice at St. Bernard's Hospital in Chicago after John had approached him in Huntington to ask him to publish an article in his paper.

Though Father Sigstein was happy to have an official residence for the Society in Santa Fe, at the same time it had its drawbacks. New Mexico was far from Chicago and it was to the Midwest and East that John knew he had to turn for both money and recruits. The first attempt at publicity by mail was not very successful. This was partly John's own fault because of his insistence on anonymity. The only address given on a leaflet or brochure was P.O. Box 334, Santa Fe, New Mexico. In those days, even as now, not many people would be inclined to reply to such a vague address. Any mail that was directed to Santa Fe was sent to Father Sigstein by Mr. Frey. Under the best of conditions John Sigstein seldom answered mail promptly, but this sending back and forth caused further delay.

As we have seen, John had some connections in the Diocese of Fort Wayne which then included all of northern Indiana. His two cousins were influential pastors in the diocese. He had relatives in Crown Point. Many parishes in the city of Fort Wayne and environs had been most generous in contributing vestments and sacred vessels to the Missionary Helpers for poor missions. Father Sigstein also knew a priest, John DeVille, whose special work was with Italians and Mexicans in the Gary area.

It was not surprising, then, that John looked to Indiana for the location of some type of training center for his Catechists. Through Father DeVille, he found it in Gary, Indiana. Gary was close enough to Chicago to make it an ideal choice. In Gary, East Chicago, Indiana Harbor, and other towns there were thousands of Mexicans who had come north to work in the steel mills. Most of them were desperately poor and were being exploited. The Catechists could do much good here and it would be a wonderful field for those in training. They could get the practical experience they needed before going to the Southwest.

Father Sigstein talked this over with John DeVille who in turn promised to discuss it with his Bishop, Herman Joseph Alerding, Bishop of Fort Wayne since 1900. It would seem that Monsignor Noll also spoke favorably of the plan to Bishop Alerding and helped influence him in giving his permission.

A Settlement House, eventually known as the Judge Gary-Bishop Alerding Settlement House, was to be erected in Gary and Father DeVille would be the director. He had been working for some time among the many foreign-born Catholics in Gary, especially Mexicans and Italians. Father Deville offered John Sigstein an apartment in the Settlement House for his young community. It was expected that the apartment would be ready for occupancy at least by Easter 1923, but it was not until early in February 1924, that it was finally ready to receive the Catechists.

Meanwhile, other things were happening, events that were evidence of God's wonderful providence.

In 1923 John Noll celebrated the silver jubilee of his ordination to the priesthood. His parishioners at St. Mary's, Huntington, Indiana, collected a generous gift of money with the suggestion that their pastor use it for a trip to Europe, more specifically to Rome and Lourdes. But Monsignor Noll said he was too busy at this time to take the trip and he arranged for his associate editor and assistant pastor, Robert E. Kelly, to go in his place. He himself would take a little time off and go to Hot Springs, Arkansas, for a vacation.

The Monsignor carried out these plans without in any way offending his parishioners. He was like that, and as a priest and bishop, it proved a wonderful asset. He could write forcefully and speak out fearlessly, but without being harsh, without hurting feelings. Appropriate indeed was the subtitle he gave his weekly paper, calling it *The Harmonizer*. It was indicative of the man himself, a follower of Jesus who "did not crush the bruised reed nor quench the smoking flax."

Indeed the Monsignor was a busy man. Besides editing *Our Sunday Visitor* which could boast at that time of a readership of 2,000,000, he published also *The Parish Monthly,* a 32-page booklet to which local notes could be added; and a special magazine for priests called *The Acolyte* which, as someone on the staff pointed out, was eventually "ordained," and became known (as it is today) as *The Priest*. As if these publications were not enough to keep Monsignor Noll busy, there was a steady flow of pamphlets, leaflets, and books coming from his prolific pen. All had as their purpose an explanation of the teachings of the Catholic Church. His style was simple, readable, and persuasive.

Speaking engagements kept him busy too. He was often invited to address both local and national groups, something he always enjoyed doing. Certainly he needed a vacation and no doubt the week or two at St. Joseph's Infirmary in Hot Springs would be more restful than sight-seeing in Europe.[3]

The Sunday after his arrival in Hot Springs Monsignor Noll was invited to celebrate Mass and preach in one of the local churches. After Mass a layman came into the sacristy and introduced himself as Peter O'Donnell of Long Beach, California. Both men were delighted at the meeting, for they had been in contact for some time without having had the opportunity to meet each other personally.

O'Donnell was active in the Catholic Truth Society and in the Catholic Instruction League. Together with some friends he had helped to establish these organizations in southern California. In carrying out this apostolate he had looked to *Our Sunday Visitor* Publishing Company for literature and this had brought him into contact with Monsignor Noll. Mr. O'Donnell told the Monsignor that he was most anxious to talk to him. They arranged for a meeting that afternoon at St. Joseph's Infirmary.

Peter O'Donnell was a former Chicago police sergeant. When he retired from the force in 1918 he and his wife sold their home and moved to Long Beach, California. They had no family nor immediate relatives. Mrs. O'Donnell's health was failing and Peter was anxious to go west where the winters would be less rigorous than in Illinois. Long Beach was at this time a very small city of 18,000 but with the discovery of oil in the area, it gave promise of becoming a boom town.

Shortly after arriving in Long Beach Mr. O'Donnell invested $3200 in land. Only after the purchase was completed did he discover that his lots were often under water. He and Julia feared they had lost their money. They prayed to Our Blessed Mother and promised that if the investment should be successful they would give half the sum to a worthy charity. Within a short time the city of Long Beach bought the property for $32,000. Subsequent investments yielded profits and the O'Donnells were anxious to keep their promise to the Mother of God.

In traveling about the area, especially in Los Angeles and in Long Beach where he distributed thousands of copies of *Our Sunday Visitor* pamphlets, Peter O'Donnell had observed how many poor Mexican children were attending public schools, when they went to school at all. He knew that these children were not given the religious instruction that they needed to preserve their Catholic heritage and he worried about it. Now with the $25,000 he wished to make available for a charitable work, perhaps he could do something constructive about it. Together with a zealous Catholic friend of his, a prominent judge in the city of Los Angeles, he made an appointment to see Bishop Cantwell.[4]

Peter told his story to the Bishop and said he wanted the money to be used for the religious instruction of poor Mexican children. Cantwell listened sympathetically but replied that he had no one to do this work. Mr. O'Donnell asked, "Don't you have priests who can be entrusted with a work so necessary?"

The Bishop said he had none available. Then Peter asked about Sisters. "Weren't there some Sisters who could give religious instructions to Mexican children?"

Again the Bishop had to say there were none. A number of religious orders were at work in the diocese but most of them were teaching in parochial schools. None could devote themselves to the type of work Peter O'Donnell had in mind. The Bishop asked Peter to give him permission to use the money for some other worthy cause, but he could not be persuaded to do this. It was soon after this interview that Peter and Julia O'Donnell made the trip to Hot Springs and there met Monsignor Noll.

Peter felt that this meeting was providential and that the Monsignor, who was knowledgeable in many areas, would be able to advise him how to help in some way to provide religious education for poor Mexican children. So it was that he confided his story, adding how discouraged he was because he had not found a way to fulfill his promise to Our Blessed Mother.

Monsignor Noll listened attentively and then told Mr. O'Donnell that in Chicago there was a priest who had just organized a community of young women whose purpose was to do the very work that he had in mind. At this time (it was May 1923) there were two members of the Society at work in New Mexico and three more in training at the Academy of Our Lady in Chicago. *Our Sunday Visitor* planned to back the new society through publicity in the paper. In fact, for many years, the *Visitor* (a non-profit institution) had been supporting twelve schools along the Mexican Border and had contributed to Maryknoll and other missionary activities. The Founding Editor and his board of trustees had just about decided to concentrate their efforts on the Society of Missionary Catechists and help provide a much-needed training school for the members. There was property already available for this at Huntington, Indiana, but *OSV* could not see the project through without outside help.

"Here is your chance," said the Monsignor to O'Donnell, "to use your $25,000."

This fitted in exactly with Peter's own idea. In his enthusiasm he told Monsignor Noll that he owned some ocean-front property that he would sell and contribute this money also. He was sure he could get a good price for it from the city of Long Beach. Not long afterward he did sell it for $90,000 and turned the amount over to *Our Sunday Visitor* for a motherhouse and novitiate for the Society of Missionary Catechists.[5]

Meanwhile, in Chicago, Father Sigstein was praying fervently to Our Lady of Victory for the financial help his Society needed so badly. He and the Catechists were making a novena for this intention, and John had invited other interested persons to join him in asking Mary's intercession. Toward the end of the novena he received a call from John F. Noll saying he would like to see him on May 25. It was the day after the feast of Our Lady of Victory.

The meeting took place at St. Bernard's Hospital. Monsignor Noll told Father Sigstein that he had just returned from Hot Springs, Arkansas, where he had met a fine Catholic gentlemen and his wife who were definitely interested in giving financial help to the Catechists. He added that with this substantial sum *Our Sunday Visitor* was in a position to sponsor the erection of a motherhouse in Huntington. The rest of the necessary funds would be solicited from the readers of the weekly paper.

Father Sigstein, deeply grateful to Monsignor Noll and above all, to Our Blessed Mother who had not failed him, said he would place the whole matter before the Board of Directors of the Society and then give a definitive answer to the Monsignor.

Most persons in John Sigstein's position would have picked up the phone right then and there, told his confreres about Monsignor Noll's wonderful offer and urged them to acquiesce without delay. But not Father Sigstein. That was not the way he operated. He must take time to pray fervently over the matter. He must consult his spiritual director.

Before accepting *Our Sunday Visitor's* proposal John wanted to be very sure that there would be no outside interference in the direction of the Society of Missionary Catechists. He had spent much time and energy, had suffered many a heartache to get the Society this far. He was adamant that it would never be turned aside from its original purpose, no matter how well-intentioned its benefactors might be. To put it rather crudely, he would accept the magnificent offer of Monsignor Noll and *Our Sunday Visitor* only if there were "no strings attached."

Someone less generous, less magnanimous than Monsignor Noll might have been tempted to drop the whole matter when John Sigstein delayed in giving him an answer. The Monsignor, however, was not only big physically; he was big in every way. He was a patient man and though he was so different from John Sigstein in many ways, he understood him.

John finally gave his answer, and toward the end of July 1923, the Monsignor was writing to him to tell him to confer with a good architect in Chicago and have him draw up plans for a building to accommodate about fifty persons. He recommended Mr. Steinbach of Worthman and Steinbach and suggested that "since you are to work among the Spanish people, the building be built in mission style."

It was about this time that Mr. and Mrs. O'Donnell returned to Chicago for a visit and Father Sigstein had the opportunity to meet them. Immediately John and Peter were attracted to each other. Their common bonds were their deep love for Our Blessed Mother and their zeal for the Church. It was but natural then that Peter would confide to Father something that he had not told before to anyone but his wife. He had not mentioned it to Bishop Cantwell nor to Monsignor Noll, but it was the reason he felt such an urgency to fulfill his promise to Mary.

Peter told Father Sigstein that not long after he and Julia had gone to California he was resting one afternoon when he became aware of a beautiful scene spread out before him. Walking along the seashore was a woman of marvelous grace and beauty. She smiled graciously and continued her walk. She seemed to fix her eyes on a certain portion of land, water-covered land that Peter recognized as his. The woman dropped a card on the shore and disappeared. Peter tried hard to read what was on the card and was saddened that the writing was not discernible. In his humility he attributed this to unworthiness on his part. It was soon after this incident that the city of Long Beach bought the O'Donnell property.

Peter had still another vision. This time it was evening. He had retired and was saying his rosary as was his custom. All at once he saw a bright light and then Our Blessed Mother carrying in her arms the Child Jesus. With them were two women who looked like religious. They did not wear the traditional black of most Sisters, however. They were dressed in navy blue. Peter understood that these religious were to do the work for which he had promised his money. Later, when he met the Catechists, he recognized them as the Sisters in his vision.

Whenever Father Sigstein told this story he would add that no one who ever met Peter O'Donnell would call him a visionary as most people conceived a visionary in those days. Father described him as being, at this time, a "hard-headed business man," one-time police sergeant.

Our Blessed Mother, Peter also recognized later, was depicted for him as Our Lady of Victory or Mary, Help of Christians. This title was given to Mary by St. Pius V after the Battle of Lepanto in 1571 when Don Juan of Austria and his men, though far-outnumbered by the Turks, routed the enemy and saved Europe to Christianity.

Devotion to Mary under the title of Our Lady of Victory is popular in many parts of the world. Perhaps the best known churches dedicated to her are *Notre Dame des Victoires* in Paris, and, in our country, Our Lady of Victory Basilica in Lackawanna, New York, a shrine made famous by the late Father Baker.

When the Victory Noll Sisters celebrated the golden jubilee of their foundation in 1972, a dear friend of the community, a Lutheran minister, began his congratulatory letter with the words: "Dear Ladies of Victory." Though he might have been unaware of the significance of the title of the Congregation — Our Lady of Victory Missionary Sisters — his manner of address was appropriate. Throughout their fifty years of existence there were victories, some large, some small, but the "ladies" well knew that they could not claim them as resulting from any work of their own. They attributed them to Mary, their Mother, their Patroness, and Intercessor, Our Blessed Lady of Victory.

Notes to Chapter V

1. San Antonio was raised to metropolitan rank in 1926, Arthur J. Drossaerts becoming its first Archbishop.

2. Father Bernard Espelage became the first Bishop of Gallup, New Mexico, in 1940. He resigned the See in 1969 and died two years later.

3. In 1988 the Sisters of Mercy will celebrate the centenary of their mission in Hot Springs, Arkansas. What was originally known as St. Joseph's Infirmary expanded into St. Joseph's Hospital (the third such), and now St. Joseph's Mercy Medical Center.

4. In 1917 John J. Cantwell became Bishop of what was then the Diocese of Monterey-Los Angeles. To meet the rapid expansion of California, the northern half of the State became the Diocese of Monterey-Fresno in 1932 and the southern area, Los Angeles-San Diego with Bishop Cantwell as Ordinary. Los Angeles was made an Archdiocese in 1936, and San Diego, a Diocese in its own right. Archbishop Cantwell died October 30, 1947.

5. Peter O'Donnell was born in County Mayo, Ireland, November 19, 1864. He and his wife Julia emigrated to the United States in 1886 and settled in Chicago. In 1918 they went to Long Beach, California. Father Sigstein and the Catechists were anxious to have their benefactors, the O'Donnells, visit Victory Noll, but they never saw it. Peter did visit the site in 1923 but was unable to return after the building was erected. In 1924 he wrote Father Sigstein that he and his wife hoped to stop in Huntington on their way to Ireland or on their return. For various reasons this plan, as well as subsequent ones, never materialized. In a letter to Bishop Noll July 30, 1938 (and preserved in the Victory Noll Archives), Peter wrote: "Thank God my health is so much improved that I may see you before you start to California, as I am anxious to see that dear Noll. I often think of the day we walked in front of it and suggested its construction and we thank God we were able to help even a little bit." Mr. O'Donnell was not able to make the trip. He died in Los Angeles on December 4 of that same year, 1938.

6

New Mexico

THE FEAST OF OUR LADY OF VICTORY, May 24, 1922, was the date set for vow day for the first band of Catechists and for their departure for the missions. However, the whole first part of that year was beset with various difficulties, real heartaches for Father Sigstein. The departure date had to be deferred.

In his good friend Anthony Blaufuss, John found a wise and sympathetic correspondent. Back and forth went the letters between Chicago and Baileyville, Kansas (where Anthony was now pastor), explaining the difficulties and delay. In January John had had a "sick spell." The next month it was the flu that put him to bed. There were financial troubles. Persons who said they would give money for burses for the Catechists, provided they sell their property, went back on their promises. One woman "promised a very substantial donation on condition that she would sell a whole block of city lots worth about $30,000. I got all kinds of prayers for her. Sometime ago she sold the lots but told me nothing of the sale until the other day. Then she did not even make mention of the fact that she intended fulfilling her promise, and so it goes with others."[1]

Of still greater concern was the "turning back" of several young women who had been attending instructions at the Academy. Anthony wisely told his friend that it was well these women backed out when they did. Obviously they did not have the qualities of Julia Doyle and Marie Benes.

One case caused the two priests much concern, however. Though this particular young woman had not had training over a very long period, it was agreed that she would accompany Julia and Marie to New Mexico anyway. She would be under their direction in the missions. John thought it would be

53

better to have three in the first band instead of just two, and the young woman would profit from the in-service training. Besides, the priest, always sensitive to the physical needs of others, thought that the climate of the Southwest would be beneficial to this young woman since she was somewhat frail of health.

At the last minute she refused to go unless she could make vows and have the same status as Julia and Marie. When Father Sigstein would not acquiesce to this, she threatened to go to Archbishop Mundelein and denounce him for deceiving her. Both Anthony and John feared the consequences. Anthony wrote his friend:

> I trust Miss ———— will enter into herself and recognize the injustice of her obstinacy. She is manifesting a bad disposition for a Catechist. God, I believe, is protecting the Society in thus permitting the various characters to reveal themselves. If she really goes to see the Archbishop, it may be a good idea to put Bishop Hoban wise, for the Archbishop may even forbid you to have anything to do with the Society, which would be very bad just now. Our Blessed Mother will plead with the Sacred Heart to bring all things out right.[2]

As if this were not enough, almost on the eve of the Catechists' departure for Santa Fe, a letter came to John Sigstein from Archbishop Daeger saying that the Catechists' first field of operation would be among the Indians, "probably in the Indian Pueblo of Zia." Daeger implied that he had given his approval to this arrangement that had been worked out between Father Dumarest and the Franciscan priests in charge of the Pueblos.

This was a real blow to Father Sigstein. It was very difficult for him to understand why the Archbishop would do this when it had been assured him that the first mission center would be in Watrous (a mission from Wagon Mound) under Michael Dumarest's direction. He had talked to Father Dumarest only a short time before the Archbishop's letter arrived and had made what he thought were final arrangements with him. The Board of Directors of the Corporation had met in Kansas City and Dumarest had acted as proxy for the Archbishop who was unable to leave Santa Fe at this time.

John poured out his heart in a letter to Anthony dated July 24, 1922: "I want to ask you to pray especially hard for me and for the Society during the next two weeks. It has pleased our most dear Lord and our Most Beloved Mother to send us some crosses lately. And just now, it seems that we are on our way to Calvary, so darkly do things loom up when there is question of our making our first foundation."

The date for leaving Chicago was finally set for August 3. The Catechists would arrive in Santa Fe two days later, the feast of Our Lady of the Snow. Father Sigstein had hoped to accompany the two women to their first field of labor but in this, as in so many other things, he was disappointed. Archbishop Mundelein would not grant him the leave of absence he asked for, much less release him from the Archdiocese for full time work with the Society.

Father Blaufuss agreed to take his friend's place and travel to New Mexico to give a retreat to the two Catechists. He had also planned to accompany them to their mission center at Watrous, but even this was not possible. Father Anthony was pastor of Baileyville, a small parish in eastern Kansas. It was difficult to arrange for a priest to replace him for even a short time.

The actual departure of the Catechists from Chicago was very quiet, almost an anti-climax after the long months and years of planning. Julia worked right up to the last minute and joined Marie at the Academy of Our Lady the night before the departure ceremonies. Very early the next morning Father Sigstein celebrated Mass. Besides the two Missionary Catechists there were present only Marie Bodin, Mother Aquinata, and several other Notre Dame Sisters. Julia and Marie received the sacrament of penance before Mass and pronounced their simple private vows of poverty, chastity, and obedience in the confessional. It was not until three years later that the Catechists made their vows publicly in chapel or church.

The vow formula was very simple. A copy of it, headed "Private Simple Vows of Obedience, Chastity, and Poverty (to be made privately before Confessor)" reads: "I N.N., promise to Our Lord Jesus Christ, through Mary His Most Blessed Mother, Obedience, Chastity, and Poverty in the Society of Missionary Catechists of Our Blessed Lady of Victory for a period of one year."

When the Catechists arrived in Santa Fe they made a Pledge of Stability in the presence of Archbishop Daeger. Later the two formulas were combined. Eventually, the Pledge was dropped. The Pledge, as made by Julia Doyle and Marie Benes and by their immediate successors, was worded:

> For the greater glory of God and in honor of Our Blessed Lady of Victory, I, N.N., pledge myself for a period of one year to consecrate my life as a member of the Society of Missionary Catechists of Our Blessed Lady of Victory to the work of imparting religious instruction and of giving a Christian training to the poor children in scattered missions according to the Constitution and Rules of the same Society. Furthermore, as a member of the Society, I pledge myself, of my own free will, to go wherever sent and to persevere in the faithful performance of all my duties, and in the exact observance of the Constitution and Rules of this Society in absolute obedience to the Reverend Spiritual Director of the Society. In the Name of the Father, and of the Son, and of the Holy Ghost. Amen.

During the Departure Mass at the Academy of Our Lady in Chicago Julia and Marie renewed their Act of Consecration to Mary according to the practice of the True Devotion of Louis Grignion de Montfort. Then, after the religious services, the little group — Father Sigstein, the Catechists, and several School Sisters of Notre Dame — had breakfast together in the Academy dining room. John left for his duties at St. Bernard's Hospital, and Julia for her home. She would board the Santa Fe train that evening at the Dearborn Station while Marie would leave from Englewood, the station closest to Longwood Academy. A streetcar strike was in effect at the time and transportation was difficult. That evening Marie Bodin and Sister Lamberta accompanied Marie Benes to the Englewood Station and put her on the nine-thirty train.[3]

At the morning ceremonies Julia and Marie wore their ordinary street clothes. Before they boarded the train they changed to their uniforms. There was very little about the uniform, however, to distinguish it from what other women were wearing. The design was simple, a contemporary dress that was common in 1922. They wore straw hats that were also in style at the time. Julia mentions later that they paid ten dollars for them. It was on the train trip that each sewed a simple little veil, dark blue with a white band.[4]

The medal of Our Lady of Victory which, suspended on a chain, would be the distinctive mark of the Missionary Catechist, was not finished until a few days after Julia and Marie left Chicago. Father had ordered the medals struck and was disappointed that they were not ready for the Catechists to receive when they made their vows. The medals reached New Mexico the following week, and Father Dumarest blessed them and presented them to the Catechists on August 12. At first the medals were worn on a short chain as one would wear a locket. Julia wrote John that it would be much better if the chain were longer. Father Sigstein agreed, and sent new chains from Chicago. Today the medal of Our Lady of Victory distinguishes a Victory Noll Sister. The chain on which it is worn is a reminder that she is bound by chains of love to Jesus and Mary, a mark of the "holy slavery" taught by St. Louis de Montfort.

The sterling silver medal is engraved on front and back. On the front is an image of Our Lady of Victory. Around the outer edge are the initials S.M.C. of O.B.L.V.; and beneath it, "Missionary Catechist." A laurel wreath is under the image of Our Blessed Mother. When the title of the Congregation was changed the lettering was changed accordingly. Since 1947 the lettering is O.L.V.M., and beneath it "Missionary Sister."

On the reverse side of the medal is a cross surmounted by a crown of thorns, and around the edge is the motto of the Congregation: *Omnia pro Jesu per Mariam* (All for Jesus through Mary). Until 1963 there was also inscribed the name of the burse assigned to the wearer of the medal, but this custom has since been discontinued.

John Sigstein, with his penchant for detail, had not left to chance anything about the type of dress the Catechists would wear. He had talked about this with some of his friends and with missionaries of long experience in New Mexico. Father Dumarest, the first pastor the Catechists would work with, strongly advocated gray material that would not show the dust. When his two sisters and niece (Mme. Berndin and her daughter Anne, and Clemence Dumarest) came in 1921 from France to make their home with their brother, he asked their opinion. Mlle. Dumarest was an artist and designer and nothing pleased her better than to draw up sketches of what the Catechists would wear. She did not confine herself to a uniform but included designs for a coat, a mantle, a veil, and two different styles of hats — a *toque* for winter and a *chapeau* for summer. She advocated the cape for summer, the coat for winter. The color was to be blue-gray such as the Daughters of Charity wore in France. The elaborate sketches are in the Victory Noll Archives with a laconic note in Julia's handwriting: "You might as well keep these. We do not need them."

The uniform (it was never referred to as a "habit") that was decided on was in keeping with the simplicity John Sigstein always insisted upon. Father Sigstein, Catechist Doyle, Catechist Benes, and Mrs. Louis (Rose) Owens visited Mandel's in Chicago and selected a style they all agreed on. Mrs. Owens, a beautiful woman of exquisite taste and refinement, was a Missionary Helper almost from the beginning. Through the years Mr. and Mrs. Owens remained faithful friends of Father Sigstein and the Society.

Perhaps the four of them — John, Rose, Julia, and Marie — visited other Chicago stores as well, but it was at Mandel's that they saw what they wanted. They did not buy the dress they liked. The color was not what they looked for. What the material was is not clear, but Julia, in describing it later, mentions a "silk sash." Mrs. Owens, an expert seamstress, made Julia's dress; and a friend of Marie's, a Mrs. Kestler, asked for the privilege of making hers. The material was navy blue serge.

In a sense, it just "happened" that the arrival of the Catechists in Santa Fe should be a feast of Mary, the feast of Our Lady of the Snow. Correspondence between Anthony Blaufuss and John Sigstein previous to the Catechists' departure from Chicago indicates that the date for their leaving depended on several things. First there was the matter of getting railroad passes for them. As late as July 25 Father Sigstein was still negotiating for the transportation.

When Archbishop Daeger's letter arrived suggesting the change of locale for the Catechists' work, John Sigstein asked Anthony to leave Kansas City Sunday, July 30. "As soon as you arrive Monday evening, see Dumarest and together with him you will get Archbishop Daeger to let the Catechists go to Watrous as per directions in my last letter to you. As soon as you have arranged the matter satisfactorily, please wire me *immediately*. By that time the Catechists will be ready to leave for Santa Fe."[5]

John was not going to let the Catechists leave unless the Archbishop acquiesced to the original plan, that they work in Watrous under the direction of Michael Dumarest.

At noon on August 1, the telegram arrived at St. Bernard's Hospital: "Everything OK — Anthony."[6] Accordingly the August 3 date was set for the vows, Mass, and leave taking.

The train was due to arrive in Santa Fe at 6 p.m. Saturday, August 5. Father Blaufuss boarded it at Wagon Mound and accompanied the women into the city. He told them later he did not recognize them immediately because he was looking for two women dressed in gray, not blue.

Nothing would have suited Julia and Marie better than to begin their retreat the morning after their arrival, but this was not to be. The three of them — Julia, Marie, and Anthony — were met at Lamy Junction (where passengers bound for Santa Fe are still discharged, there being no rail line into the city that gave the road its name) by Will Frey and taken to the house prepared for them near the Cathedral and not far from Archbishop Daeger's residence. Will had been acting as Father Sigstein's agent in New Mexico for two years, living first in Wagon Mound and then occupying bachelor's quarters in Santa Fe in what was for a short time quaintly referred to as the Catechists' motherhouse.

Will "had the potatoes cooking," Anthony reported later to his friend, and supper was ready shortly after the little group arrived. They had hardly begun to eat when the Archbishop came to give them a hearty welcome. He suggested that rather than begin their retreat the next morning, the Catechists rest a little and then see something of the city. Accordingly they spent Sunday seeing the Cathedral, Loretto Academy, St. Vincent's Hospital where Father Sigstein had a number of friends among the Sisters of Charity of Cincinnati who staffed it, and patients whom he had met on previous visits to New Mexico. They also visited the families of two other good friends of John's, Theodore Thoma and Charles Eckert. Both of these men had generously helped Father on a number of occasions and like so many others, they remained loyal friends of the Society throughout their lives.

That night Julia and Marie began their retreat. It closed Thursday and Father Anthony had to leave immediately for Kansas. He regretted that he could not accompany the Catechists to Watrous but he had gone there with Father Dumarest so he could report on the condition of the mission center in a letter to his friend John. Michael Dumarest would drive from Wagon Mound to Watrous and be there when the Catechists arrived.

Though Father Sigstein was prevented from actually being with the two Catechists as they began the foundation of the Society in New Mexico, he was with them in spirit, thinking of them each moment during the days ahead. On August 5 he sent a telegram that read: "Congratulations and blessings of O.B.L.V. Wire me immediately when the retreat ends and when you expect to leave for Watrous."

It was with relief and gratitude that John read his friend's detailed account of the beginnings in Santa Fe. He wired the faithful Anthony: "May Our Blessed Lady of Victory bless you and all your good work for her Society in New Mexico. Hope Archbishop OKs the Constitution and Rules."

This was another mission Anthony had been entrusted with — presenting the Constitution and Rules to Archbishop Daeger for his approval. Evidently this entailed no great difficulty though at this distance we might be surprised at the things the prelate singled out for comment. Father Blaufuss reported:

His Grace finished the reading of the Constitution and Rules the evening before we left. One suggestion he made was that you did not mention explicitly the practice of Spiritual Communion. This is just an oversight which the Catechists will practice as you taught them in your principles of the spiritual life. His Grace found no other objection. He, however, expressed his opinion repeatedly that you expect too much of the Catechists spiritually. I gave the principal reasons why Catechists must be strongly grounded in virtue, even more so than other Sisters. He seemed to catch the point and, I believe, on the whole he is rather pleased that they have received a good religious training. He was proud to introduce them to different priests that came. From the expressions of good will I heard from the different Fathers, all were sorry that you had sent out only two and not a carload.[7]

John Sigstein was to insist again and again on a deep spiritual life for the Catechists. They would be working principally in places where they would not have ready access to sacramental helps, could not consult spiritual directors but must put all their reliance and trust in their heavenly Father. In the course of time some found this too difficult and either separated themselves from the Congregation or asked for a change of mission where they would not be so isolated and thrown on their own.

That Father Sigstein had been able to draw up the Constitutions in time for Anthony to present them to Archbishop Daeger was a miracle of sorts. In a letter dated July 15, 1922, he told his friend he had not yet drafted them. What he wanted to put down in writing was still in his mind and on various scraps of paper, scrawled in pencil in his all but illegible handwriting.

Writing to Anthony in the middle of August John said that he had had to "crowd two months' work practically into a week's time and had it not been for the helpful service rendered me by my friend Ronald Fahey, I would never have succeeded in getting out the Constitution and Rules in time."

Fahey, a young man whom he had known since his years as curate at St. Pius' parish, had just begun his duties as public relations director for the Society of Missionary Catechists.

As might be expected, after the work and worries of the past months, John suffered nervous exhaustion and was "on the sick list for some days." However, he could also tell his friend of his happiness. "Calvary is past," he wrote, "and now we are on Mount Tabor. With St. Paul I can truly say that I was in labor until this Society could be born in Jesus and Mary. Now that it is a reality, I can see, as indeed I saw from the beginning, that Our Blessed Mother was shaping and directing all things for her own end. First the trials, which would not only serve to give the work a divine character, but would cause us, as it were, to throw ourselves into her maternal arms."[8]

Then John reminded Anthony of the important part he had taken in laying the foundation, and not only voiced his deep appreciation but took advantage of the opportunity (as he had done in the past and would continue to do) to point out to his friend that if he would join him in working full time for the Society, he would be able to reach out to thousands and tens of thousands of souls instead of continuing as a simple pastor of a small country parish.

In reply, Anthony told John that it had been a privilege to help with the foundation in New Mexico. "You give me altogether too high credit for the little I could do in Santa Fe. I felt all along that you should have been there to introduce the Catechists into their field of operation. How great a pleasure it would have been for you. No doubt God and Our Beloved required this sacrifice on your part as the price of more abundant blessings they wish to shower upon the Society."[9]

Then, practical as always, he reminded John that in the beginning there would be little revenue and the going would be rough. He advised him to start with a rented building for a training school. Some parish building might be available without rent being required. Only when the number of candidates would increase greatly should there be any plans for permanent quarters for a training school.

Anthony was not at all surprised that the feverish pace of the past weeks had exhausted John and sent him to bed. "Your breakdown came just as I expected, but our dearest Mother has a special care of you to make you rise again as quickly as you went down, to continue and finish her work."

The important thing to both men was that the work had at last come to fruition. A foundation had been made. Now they trusted Our Lord and Our Blessed Mother to continue to watch over it.

Notes to Chapter VI

1. Letter to Father Blaufuss June 24, 1922.
2. Letter from Father Blaufuss to Father Sigstein July 26, 1922.
3. Father Sigstein wrote his friend Father Collins a detailed account of the Mass, celebration of vows, departure from Chicago, and arrival in Santa Fe. The letter, dated September 17, 1922, is in the Victory Noll Archives.
4. It was Father Sigstein's original idea for the Catechists to wear hats except when they were actually conducting religion classes. Then they were to wear veils. The prospect of constantly having to change headgear was too much for the practical Julia and she convinced Father Sigstein that it would be very inconvenient, to say the least. The hats had cost ten dollars each. Since they were not going to wear them, they sent them back to Chicago to the department store where they had been purchased. Their money was refunded in full!
5. Letter to Anthony July 24, 1922.
6. Father Sigstein kept this telegram from Anthony Blaufuss. It is in the Victory Noll Archives.
7. Anthony's letter of August 12, 1922.
8. Father Sigstein's letter is dated August 17, 1922.
9. Both priests in their letters to each other used many such terms of endearment for Our Blessed Mother to whom they were so greatly devoted.

7

Watrous

RAVELERS ON THE Old Santa Fe Trail knew Watrous well. Two rivers
come together here, the Mora and the Sapello, and this made the place
a mutual camping ground for both Indians and adventurers. Many a
coach robbery was staged here, for often the wagons were loaded with
valuables, not the least of which were furs. Fur trappers met at the *Junta* (the
Spanish called the place *La Junta de los Rios,* the Meeting of the Rivers) to do
their trading. The site became known as Watrous only much later when the
town was laid out and named for one of its pioneer citizens, Samuel Watrous, an
early trader and land grant owner.

Watrous today is only a name to one who travels along Interstate 25 and it is
little more than that to motorists who turn off the highway at this point. The
small Catholic church is still there and Mass is offered once a week. The only
other buildings close by are a filling station and one store. But tourists who go a
block or so beyond the main street will see reminders of frontier days: a few
homes, stone corrals, and buildings that were very much a part of the era when
it was in its heyday — the hotel, Masonic Hall, Methodist church, the school
house.

In 1922 Watrous was anything but a metropolis. For years there had been
nothing to contribute to its growth. The railroad had long since come to New
Mexico but only a branch line went into Watrous. Lying halfway between Las
Vegas and Wagon Mound, Watrous was typical of the many places in which
the Catechists were to work in the years to come. Some of the families lived up
in the hills, miles from the town itself. They came to Mass and school in wagons
or, more likely, on foot.

The building designated for the convent was next to the little mission church. We wonder what Julia and Marie thought when they learned that part of the house was occupied by a widow with three children. For a time Father Dumarest had made his residence in Watrous. Whether the widow kept house for him we do not know, but when he moved to Wagon Mound he no doubt wished the church property to be occupied and asked her to live there. The widow would probably have been hard pressed to find a home for herself, so the arrangement was mutually helpful.

Father Blaufuss, in describing the place to Father Sigstein, said that "there remain the kitchen, dining room, parlor and two sleeping rooms, but nothing for Mr. Frey." He did not seem to think the presence of the tenant would cause inconvenience. He wrote: "The Spanish lady seems to be agreeable enough. May become helpful to the Catechists in picking up Spanish."[1]

Dorothy Day often pointed out that one of the most difficult aspects of poverty is lack of privacy. The poor can never enjoy the luxury of being alone. This lack of privacy must have been especially trying for Julia. She was forty-seven years old. All her adult life she had managed her own affairs and had lived in her own apartment. We can be sure her living quarters were never sumptuous but at least she had privacy. Now it was very different and would be different for years to come. Only in comparatively recent times have bishops and pastors recognized the fact that women religious are entitled to a room they can call their own. And even if some priests years ago acknowledged this right, very few convents occupied by the Catechists were large enough to make it possible.

Things were still more complicated in the Watrous house because of Mr. Frey. It was not simply that Will, if he were to live in the same building, would use part of the house, a house already occupied by six people; but it was a delicate situation. In one of her first letters from Watrous Julia asked Father Sigstein to let her know exactly what Mr. Frey's status was. And in a letter to John dated September 23, 1922, Anthony wrote: "My opinion is that Mr. Frey ought to find a rooming place apart from the Catechists' house. There is possibility that too intimate association with the Catechists would reflect on their character. Evil tongues could find a ready occasion to do harm. In fact, I even suggested as much to Mr. Frey when I was in N.M. Of course, this is matter for you to regulate. I believe the Catechists would much prefer to be left to themselves."

Will Frey's position was unique. He had been closely associated with John Sigstein since 1902 when he began to work with him and Francis Collins at the Mission in Chicago. Will was a deeply religious man, dedicated to the apostolate, so much so that he continued to work among the poor men even when the work became more and more difficult to carry out. After Father Sigstein's ordination and the official transfer of Our Lady of Victory Mission to the Paulists, Will continued to serve the poor there. Through the years John kept in close touch with Will, solicitous for his welfare and especially concerned about his health which was never robust. In 1920 he asked him to go to New Mexico to prepare for the coming of the Catechists.

Both men anticipated that it would be but a short time until the foundation would be made and the work actually begun, but the weeks went into months and the months added up to almost two years. Meanwhile, Will lived for a time in Wagon Mound and then in Santa Fe in the frugal quarters that it was thought would be the Catechists' motherhouse. He put the house in shape and carried out Father Sigstein's directives regarding several abortive campaigns for funds. He was often lonely, but his faithfulness in living the life of a Franciscan Tertiary helped him meet his difficulties. His natural optimism also proved a wonderful asset.

John Sigstein knew Will as no one else did. Incidentally he seemed to be the only person who consistently called him "Will." Even the early Catechists who knew him so well, still refer to him as "Mr. Frey." John loved Will and revered him. He appreciated his worth and assured him again and again that the Society would always care for him. Besides, he looked on Will as the first member of the Society of Men Catechists though this was one of the many organizations that never came into existence in spite of Father Sigstein's earnest efforts. It was John's idea that Will and others like him would teach older boys; and not give them religious instruction only, but teach them crafts that would enable them to find work and help their families.

Will was an all-round handy man and proved his worth over and over during the years between 1921 and his death in 1950. He was forty-eight when he went to New Mexico, two years older than John and Julia. During the first year or two after the Catechists began their work Will was their chauffeur. As one of the Sisters said, when he was not out with the car, he was under it, keeping it in good running condition. When provisions ran low, supplies usually had to be brought in from distant points, and Will always made the trips.

A simple man with little or no formal education, Will struggled to learn the Sign of the Cross, the Our Father, and the Hail Mary in Spanish so that he could teach the very small children these prayers. He loved children and always had a bag of candy in his coat pocket. The candy was intended to be distributed when his prayer class ended, but very often by that time there were fewer pieces in his pocket than there were at the beginning of class. Very small children — even three-year-olds — liked to tag along when their older (those who were five or six) brothers and sisters went to class. Not infrequently the three-year-old got bored and set up a wail. Mr. Frey restored order quickly by pushing a marshmallow into the little mouth. If the wail was resumed, he repeated the treatment.

Even when the number of Sisters increased to such an extent that Mr. Frey was no longer needed as catechist, his love for children made his quarters a very popular place. He bound up their wounds when it was necessary and repaired their playthings. As one of the Sisters remarked, his simplicity made it easy for him to grasp the make-believe world of childhood. His way with children of all ages was ingenious. Once when some little boys stopped their ball game to ask Mr. Frey for a drink of cold water, he filled empty pop bottles with drinking water and solemnly inquired of each ball player what flavor he preferred.

In the fall of 1922 things were very different; they had not reached this stage. Will must have been overjoyed at the arrival of the Catechists. He had known Julia in Chicago and was acquainted with Marie. He shared their ideals and was anxious to help in every way possible to further the work Father Sigstein had begun.

To say that Mr. Frey was garrulous would not be right. Certainly he was not garrulous in the strict sense of that word, meaning one who talks much about unimportant things. He was outgoing, had a quick mind, and was good at repartee. Everyone who knew him describes him as a perfect gentleman, a very saintly man with high principles, and one who could come right back with a witty rejoinder but without ever giving offense.

Julia gently complained to Father Sigstein that Will's presence was a deterrent to their being able to keep the rule of silence. It can be assumed that Will had not been taught to observe "religious silence" as the Catechists had, especially the kind of silence that was upheld as the ideal in convents at that time. Perhaps, after having lived alone in New Mexico for over a year, he was making up for not having anyone around to talk to. And after all, he had much in common with Julia and Marie.

John had given Julia very specific directions about writing him every week and reporting on the work, living conditions, and above all her spiritual progress. In a letter dated only a week after arriving in Watrous Julia came to the point about Mr. Frey.

"Tell me, Father," she wrote, "the status of Mr. Frey. He has his meals with us, does all the work possible, is never idle a moment. He is a perfect gentleman, willing to do anything at any time. But we are never alone. There is too much talk, talk, talk all day. I feel there is some mistake here. Mary has spoken to me too about this. She is well and apparently happy, efficient, zealous and very, very spiritual, but we have not been able to carry out all the exercises of the day. Sometimes one is omitted, sometimes another. Mr. Frey is perfect but I fear he is with us too much."

John's reply did not come until almost three weeks later. Meanwhile other questions had been sent off by Julia, questions concerning the catechism they should use, whether or not they should appeal to the Missionary Helpers for clothes for the poor and for small donations, and what should be done about the High Mass called for by the Rule, to be offered on the first Tuesday after the first Monday of each month. "There is no resident priest, no organist, and no way of getting to Wagon Mound."[2]

There were questions also about getting another uniform and about the style and material for capes. Cold weather would come soon and the Catechists had no outer wraps. Mlle. Dumarest favored getting the goods from France. Julia, practical as always, suggested getting material at Field's in Chicago.

When John Sigstein did answer Julia he wrote five and a half pages, meticulously taking up each item for comment. He asked her to make out her work and financial reports every Friday evening, to write an accompanying letter and put everything in the mail Saturday morning. "Your letter will reach me Monday evening or at the latest, Tuesday morning. I can then reply on Tuesday and you will receive my letter every Thursday. In this way we can keep up our correspondence and reports, regularly."

It is not hard to guess that this arrangement did not work out so well. For her part poor Julia tried faithfully to carry out the directive but she often found it impossible. And characteristically, Father seldom answered even the same week he heard from the Catechists, much less the same day!

In his long letter of the first of September John rejoiced that things were improving insofar as religious exercises were concerned, that the Catechists were finding it easier to meet their obligations. He cautioned against the temptation to extend their class periods beyond an hour even though the children might ask for it. "The main point is to keep them interested. If the class time runs over, they will grow tired or their parents may object, and so they will end by remaining away from classes altogether."

He mentions several techniques to arouse and keep interest: a contest somewhat in the nature of an old-fashioned spelling bee, the use of slides (he is trying to obtain a "steriopticon" for them). They were to use the Spanish catechism which followed closely the format of the official Baltimore Catechism. The rest of the long paragraph is devoted to the need for prayer and study in order to reach the hearts of the children.

Father called attention to the fact that on the reports so far there was no mention of visits to the sick poor in their homes. He hoped that now that things were running more smoothly "you will no doubt be able to make these visits according to your Rule." Again, detailed prescriptions how the Catechists should conduct themselves, reminding them how privileged they were to serve Jesus and Mary in the person of their poor. They should never tire of meditating on the invocation in the Litany of the Holy Name: "Jesus, Father of the Poor, have mercy on us."

Next followed admonitions regarding the care of mission chapels, training of altar boys, and the importance of carefully preparing everything for the celebration of Mass. John hoped the Catechists were finding time to practice the organ so that they "can not only accompany the children in their hymns but also be able to play Requiem Masses, simple High Masses for the missionaries, and hymns suitable for Benediction of the Blessed Sacrament."

Father Sigstein told the Catechists that for the present they were not to worry about the weekly, monthly, and yearly Masses prescribed by the Rule. He would take care of them himself. Eventually, when they could set aside some funds, he preferred that the stipends be given to poor missionaries. Ideally such offerings should be "the result of self-denial on our part. These add to the merit of the work and bring a special blessing."

He was pleased to hear that Julia was acquiring a knowledge of Spanish. She had confided to him that though she had worried much about this, it was turning out to be easier than she expected. "The study of Spanish, as well as your instructions on the spiritual life and your lessons in catechetics must occupy the major part of your study periods during the day."

Before taking up the questions about uniforms, John asks the Catechists to write to the Archbishop at stated times and also keep in touch with the Missionary Helpers Society back in Chicago.

Not at all sympathetic toward the blue-gray material Mlle. Dumarest advocated getting from France, Father said he would have Mrs. Owens obtain samples of goods from Marshall Field's and send them to New Mexico.

A shipment of rosaries, medals, etc., was being sent to Mr. Frey with instructions to clean the chains before any of these articles were given out to the children.

Finally came the important question of Mr. Frey's status in the Society and "how yourself and Mary can enjoy more privacy in the routine of your daily life." (Both John and Julia used "Mary" more than "Marie" in referring to Catechist Benes. It would seem that her immediate family called her Marie, having used this name in Europe, while most of her close friends in Chicago preferred "Mary." Eventually, throughout her religious life, she was known as Catechist Marie Benes.)

John himself wrote to Will and sent a copy of his letter to Julia. Though this letter was lost, we can be sure it was a model of diplomacy, for Father would not for the world hurt his friend in any way. From his letter to Julia we can deduce pretty well what he told Will himself.

"In reading this letter," Father wrote Julia, "you will note carefully that Mr. Frey, in addition to his ordinary duties of locating the house of your various mission centers, of arranging for your housing, the transportation of your goods, driving you about from place to place — he is also to teach catechism to the OLDER AND LARGER boys. It is not fitting, I stated to him, that the Catechists should be called upon to deal with the older boys who are really young men."

Directives such as these (regarding older boys) would be given again and again to the Catechists through the years. This was, perhaps, not a characteristic of Father Sigstein exclusively, but seemed to be peculiar to the era, especially where women religious were concerned.

John then reminded the Catechists that "should it please Our Blessed

Mother, there will be a Society of Male Catechists formed to take care of this class of subjects." Meanwhile, Will has a special place, an important place, being Father's own assistant in those things that require the attention of a man!

However, he is not to take his meals with Julia and Mary. "You can therefore have Mary serve Mr. Frey first in his own quarters before you partake of your own meals. I know that you will always be good and kind and agreeable to this good soul. Serve him well. He is entitled to the very best treatment for like yourselves, he has left all to serve Jesus and Mary in the person of their poor. I feel sure that if you explain to him that your rules call for silence at certain times, he will readily understand the situation."

The rest of the long letter was concerned with admonitions for their spiritual progress. There was a bit of news of mutual friends in Chicago; the sad report of the sudden death of the father of a young woman who had begun her training at the Academy but subsequently did not persevere. Julia and Mary were to offer special prayers for the repose of his soul and also should write to Irene as soon as possible. And they must not forget to write to Irene and Marie (Bodin) as frequently and regularly as possible. "They need such letters to encourage them and console them in their preliminary training course." A final plea was for prayers for the latest plan for raising funds for the Society. They must get the children to pray hard for this intention.

Serving Mr. Frey separately might have solved the question of privacy, but it must also have put an extra burden on the two women. It meant setting a separate table, having extra dishes, etc. Julia never mentioned this, for she was never one to complain without good reason. No doubt the added work was compensated for in other ways.

The days must have been very full indeed what with spiritual exercises, study periods, daily classes for the children, daily visits to the homes of the poor and the sick, not to mention necessary household chores and the never-ending round of letter writing: letters to Father Sigstein, letters to benefactors, to Marie Bodin and the other "subjects" back at the Academy who came but did not stay. Besides, poor people from miles around came to the mission center for help of various kinds. It was sometimes very late at night before Julia could get to her reports and letters.

Father Sigstein's own letters were coming quite regularly now. Not exactly every week as he optimistically aimed at, but he did write frequently. With his penchant for detail, he outlined a plan for putting "real system" into his own letters and Julia's replies. Each of his letters would be numbered. Julia's reply would bear the same number. And each subject treated in the letter would also be numbered. Julia was to use the corresponding number when she wrote. John hoped this would save both of them a great deal of time. On a separate sheet he would treat of her spiritual progress and answer whatever questions she had.

The system seemed to work surprisingly well. The numbered letters went back and forth between Chicago and Watrous for the rest of the year and throughout most of 1923. Not every week, perhaps, but they were spaced every ten days or two weeks, sometimes oftener. Two more unlikely correspondents, however, would be hard to find. John Sigstein and Julia Doyle shared the same vision, the same ideals, but their manner of expressing themselves was totally different. Father's letters were usually long ones with wordy and sometimes involved paragraphs, detailed directives. His expressions were sometimes flowery and formal. The letters were dictated and neatly typed. Sometimes he made corrections in his own hand, a word inserted here or there. Julia's letters were written in longhand and she said what she wanted in very few words. When it was possible she answered John's questions in one word only, carefully numbering the word so that he could refer back to his own letter and know what she was answering.

How Father Sigstein managed to carry out his part of the arrangement is amazing. Besides directing every aspect of the work of the Society, he meticulously carried out his duties as chaplain at St. Bernard's Hospital, kept in close touch with the Missionary Helpers and attended their monthly meetings. He gave instructions to Marie Bodin and to the others who came to the weekly gatherings at the Academy but did not continue in their resolve to be Catechists.

One *did* persevere, however — Sophie Mary Renier of Chicago. Sophie and her mother were Missionary Helpers, having first heard of this organization shortly after it was founded. One of the members, knowing Sophie's talent for sewing, brought her an altar cloth to embroider. In May 1918, Father Sigstein called at the Renier home and invited Mrs. Renier and her daughter to become permanent members of the Helpers' Society.

John became Sophie's spiritual director and she visited him "when he sent for her" at St. Bernard's Hospital. Recognizing her sterling qualities and her inclination to a devout life, Father Sigstein introduced her to the practice of the True Devotion of Grignion de Montfort. She consecrated herself to Jesus through Mary in a formal way on the feast of the Annunciation 1921.[3]

Whether either of them discussed Sophie's becoming a Catechist we do not know. It would seem that neither thought it would ever be possible. Sophie was thirty-five at the time but it was not her age that was the barrier. Julia was still older. Sophie had a physical handicap. As a child she had injured her knee. Deterioration of the bone followed and several surgeries were not successful. The knee was rigid and she walked with a slight limp.

Perhaps Father Sigstein thought this would be a great handicap in New Mexico. At best, living conditions would be primitive and it might not be fair to expect Sophie to do missionary work under such circumstances.

Subsequent events were to prove that Sophie's handicap was no barrier to her becoming a dedicated, generous Missionary Catechist. John Sigstein was never to regret his decision to accept her as a member of the new Society. The day after Christmas 1922, after much prayer and a long conversation, Father advised Sophie to make a novena to Our Lady of Victory and then tell her mother and family that she wished to be a Catechist. She took up residence at the Academy of Our Lady, joining Marie Bodin there on January 18, 1923.[4]

Notes to Chapter VII

1. Father Blaufuss' letter is dated August 24, 1922.
2. Julia wrote in September 1922, less than a month after they arrived in Watrous.
3. Sister Madeleine Sophie Renier's own account of her friendship with Father Sigstein was written in 1966 at the request of Sister Margaret Ann Harrison, General Secretary of the Congregation at that time.
4. Sister Madeleine Sophie (Sophie Renier) was born October 27, 1886, in Pierceton, Indiana, the second oldest of ten children. The family moved first to Avilla, Indiana, and then, in 1908, to Chicago. Sophie became a Missionary Helper in 1917 when she was recuperating from surgery on her knee and someone brought her an altar cloth to embroider. Throughout her religious life she endeared herself to all her Sisters by her kindness, her thoughtfulness, and her courtesy toward everyone. Sister Madeleine Sophie died May 25, 1976. It was the feast day of her patroness, St. Madeleine Sophie Barat.

8

FIRST YEAR

JULIA AND MARIE BEGAN their mission life in Watrous, New Mexico, at a time of *fiesta*. *Fiesta* is a celebration of the gift of life. It plays a significant part in the life of Hispanic people. The parish *fiesta* is celebrated with Mass, with a carnival especially for children, and with songs and dances.

The little mission church in Watrous was dedicated to the Sacred Heart of Jesus, but the mother church at Wagon Mound was under the patronage of St. Clare of Assisi whose feast at that time was kept on August 12.[1] The Catechists had gone to Watrous on August 10 and they spent the rest of that day and most of the next putting their little house in order. On the evening of the eleventh they joined the parishioners of Santa Clara Church in Wagon Mound for First Vespers of the patronal feast.

A large crowd had come for the occasion, having assembled from all the little missions and stations served by Father Dumarest. The festivities included a warm and hearty welcome for the Catechists. Julia was somewhat startled but touched when the women asked her for her blessing. With good judgment and sensitivity for the petitioners she placed her hand on the head of each with a simple "God bless you." Afterward Father Dumarest assured her that this was exactly the right thing to do.

Hispanic people are profoundly religious. They accept life as it truly is, a gift from God. They have a strong sense of a personal relationship with their heavenly Father and almost an intuitive reverence for things religious. Their sense of family ties, of *familia*, is strong.

The word "Mexican" has been used indiscriminately to describe Hispanic Americans regardless of their origin or where they live. Today we are more precise in our terminology. In its restricted sense a Mexican is a native of Mexico. On the other hand, the Mexican American has lived in the United States for many years, even centuries. In the earlier part of this century Mexican Americans were more apt to live in our Southwest, especially in the States of Arizona, Texas, New Mexico, and California. Today, like other North Americans, these people live in practically every part of our country.

Hispanic people in New Mexico are for the most part descendants of the *conquistadores* who came to our Southwest in the sixteenth century. The Spaniards did not make the same mistake that other colonizers in North America made. They intermarried with the natives and adapted their culture so that a whole new race developed, a people with a rich heritage: European (from Spain) and Indian.

In Mexico the natives whom the Spanish conquered were mostly Aztecs. In New Mexico they were the Pueblos — Indians with a highly developed culture of their own.

Virgilio Elizondo gives one of the best descriptions of the origins of Hispanic Americans in his *Christianity and Culture*. Especially significant is his insight into their religious heritage.

> The Missionaries accepted the Indian as he was, and began what may seem a superficial and inadequate process of conversion. But when seen from the vantage point of history several hundred years later, this was an authentic process of evangelization. The natives were not given a burden of doctrinal facts, but were initiated into a knowledge of the one God, who was the creator and provider of all things; of His Son Jesus Christ, who had freely sacrificed Himself so that man would no longer have to offer himself in sacrifice to the gods; they were introduced to Mary, to the Christian concept of heaven and of hell . . . The seed of the Faith was planted in Latin America in the early 1500s. It had been brought from the outside, but the soil in which it was to grow and from which the Faith would receive its unique expressions was the soil of the newly discovered continent. The dialogue of culture and Gospel was begun.[2]

It is not to be wondered at that the natives of New Mexico should endear themselves so quickly to Father Sigstein and the Catechists. Mexican Americans living in California, Texas, and other southwestern States shared the same characteristics of the Hispanic people of New Mexico and likewise had a rich cultural heritage. They migrated to the Southwest under varying circumstances and, in more recent years, have spread out to every part of the United States.

Early in the present century some of the people of New Mexico moved into Texas and Colorado in the hope of finding work on the expanding railroads and in other industries and thus better their economic condition. Others envisioned opportunities in California, especially in agricultural work in the San

Joaquin Valley, the Imperial Valley, and in Los Angeles and its environs. Here they were too often exploited as cheap labor.

Religious persecutions in Mexico accounted for a large influx of Mexicans of all classes. Many of these people thought the 1910 Revolution would be a short-lived affair. They fled across the border into El Paso and other towns, expecting to return in a week or ten days. Most of them never returned. With little or nothing in their possession, they had to make a new beginning in the United States.

Still more Mexicans migrated to the States at the time of the fierce persecution of the Church under the Calles regime in the late twenties. Many suffered death in Mexico because of their religion, the best known being Padre Miguel Pro, the Jesuit martyr.[3]

Though for a number of years the Catechists worked principally among Hispanic people, first in New Mexico, in Gary and Indiana Harbor, and later in California and Texas, Father Sigstein never intended that they should work exclusively among them. In fact, even during the first decade of the Society the Catechists labored also among Italians and Portuguese in California, especially in the San Joaquin Valley; and among Slavs in northwestern Indiana.

No mention is made in any early records about nationality or race of those to whom the Catechists would minister. One requirement, one condition *is* always present, however, and that is that the people must be *poor*. There can be no denying that this comes through over and over. The Catechists are to labor among the poorest of the poor. They are to go to people too poor to support parochial schools. When a choice must be made between two mission centers, they should choose the poorer one. John Sigstein was adamant in this.

Likewise he insisted that the Society would never staff schools, hospitals, or institutions of any kind whatsoever. He was ever fearful that this might happen. He saw it as a threat to the special end of the Society: "The imparting of sound, religious instructions and giving of a practical Christian training exclusively to poor neglected children in mission places and settlements, wherever found."

It was in 1927 that Father Sigstein revised the pledge of stability to include the phrase: ". . . and to hold fast to the original spirit and work of the Society among the poor." The Catechists were to receive no remuneration whatsoever from the poor among whom they would labor. They were not to work among those who could pay for services.

Much more will be said of this in later chapters. Suffice it to say now that this predilection for the poor, this requirement that the mission of the Catechists was to seek out the poorest of the poor was certainly met with by Julia and Marie in their little center in Watrous.

Julia wrote to the Missionary Helpers shortly after the Catechists' arrival in Watrous: "Children come to our catechism classes with scarcely enough

73

clothes to cover their poor bodies. You would feel sorry to see little girls who actually have neither underclothes, nor shoes, nor stockings. There are children so poorly clad that they have to stay indoors in inclement weather."

Nothing saddened the Catechists so much as to be unable to help the poor who came to them. Julia lamented that "there is no charity service out here to turn to as we have in the big cities back east."

Those who came to them for help often needed more than the simple remedies they could supply. There was an old doctor in Watrous who was kind and willing to do what he could, but he could not afford to supply medicines that were needed. The people did not have the means to go to Las Vegas where they might get better medical service. Julia and Marie suffered with the poor man who took his very sick child to Las Vegas but had to return home with her. The doctor did not treat her because the father could not pay him.

Julia was too humble and self-sacrificing to exaggerate the hardships required of Marie and herself in their mission work, but it comes through in many of her reports and letters. On their first Christmas they were deprived of Mass and Holy Communion. The weather was twelve degrees below zero and the wind so fierce that they did not venture out for a visit to church until afternoon. They had scarcely knelt down to pray before the Blessed Sacrament when they were summoned to attend a sick woman. "Christmas was indeed, a very busy day for us," Julia wrote. "We gave medical treatments to seven different people and gave out twenty-five articles of clothing to two poor girls who had come in on horseback in the below-zero cold."

No wonder she advised Marie Bodin and Irene (who did not persevere) back in Chicago to "pray intensely to persevere, but do not come out here if you want to be a Sister within convent walls. We cannot pray when someone wants medicine for an ache or pain. The children cannot come to us; we must go to them and bring along with us not only our catechism and Bible history but all the patience and mildness that we can beg from God to keep us from 'flying off the handle' at their ignorance or listlessness."

In many letters Julia warns that if the women who want to be Missionary Catechists think they can pattern their lives on those of Sisters who teach school back East, it would be best for them not to come to New Mexico. Julia herself was probably not very familiar with convent life and she sounds rather naive in expressing herself this way. However, she did not hesitate recommending to Father Sigstein that he send would-be Catechists immediately into the field so that they can find out for themselves what mission life is like! Otherwise she felt that many of them would not persevere. They could not face the hardships day after day.

John did not agreee with this idea at all. He insisted that "subjects" (as he always called them) should be thoroughly grounded in the spiritual life before they went to the missions.

Certainly Julia and Marie had turned their hands to the plow and were not looking back, not even when the roof leaked in two places — over the stove and over a bed. They put a bucket on the stove to catch the water and moved the bed to make room for another bucket. For a time the window panes were out in Marie's room.

They must have suffered from cold, for winter comes early in the windswept mountain area of northern New Mexico. In October Julia wrote Father to remind him that they had no winter wraps, only sweaters. He had promised to have Rose Owens make capes and also coats but there was a delay. After waiting awhile, Julia wrote again telling him not to worry about the wraps, that they were wearing old coats that had come in a box of clothing for the poor. "Out here no one minds being out of style."

It would seem that most difficult of all, much more difficult than being deprived of material things, was to be so completely dependent on Father Sigstein for everything. They had only the money that he was able to send them. Sometimes the money to pay the bills was not forthcoming and then Mr. Frey had to come to the rescue by dipping into his own meager resources. This "galled" Julia — the word she used. As early as September 15, 1922, she was writing John that they had had to borrow from Will. She was of the opinion — and there is every reason to believe it from what is known of Julia — that "when we control the purse we may be able to do better."

An arrangement was worked out but still they were dependent on money from Father. Every week Julia was to send to Chicago an itemized account of current expenses. John would send a check to cover this amount. The check did not always reach the Catechists on time, either because Father's own account was overdrawn or he delayed sending it. He often expressed his regrets that he could not include a reserve fund.

This money arrangement must have been hard enough but it must have been still more difficult to have everything regulated by John Sigstein. Surely there were some things besides food that the Catechists could have purchased locally and to their advantage financially.

Perhaps it was a combination of many reasons why things were handled in this way. It was in keeping with Father Sigstein's usual manner of acting and it probably never occurred to him to do things differently. Male chauvinism might not have been so distasteful then as now. And Sisters were not encouraged to make their own decisions. Julia was very humble and submissive and yet she asserted herself when she was convinced she should. She even insisted on some matters.

For example, the Catechists knew from experience what kind of material they needed for "work uniforms," though John thought it would be better to wear a type of apron that would cover their usual uniform. For a time they seemed to get nowhere when Father saw no reason to have a veil made of washable material that the women could wear when they "cleaned the flue, swept the sand that blows in constantly," etc. Finally, Julia wrote in one of her letters: "I have nothing more to say on the veil question."

All this must have been trying and it is a tribute to the humility and faith of Julia and Marie that they did not protest many of John's decisions and arrangements, especially when they thought some were very impractical.

Though John Sigstein certainly controlled everything, he was solicitous for the welfare of the Catechists. Time and again he asked them not to be frugal about meals. It was essential that they eat nourishing food. He subscribed to *The Messenger of the Sacred Heart* and to *Ave Maria* for them. He sent them books. Julia and Marie were touched by these "extras" and protested they could do with one magazine, for they well knew that John used his own meager funds for anything he sent them.

Every day was filled to the brim. There never seemed to be time enough for the Catechists to do everything that had to be done. Poor Julia! Besides trying to find time for prayers, classes, visits to the sick, the housekeeping, and other daily duties, she was being reminded by Father to write regularly to the Archbishop to inform him of the work of the missions, keep in touch with Father Blaufuss and Father Hurley, write to this benefactor and that one, take pictures of the children, of the poor people, their poor homes, and a multitude of other things; not to mention the weekly detailed reports she was to send him: expense accounts, work reports, reports of her spiritual progress. She was expected also to keep a diary of mission happenings.

Fortunately Julia's health was robust but she worried because Marie was often exhausted. She tried to spare her the heavier work but she knew that her younger companion was better equipped than she to look after the sick and to teach the children. Sensibly, she did not prevent her from these ministrations.

However, all this was nothing compared with the problem that from the beginning confronted both the Catechists, but Julia in particular because she felt more responsibility in the matter. This was the "problem of Loyola."

Loyola, a native of New Mexico, had spent eighteen years in two separate religious communities, working most of this time in Puerto Rico. She was now dispensed from her vows but she continued to wear a habit and evidently still considered herself a religious. She had returned to New Mexico hoping to work among her own people there. Michael Dumarest thought of her as a possible candidate for Father Sigstein's Society and arranged for John to meet her when he visited New Mexico in 1920. John was favorably impressed with Loyola but he did not commit himself to any promise to accept her as a member of his community.

For a year before Julia and Marie went to New Mexico, Sister Loyola, as she was called, and another woman, Eula Lee, had been trying to keep in operation a very small school under the half-hearted direction of Father Dumarest. The priest did not believe that a parish school was practical. His many years in New Mexico had convinced him that Father Sigstein's idea was better; that is, have the children attend public school and let the Catechists give them religious instruction. Nevertheless, he did let the two women give it a try.

It began with twenty-five pupils, all girls. Later a few little boys were added. According to Miss Lee who was the ardent promoter of the project, the enrollment climbed to seventy-eight in the spring but it dwindled to twenty-three before the end of the school year.

Eula Lee had gone to New Mexico at the same time as Will Frey, and somewhat in the same capacity, as "advance agent" of the Society of Missionary Catechists. Miss Lee knew Will in Chicago but her friendship with Father Sigstein was not of long-standing and certainly not so close as Will's.

In the correspondence that took place between John Sigstein and Eula Lee from 1920 to 1922 there is no intimation that either of them considered her as a candidate for the Society, but she was familiar with the Missionary Helpers and she had belonged to Father Lyons' Catholic Instruction League. Before going to Chicago she had been a newspaper woman in New York; and somewhere along the line she had taught school for a number of years. Exactly where she was from originally is not clear. Hardly New York or Chicago, for she writes in one of her letters that she is teaching Will Frey to milk Father Dumarest's cow!

At one time Father Sigstein's plans were for her to be President (organizer) of the Associate Catechists of Mary. Later he thought her talents and experience could better be used as a lecturer, a kind of field representative for the Society. In 1921 he was planning to send her to Northwestern University School of Journalism so that she could edit "our little journal that we hope to launch soon." This was the magazine, *The Missionary Catechist,* that began publication in 1924. By that time Miss Lee had dropped out of the picture almost as mysteriously and abruptly as she had entered it.

When she first arrived in New Mexico Eula Lee went to Wagon Mound where she did all the things a zealous lay missionary would be expected to do, ministries such as Father Sigstein envisioned for his Catechists. She lived in a little adobe house across the road from the church. Will made his home with Father Dumarest and was handy man in the parish.

Besides teaching catechism, playing the organ (she was a gifted musician), training altar boys, organizing the Children of Mary Sodality, and preparing altar and sanctuary for Mass, Miss Lee, for a time at least, served also as priests' housekeeper, for she writes:

Caring for my family of three hearty men [Father Dumarest had the luxury of an assistant for a short time] and trying to clear our camp of the dust which these New Mexico winds persist in forcing through every crack and crevice, all take so much of my time that there is very little left for the children. Mr. Frey looks after the instruction classes nearly altogether during the week. On Sundays I take the advanced children in a Bible History class and the time passes all too quickly.[4]

Some of Miss Lee's descriptions are so delightful and so typical of the experiences the Catechists had later that it is a temptation to quote them at length. We will include here only an excerpt from her story of a *fiesta* at Ocate in honor of Our Lady of Guadalupe, the patroness of the little church.

Last Saturday Father Dumarest took me with him to Ocate to sing Mass Sunday, it being their patron feast of Our Lady of Guadalupe. Saturday evening was the Vesper service. I never sang Vespers before, and watching notes and words was quite some task. One of the school teachers was helping as best she could and we proceeded fairly well when suddenly a shot sounded under the choir window, followed shortly after by another. By this time I began to lose my place in the chant and was singing Father's part. A third loud report and I was wondering why the congregation remained so unmoved. What band of outlaws was that disturbing the sacred service? After it was over and we had entered the automobile I inquired the meaning of the shots, to be told that it is the custom on the eve of feasts and that at that moment I was sitting on the gun. Sure enough; the muzzle of a shot gun was pressing against my side. Father then told how once on one of the Indian missions a visiting priest from the East was officiating at Vespers. At the right moment there came a tremendous firing of guns and beating of drums. The poor priest ran into the sacristy. He thought surely the Indians were on the war path. When he was coaxed to return and proceed with the service, he was ashamed to go back into the church. The other priests comforted him with the assurance that the people would consider it all a part of the ceremony.[5]

In September 1921 Loyola wrote to Father Sigstein formally asking admission into the Society of Missionary Catechists. He answered that he would admit her provided she was willing to give herself exclusively to teaching religion. She acquiesced and yet very shortly after, she was helping Miss Lee to open the school in Wagon Mound. John wrote her that he was disappointed in her decision. He was in touch with Miss Lee and expressed his surprise and disappointment to her also. However, with characteristic generosity he offered to help them obtain the necessary furnishings and funds for the school. They were starting without any supplies whatsoever.

Eula replied that her heart was not in the undertaking. She gave John the impression that it was Father Dumarest who wanted the school. This puzzled Father Sigstein because he had just returned from the meeting in Kansas City of the Board of Directors of the Society's Corporation and had talked over final plans for the Catechists' work in Wagon Mound and the missions. Michael Dumarest had attended the meeting as proxy for Archbishop Daeger who was prevented from being present. He had said nothing at all to John about opening a school. He had told him that he thought Loyola would make a good Catechist and that her knowledge of her people and of the Spanish language would be an asset.

Eula Lee's last letter to John Sigstein was written from Las Vegas, New Mexico, and dated July 7, 1922. By this time it had become more and more clear to Father that Miss Lee was the kind of person who only seemed to be in agreement with him. She had her own ideas about the work she wanted to do and was determined to swing everything her way. She played one person against another. No doubt she was sincere in her love for the people, in her admiration of the missionary priests, but she continuously vacillated, went from one place to another, from one idea to another. She had first acquiesced with enthusiasm to Father Sigstein's offer to attend Northwestern University to study journalism; then found all kinds of excuses for not going to Chicago. John investigated correspondence courses and sent her a check to enroll for such a course at Columbia. After a lesson or two she dropped it.

It is a tribute to John Sigstein's patience that he continued to put up with her as long as he did. None of the early Catechists except Julia, Marie and Marie Bodin ever met her but from the little Father Sigstein had to say about her, she made a tremendous impression on all who met her and it was easy to be "taken in" by her. John Sigstein terminated the whole episode of Eula by writing tersely in heavy pencil on her last letter: Not Answered. Always charitable, he wrote Julia that he prayed that "Jesus and Mary may inspire her to do well in whatever field of work she may next take up."

Though Julia and Marie had little actual contact with Miss Lee, they had to deal with her indirectly because of Loyola. When the Wagon Mound school collapsed, Loyola once again asked to be admitted to the Society. Father Sigstein asked Anthony Blaufuss to interview her when he went to New Mexico in August 1922 to give the Catechists their retreat. He reported that he was favorably impressed with her and that she had a submissive spirit. "From what I gather," he wrote, "she obeys and submits to Miss Lee."

Anthony told his friend that the two women had been carrying on against odds for "it seems to me Father Dumarest gives very little encouragement and would just as well see the parochial school go under." Like most pastors from well-populated dioceses Father Blaufuss favored parish schools; his sympathies were with the two women. "They are carrying on the work alone; that is always hard when there is not the encouragement and hearty cooperation of the pastor. If she fails in this attempt I believe she will gladly become a Catechist . . . I would advise you to rest her case for the time being. I told her that she would have to submit to the training of a probationer, the same as the others."[6]

John thanked Anthony for his report on Loyola and expressed surprise that "she clings so tenaciously to the idea of establishing a community to do parochial school work among her own people."

A few weeks later Anthony again wrote about Loyola. He believed she would have to come to a decision soon. The Archbishop said he would not allow her to continue to wear the religious garb since she was no longer under vow and he definitely refused to hear of a new Sisterhood such as Sister Loyola wished to establish.

Father Sigstein relayed this information to Loyola and told her she must come to her own decision. In her reply Loyola asked permission to spend a few days with the Catechists at Watrous. John readily gave the permission provided this was agreeable to Father Dumarest. The visit worked out to their mutual edification. The Catechists were favorably impressed with Loyola and she with them and their way of life. However, she hoped she would not have to go to Chicago for training.

Julia favored waiving the Chicago training for Loyola in view of the fact that she had been in religious life so long and knew and understood the culture of her people. Confident of Julia's good judgment, John agreed to this but he warned that Loyola would have to "unlearn her institutional ideas."

This was the situation, then, when Loyola wrote Father Sigstein that she definitely wanted to join the Society, that she had put aside any idea of establishing an organization of her own. After hearing she would be accepted, she went to her own home to spend a short time with her parents. John wrote to Julia with all kinds of instructions for receiving Loyola. He would send conferences that she herself could read during the retreat before reception. At this time she should not have to do any housework but devote herself to prayer and silence.

At the close of the retreat Julia was to preside at the reception ceremony if Father Dumarest was unable to come. (He did come, much to the happiness of all concerned.) Father Sigstein intended to consult Mother Aquinata as to "the patterns, materials, etc. of uniforms for both the Probationers and Juniors. Mlle. Dumarest can make the uniform when you receive the material. You stated in your last letter that they have no machine, so I presume they are accustomed to sewing by hand which will, of course, take a little longer."

The decision was for black for the probationers' uniform and white veils "such as novices wear." A black veil was out of the question because "it gives the wearer a funereal appearance just like some Sisters who wear a black crepe veil." The practical Julia must have pressed for black, however, for she knew how difficult it would be to keep a white veil presentable.

Loyola began to live with the Catechists in October 1922, but was not formally received until November 21, feast of the Presentation of Mary. Perhaps it took that long for the Dumarest women to sew the uniform by hand! Meanwhile Loyola took "mail order music lessons" and was progressing slowly.

At first Loyola seemed to enter into her new life with enthusiasm, but as the weeks passed, it became more and more apparent that she was not the type of "subject" John Sigstein wished for. Perhaps she cannot be wholly blamed for thinking herself superior to Julia and Marie in the ways of religious life. After all, she had lived as a religious — and in two different traditions — for eighteen years.

Julia was extremely patient with her, always ready to chide herself, wondering whether she was to blame in some ways for the other woman's attitude toward her and the work. Julia wrote frankly to John of her own actions, how she handled each situation.

In February Miss Lee (with whom Loyola had been in almost constant contact though she was not always open about it) became ill and Julia allowed Loyola to go to Wagon Mound to care for her. Father commended Julia for this: "Your action in the matter of giving permission to Loyola to go to Wagon Mound to nurse Miss Lee was perfectly proper. In a matter like this, charity is the great law for every member of our Society to observe. I know that Loyola's absence, together with Mary's illness, will make matters hard for you at the present time. However, you may surely count upon the help of Our Beloved Mother for the strength you need to carry on the various works of the Society."

Both John Sigstein and Julia Doyle were much concerned about Mary's health. The high altitude and her zeal for the work were taking their toll. Julia indeed needed all the strength she could muster at this time. Coping with the inconveniences and the demands made on her for carrying out her ministry was nothing compared with the strain of dealing with Loyola. Father Sigstein hoped the woman would leave of her own accord "rather than remain as a dissatisfied member." At the same time he assured Julia that Loyola could not possibly find any just ground for complaining against her, for she had borne with her patiently. Then he added:

> I cannot understand why a woman like Loyola would fail to grasp the true significance of the high and holy work she is called upon to do in the Society. I tried to make it crystal clear to her in the conferences I gave her for her retreat. Why should she grasp at the empty shell of a Sister's habit which after all does not signify anything in itself, when she could gather the fruit so precious that grows on the tree of Divine Charity?"[7]

In April Father Sigstein wrote Father Dumarest asking him to advise Loyola to leave the Society. A brief note in the Watrous diary states that on Monday, May 14, 1923, Loyola left for Wagon Mound.

To put it mildly, Loyola had not measured up to the great expectations John and Julia and others had of her. What happened to her is not certain, but her leaving must have been a great relief for Julia though she never again referred to the painful episode that put such a burden on her first months as a Missionary Catechist in New Mexico.

Notes to Chapter VIII

1. After Vatican II and the reform of the calendar of saints, Clare's feast was changed to conform to the actual date of her death, August 11, 1253.

2. Virgilio Elizondo, *Christianity and Culture,* An Introduction to Pastoral Theology and Ministry for the Bicultural Community (Our Sunday Visitor, Inc., 1975) pp. 120; 122. Used with permission.

3. Father Pro and his brother Humberto, a layman, were executed before a firing squad in Mexico City November 23, 1927. The cause of Miguel Pro's beatification was begun in 1952.

4. Letter of August 27, 1920.

5. Letter of December 13, 1920.

6. Letter of August 17, 1922.

7. Letter of February 15, 1923.

9

Victory Noll

BACK IN CHICAGO GOOD THINGS and not-so-good things were happening. The "splendid subjects" Father Sigstein optimistically wrote about to Julia and Marie came and went, leaving only Marie Bodin and Sophie Renier at the Academy. In fact, most of the women who showed interest in joining the Society and attended a number of instructions, dropped out. Only "our dear little Helen" actually joined the other two women at Longwood. Her entrance had been delayed until she could obtain her mother's consent. The mother finally did acquiesce but Helen's stay was a brief one.

(Father Sigstein always used such expressions as "our dear little Marie," "good little Sophie," "our good Bishop," "dear Mrs. Smith," etc. He did not mean to be patronizing. It was just the way he expressed himself in writing and in speaking. He referred to a Catechist or spoke to her as "my dear Child." Julia he often called "my dear Spiritual Daughter." As for himself he preferred that the Catechists refer to him as their "Spiritual Father" or simply "Father." Seldom did they call him "Father Sigstein.")

Plans for the Preparatory Training Institute in Gary were taking shape but very slowly. Father DeVille had hoped the building would be ready for occupancy at Easter, but because of labor troubles it was not completed until February 1924. John DeVille was the priest who worked with Italians and Mexicans in the Gary area and was supervising the erection of the Gary-Alerding Settlement House. With the permission of Bishop Alerding he planned to make available some rooms to be used as a training center for the Society of Missionary Catechists. The apartment would be rent free and utilities paid for. For their part the probationers would assist Father DeVille in catechizing and in visiting the poor who lived in the Gary/Indiana Harbor area. This would not only give Father Sigstein a home for his probationers but also provide a valuable opportunity for them to put into practice the training they had had in Spanish, catechetics, and simple home nursing.

Shortly after the Society of Missionary Catechists was incorporated in New Mexico in July 1921, John Sigstein contacted John F. Noll, editor of the weekly paper *Our Sunday Visitor* at Huntington, Indiana, asking him to give publicity to the new community. Father Noll gladly gave space to the article submitted by Father Sigstein. It was a very lengthy piece of 1200 words. Not a word of who the Founder was, but within the article in boldfaced type was a glowing endorsement by Archbishop Daeger of Santa Fe.

The news story was entitled: "New Society of Religious Women." The reader would envision at least dozens of these women in the mission field and dozens more in training. Archbishop Daeger is extolled for having provided "gratis a suitable building as a Novitiate or Training School for the Catechists."

The article appeared not only in *Our Sunday Visitor* but in many other Catholic papers and magazines as well. Most of these reprints were considerably shortened versions. As a result inquiries came in from all parts of the United States but because Archbishop Daeger's name was the only one mentioned in the story, they were sent to him in Santa Fe. Mr. Frey redirected them to John Sigstein. Unfortunately most of the would-be applicants were too old or they offered their services for a few months only or for a summer at most.

Subsequent publicity resulted in more inquiries. Some of these women John considered promising, among them Blanche Mary Richardson of Indianapolis. A small item in *The Sentinel of the Blessed Sacrament* had caught Blanche's eye. This type of apostolate appealed to her. She herself was a convert to the faith, having become a Catholic at Immaculate Conception Academy, a boarding school for girls at Oldenburg, Indiana, where she attended high school.[1]

Blanche read the leaflets and descriptive material she received from Father Sigstein but she did not commit herself in any way until a year later when, after prayerful consideration, she wrote to ask for an interview. Father asked her to come at once to Chicago. This was in March 1923.

Sister Blanche Marie, as she is known today, visited John Sigstein at St. Bernard's Hospital. He spoke with enthusiasm about the missions in New Mexico and the work of the Catechists, but Blanche was somewhat surprised when she inquired how many were in the field and was told "Two." John mentioned that women who were preparing to join them were at the Academy of Our Lady in Chicago. She concluded that there must be at least twenty-five or more making their novitiate but for some reason it did not occur to her to ask how many there actually were. Perhaps it was just as well. She would have been astonished to get the same answer: "Two."

Father Sigstein did not at first give Blanche a definite answer that he would accept her for training as a probationer in the Society. He simply commented that "the life of a Missionary Catechist is not child's play." Blanche was not sure just how to interpret his remark but she did manage to ask, "Father, if you think I am a suitable subject, how soon would you want me to come?"

John did not reply directly but appeared to be considering the matter. "You would not have to give the company much notice, would you?" he asked.

Sister Blanche Marie said she returned home expecting to be called any day and yet not really sure of it. Four weeks later the summons came. She was to come to Chicago *immediately*. The set date was May 13. Father Sigstein and Caroline Meister (who was the next woman to join the Society) met her and took her in a cab to the Academy of Our Lady where Mother Aquinata gave her a kind welcome. "Imagine my surprise," she recalls "when I found this convent peopled not with Missionary Catechists but with School Sisters of Notre Dame, and only two candidates in training as Catechists, Marie Bodin and Sophie Renier, both in secular dress."

Two days later Marie and Blanche began a nine-day retreat under the guidance of Father Sigstein who managed to get away from the hospital a couple of hours every day to give conferences to the young women.

On May 24, feast of Our Lady of Victory, Catechist Bodin renewed her Act of Consecration to Our Blessed Mother and became a junior in the Society. Blanche consecrated herself to Jesus through Mary according to the practice of the True Devotion of Louis de Montfort. At this ceremony Marie wore her uniform for the first time. That evening Sophie and Blanche went to the railroad station with Marie Bodin who boarded the train for New Mexico where she would join the other two Catechists at Watrous.

This feast of Our Lady of Victory in 1923 and the day following were especially joyful for John Sigstein. It was on May 25 that Monsignor Noll made his generous offer to sponsor the Society and with the help of readers of *Our Sunday Visitor* and of Peter O'Donnell of Long Beach, California, to build the motherhouse and novitiate at Huntington, Indiana. It is doubtful whether John shared the good news immediately with the Catechists nor with anyone else, however. He at first kept it to himself.

Other good things were happening. Early in June Father Sigstein once again called on Archbishop Mundelein and begged him to free him from duties in the Archdiocese of Chicago so that he could devote all his time to the Society of Missionary Catechists. The Archbishop received him graciously but again refused his request, pointing out the shortage of priests. John pressed his cause and told Archbishop Mundelein that Archbishop Daeger was willing to incardinate him into the Archdiocese of Santa Fe if he would release him. Finally, Archbishop Mundelein told Father to return in a week and he would give him a definite answer.

A week later John Sigstein's friend, Bishop Hoban, told him that the Archbishop would release him upon receipt of incardination papers from Santa Fe. Father Sigstein lost no time in getting in touch with Archbishop Daeger who was visiting his family in New Alsace, Indiana, at the time. They set up a meeting at St. Peter's rectory in Chicago to discuss arrangements.

John asked not to be appointed to any parochial duties in Sante Fe but to be free to devote himself exclusively to the work of the Society. Wisely he stipulated that he would not be under any expense to the Archdiocese. He would support himself. Accordingly Archbishop Daeger sent his document of incardination to the Archbishop of Chicago. It was not until September 8, however, that Father received his *exeat* from the Archdiocese of Chicago and the final papers were signed.[2]

In July Caroline Meister of St. Martin of Tours parish, Chicago, joined the Society. At the end of the month John went to New Mexico for a Corporation meeting and a visit with the Catechists at Watrous. He returned to Chicago August 7 bringing with him Marie Benes whom he appointed directress of the little band at the Academy. Before settling down at Longwood, however, Marie represented the Society at the Catholic Students Mission Crusade Convention held at Notre Dame University.

This would be a good place to explain the various terms that were used to designate the members of the Society. They were names that differed from the more conventual ones such as postulant, novice, etc.

In the very beginning Father Sigstein referred to the women who entered the Society as "probationers," but this was later changed to candidate. The newcomer was a candidate only for a month. She then made her Act of Consecration and was known as a consecrate. The candidates wore a plain dress, preferably of a dark color. It was described as an ordinary "secular" dress.

It was not until the fall of 1929 that this initial period was lengthened to six months. The candidates during this time wore a simple washable uniform. They put on a net veil only when they went to chapel. At the close of this period they made their Act of Consecration and were given a bright blue uniform with white collar and cuffs. The veil was white, made exactly like the one a professed Catechist wore.

At the end of another period of six months the young women became probationers and wore a black uniform with small white collar and white cuffs but continued to wear the white veil. They were probationers for a year. Then they became juniors and were given a dark blue uniform and veil such as the professed wore but with this difference. They wore a pin with the image of Our Lady of Victory on it. The medal and chain were given on profession day.

As juniors the young women were eligible to be sent to a training center for practical experience under supervision. Not all left the motherhouse, however, It depended on the background of the Catechist and the work she was doing at Victory Noll.

The superior of the mission center was called Senior Catechist, while the superior of the motherhouse was known as the Catechist Directress. Though there was a Head Catechist, her powers differed greatly from those of a superior general. There was a board of governers that in a manner paralleled the General Council of religious communities, though it also differed greatly in many respects.

After canonical elections in 1938 these terms conformed to the more traditional ones of postulant, novice, superior, habit (instead of uniform), though certain monastic terms and practices were never adopted: chapter of faults, penances for exterior faults, etc. Father Sigstein always deplored such practices and would not tolerate them.

In the beginning the women called themselves by their first names: Julia, Mary (or Marie), Sophie, Marie, Blanche, Caroline. In New Mexico the priests and people referred to them as Miss Doyle, Miss Benes, etc. Julia often expressed her dissatisfaction with this manner of address for she felt that because of their vows, they should be given a title that denoted their calling.

When Marie Benes returned to the Academy in the summer of 1923, the others asked her how they should address one another. She said that in New Mexico she and Marie Bodin had begun to call themselves Sister and Julia, Mother. They decided to consult Father and he told them to use the title Catechist with their family name.

This seemed a natural thing for John Sigstein for he had served as chaplain to two congregations of women who used their family names: Religious of the Sacred Heart (with the title Mother or Sister) and Religious Hospitallers of St. Joseph. To others, however, this mode of address seemed very strange and was interpreted by many as another indication that the Catechists were not women religious. Besides, most people — even Catholics —found the title Catechist very puzzling. They had no idea what it meant and could not pronounce it, much less spell it correctly. The Sisters who taught in their parishes used first names only, even if they were men's names. Catholic school pupils loved to "discover" their teacher's family name, something that was formerly kept secret by most Sisters.

In 1947 the Catechists changed their title to Sister and no longer used their surnames. At the same time the name of the Congregation was changed to conform to the dropping of the title Catechist. The community was no longer called the Society of Missionary Catechists of Our Blessed Lady of Victory, but Our Lady of Victory Missionary Sisters. These changes, and others that followed, will be pointed out later.

In the fall of 1923 Sophie Renier went to New Mexico to join Julia Doyle and Marie Bodin. This left at the Academy Marie Benes, Blanche Richardson, and Caroline Meister. In November a young woman joined them and became a professed member, but later withdrew from the Society.

Other would-be applicants were deferred until the little band could move to Gary. Finally, the Settlement House was finished and February 10, 1924, was designated as moving day. The following day, feast of Our Lady of Lourdes, Mary Stickling of Ambia, Indiana, was accepted. In March Catherine Olberding and Helen Srill entered. Catherine came from Father Blaufuss' parish in Baileyville, Kansas. She was to become the first canonically elected Superior General of the Victory Noll Sisters in 1938. Helen Srill, who belonged to St. Catherine of Siena parish in Oak Park, Illinois, was the first of three sisters in her family to become Catechists. A month later Catherine and Helen were joined by Edna Like of Farina, Illinois. Hannah Barthen was the next one to come to Gary. Like many of the others, she too was from Chicago.

In the late summer and early fall a half-dozen other women entered the community. The three who stayed were Agnes Kozla, Bridget Hynes, and Rafaela Mendoza. They came to Gary from Chicago, but only Agnes was a native of the city. Bridget had come to the United States from County Clare, Ireland, and for some years had been working as a practical nurse in Chicago. Rafaela was from Old Mexico, having come to Chicago with her parents when she was a child.

The quarters Father DeVille had provided at the Settlement House for the Catechists proved too small. A house in the same neighborhood, but five blocks away, was secured for living quarters and referred to as the Annex, with Caroline Meister in charge.

Gary was unique in that it had had released time for religious instruction of public school children since the year 1917. Called the "Gary Plan," it remained in effect until the decision of the Supreme Court in the McCullom case called a halt to released time in 1948.

Two members of the Congregation of Poor Handmaids of Jesus Christ taught religion to the children who attended schools in the area of the Settlement House. The Sisters lived at St. Emeric's convent with the members of their community who staffed the parochial school in the parish.

When the Catechists came to Gary it was with the understanding that some of them would assist the Sisters in catechetical instructions. The Poor Handmaids generously supervised the young recruits who, for the most part, had little or no teaching experience. It was on-the-job training. Staggered classes were held from nine in the morning until three in the afternoon in order to accommodate the children at the various centers near the public schools. These centers or buildings were referred to as "catechism huts."

The Catechists who taught the Gary boys and girls under the supervision of the Poor Handmaids remember Sister Mary Caritas and Sister Mary Clarissa with affection. Their expertise, charity, and patience made a lasting impression on their apprentice teachers.

When the Catechists were not teaching, they spent their time visiting the homes of the many Spanish-speaking families whose wage earners were employed by the United States Steel Corporation. These contacts gave the young women the opportunity to use the Spanish language and prepared them for their work in the Southwest.

Though the Catechists had moved to Gary in February, Father Sigstein was not able to take up his residence there until September. He had been assured of his release from the Archdiocese of Chicago, but it was not until the end of August that he could leave St. Bernard's Hospital. The priest of the Society of the Precious Blood whom he had engaged as his successor, could not begin his duties until the last week of August.

Traveling back and forth between Chicago and Gary was wearisome, so it was with much gratitude that John was at last able to take his mother to Gary where they would live in the little apartment provided for them. He could look forward now to the next milestone, the building of the Preparatory Training Institute at Huntington.

In a letter to Julia written September 6, 1923, Father Sigstein tells her that ground will be broken the following week. He added:

> I have specified very plainly that the Catechists are to have only bare living rooms. May our sweet Mother keep us always wholly detached in our life and our living quarters at both Huntington and Gary so that our probationers and juniors may become accustomed to the manner of life that will fit them for the poor life they are to live in the missions. I cannot tell you how happy I am, my dear Spiritual Daughter, that both my mother and myself, who have always been accustomed to living a plain, simple life will have only small and simple living quarters in our flat at Gary. Let us always pray that the poverty of Jesus and Mary may be our happy portion here upon earth, so that we may enjoy their riches forever more in Heaven.

From the time that work was actually begun on Victory Noll until the Catechists moved there on December 7, 1924, Father Sigstein was busy running back and forth between Gary and Huntington. In the spring of 1924 Monsignor Noll went to Europe for several months, leaving Robert Kelly, his assistant, in charge of St. Mary's parish. Father Sigstein helped Father Kelly every weekend until the pastor returned.

It was during this time that John decided on the name "Victory Noll" for the training center. The site on which the building was being erected was on a hill overlooking the Wabash Valley. It was the highest point for miles around. Monsignor Noll's name lent itself to a play on the word "knoll." The Monsignor himself often recalled that he was not consulted about the name, but obviously he was pleased with it. And what could be more appropriate than to link the name of the Society's beautiful patroness with its greatest benefactor?

The Preparatory Training Institute, as it was then usually called, was to be large enough to accommodate eighty women. It was thought that this would take care of the community for many years. Monsignor Noll thought Father was planning for too large a building, but John did not agree with him.

A special apartment was provided back of the chapel for John and his mother. On November 29 Blanche Richardson and Caroline Meister took Mother Sigstein to Victory Noll. The next day Julia Doyle and Hannah Barthen joined them. Catechist Doyle and Catechist Richardson had come to Gary from New Mexico for retreat and Blanche's profession of vows. While they were in Indiana, John was anxious for them to see Victory Noll.

On December 7 Father Sigstein, nine Catechists, and Ida Keller arrived from Gary by train. Ida was the first "probationer," as she was called then, to enter at Victory Noll. She had gone to Gary from her home in Chicago to make the trip to Huntington with the Catechists.

Victory Noll was far from completed but it was livable. One whole wing was still open but fortunately the weather was comparatively mild. The boiler gave trouble and sweaters were a necessity. But the inconveniences did not bother the Catechists. At last they had a home and it was with joyful hearts that they sang a *Magnificat* in thanksgiving. Their first supper, served on a carpenter's table in the kitchen, was a happy meal indeed.

After supper Monsignor Noll, Father Kelly, and Clarence Dougherty came out to see the Catechists.[3] And lucky they did. The trucks that had left Gary forty-eight hours before the Catechists themselves left, had not yet arrived. Evidently they were marooned somewhere between Gary and Huntington. On the trucks were household furnishings including bedding. Victory Noll had beds and mattresses but no blankets nor pillows. The Noll family had what they called a summer cottage on Victory Noll hill so Monsignor and Clarence went over to the house and brought back bedding for the Catechists.

When the guests left, Father Sigstein and the Catechists went in procession through the second floor, east wing, and John blessed the bedrooms. Then each Catechist, "according to vocation" (order of entrance into the Society), selected her room.

The next morning the little community assembled in the still unfinished chapel to offer with Father Sigstein the first Mass in their new home. It was the feast of the Immaculate Conception, a feast which celebrates the victory of the Woman who crushed the head of the serpent; a fitting day for the Catechists to dedicate themselves and their new home to Our Lady of Victory, the Mother of God and their Mother.

The community consisted of Caroline Meister (Catechist Directress or superior), Mary Stickling, Helen Srill, Agnes Kozla, Bridget Hynes, Rafaela Mendoza, Ida Keller, and several others who did not persevere. Marie Benes, Sophie Renier, Catherine Olberding, Edna Like, and Hannah Barthen remained for the time being in Gary. Marie had suffered a severe heart attack and was hospitalized. Sophie Renier, who had come East with Julia and

Blanche, replaced Catechist Benes as Directress of the Gary house.

Catechist Meister, following Father Sigstein's orders, kept a daily record of events. The Victory Noll diaries, continued through the years, are a priceless source of information. During the first year Marie Benes and others took their turns at keeping the journal. Depending on the chronicler, some entries are very detailed; others very brief. Caroline and Marie, fortunately for us, wrote expansively.

Victory Noll is just short of two miles from the center of Huntington, and yet walking into town was a regular thing. The Catechists had no car. Caroline Meister and Helen Srill seemed to think nothing of walking to Huntington even twice in a day when something unforeseen was needed.

Every day was a busy one. Men were still at work in the building and the Catechists tried not to mind the sawdust, the smell of varnish, and the sounds of hammer and saw. Caroline, in the diary, always referred to the chapel as "our beautiful chapel," but she admitted also that for weeks they knelt on the floor amid boards and pipes and tools of various kinds.

On December 16 Father Sigstein began a three-day retreat for the probationers and consecrates. Monsignor Noll celebrated the investiture Mass December 20. Besides the Catechists, the ceremony was attended by Mother Sigstein, the Monsignor's housekeeper, and several women who lived not far from Victory Noll. All the guests stayed for breakfast.

The next day the community settled down to what Caroline always referred to as the "regular routine," but it was interrupted by the serious illness of Mary Stickling. She had become ill December 17 but later had showed signs of improvement. Now she had a relapse and the doctor pronounced her condition critical.

Christmas was a happy time, clouded only by Mary's illness. Monsignor Noll furnished the turkey, and the Rotary Club of Huntington sent out several baskets of fruit and vegetables. On the twenty-third John Sigstein went to Chicago by train to purchase a crib. It arrived late Christmas Eve. There was just enough time to set it up before Midnight Mass. The tree was also a last minute thing. Caroline and Helen walked to Huntington the afternoon of Christmas Eve to get it.

After Midnight Mass all gathered together in the community room where Father Sigstein distributed the gifts that were piled under the tree. This was a tradition that he continued during the years he lived at Victory Noll. After a light breakfast all retired for a few hours, then arose for morning prayer and two more Masses that Father celebrated beginning at six-thirty.

Mary Stickling's condition became more grave each day. She had suffered a stroke and was unable to swallow. Father had given her the Sacrament of the Sick when she first became ill. Now she was unable to receive Holy Communion. Her throat was paralyzed. Shortly after one o'clock in the afternoon of

January 7, 1925, Mary Stickling died.

A few hours before her death John invested her as a junior in the Society. We can only wonder now why she did not make vows. Perhaps Father Sigstein thought it might not be regular, for until this time the Catechists had been making private vows in the confessional. In another year the Catechists made public profession of vows. Monsignor Rempe, who was vicar for religious in the Archdiocese of Chicago, came to Victory Noll to preside at the ceremony of investiture and profession on the feast of the Annunciation 1925. He told Father Sigstein there was no reason whatsoever why the Catechists could not make public vows.

Catechist Mary Stickling was buried in what is now referred to as "the woods." Four years later her remains were transferred to the present Victory Noll Cemetery.

Though the chronicler often wrote "regular routine" in the diary, to us the days sounded far from routine. Or perhaps it had become routine to have guests for meals, guests visiting for an afternoon and evening, overnight guests. Father Sigstein, always hospitable, welcomed all who came. Monsignor Noll brought all his visitors to Victory Noll. He often brought Fort Wayne priests for supper.

Even the Rotary Club had their monthly meeting at Victory Noll in June. It was not enough to serve dinner for the forty-five men. The meal was followed by a program given by the Catechists. This, too, was typical of John Sigstein. He expected the Catechists to entertain guests with music and song and skits.

Classes in catechetics, pedagogy, nursing, social work, singing, and sewing were called off for the last week in June. Monsignor Noll was to be ordained (or consecrated as it was then called) Bishop of Fort Wayne on June 30. He had been apppointed to succeed Bishop Alerding who had died in December. One of the first public ceremonies the new Bishop would perform would be the dedication of Victory Noll on Sunday, July 5. And yet with all the "goings on," there was an investiture ceremony and renewal of vows that week. Father Blaufuss came to Victory Noll to preach the retreat.

Thirty guests — relatives of the Catechists in the ceremony — arrived the afternoon of July 3. The Investiture Mass was at six-thirty the morning of the Fourth of July. Bishop Noll and his family joined the other Victory Noll guests at supper that evening. It was followed by a special program and presentation of a vestment made by Catechist Renier for the Bishop.

The next morning there were six Masses in the Victory Noll chapel beginning at five-thirty. (Concelebrated Masses were still decades away.) The celebrants were Bishop Noll, Father Blaufuss, Father Bonet from Colorado, Father Young from Chicago, Father Collins from Sour Lake, Texas, and Father Sigstein. The Bishop celebrated the last Mass and it was followed by Benediction of the Blessed Sacrament! At nine-forty-five breakfast was served to "clergy, visitors, and Catechists."

At three that afternoon the formal dedication of Victory Noll took place. Taking a special part were the Knights of Columbus, Daughters of Isabella, city officials and other dignitaries, besides people from Chicago, Huntington, Fort Wayne, Marion, Elwood, Kokomo, and other northern Indiana towns.

The Fort Wayne *Journal-Gazette* reported that seven thousand persons attended the dedication. The Erie Railroad ran a special car down from Chicago. "A distinguished prelate attending the event," wrote the staff writer, Helen Irwin, "was the Most Rev. Elie Joseph Morel, Archbishop of Pondicherry, India, who was accompanied by Rev. Gavin Duffy, the famous missionary. Interested in the work of the Missionary Catechists, they came from abroad to study the plan so that it may be adopted in India."

At the flag raising, besides the National Anthem, the crowd also sang "America." Helen Hartke, who came to Victory Noll every week from Chicago to teach singing to the Catechists, sang "My Own United States." Francis Young, Father Sigstein's friend who was known at the time as the Poet Priest of Chicago, recited his poem, "Our Nation's Prayer." Then, according to Miss Irwin, he presented Bishop Noll with an autographed, illuminated copy of the poem.

There were speeches by Bishop Noll and several other dignitaries. The crowd sat in the shade of the oaks and maples on Victory Noll's hill. Refreshment stands dotted the grounds and the people enjoyed ice cream and cold drinks. At six-o'clock a special dinner was served to the Bishop, seventy-five priest guests, and other special guests of the Catechists. A group of women from Huntington, Our Lady of Victory Circle of the Associate Catechists of Mary, helped to prepare and serve the meal.

More was yet to come — an entertainment. There were songs in both Spanish and English. The principal address was by Catechist Madelon LoRang who described the work of the Missionary Catechist as helper to the missionary priest. She emphasized that "the Catechists place no hampering limitations on the extent of their activities save to confine them within the broad sphere of personal service — working, like Christ, as individuals with individuals. As Catechists, we instruct the poor and neglected in the truths and practices of our holy faith, bringing into their homes as visiting nurses the blessings of health; and as experienced social workers, training them for good citizenship through a realization of their opportunities and privileges."[4]

It can be doubted that there was much sleep at Victory Noll that night, for Catechist Benes' diary entry notes that many of the Chicago friends left on the three-seventeen train in the morning. And John Sigstein would not think of letting his guests leave without a hearty breakfast.

Bishop Noll left immediately after a later breakfast. The other priests left after dinner, and Father Sigstein went to Chicago on the afternoon train with some of his friends.

By this time the Catechists must have been ready to collapse. Marie Benes wrote: "During the hours of 1:30 and 5:20 all the Catechists will rest every afternoon of this week. There will be no classes this week."

How so few women (not even two dozen) could manage to hold to such a fast pace astonishes us now, but all except one or two were in their twenties and early thirties. A half-dozen were still in their teens. They were fired with enthusiasm and most anxious to prepare themselves well for their work in the mission field. They knew how fortunate they were to have a training center, a beautiful motherhouse such a short time after their foundation as a Society. John Francis Noll, their friend and benefactor whose zeal and generosity had made this possible, was now their Bishop.

Notes to Chapter IX

1. Sister Blanche Marie Richardson died April 5, 1980, early in the morning of Holy Saturday. She was buried on Easter Monday. Though Sister died before this history was published, she had read the manuscript and had verified the events of the early days of the community. It was appropriate that Sister Blanche Marie first heard of the Catechists in *The Sentinel of the Blessed Sacrament*. She had special devotion to the Blessed Sacrament and made a holy hour every day. In her early years in New Mexico one of her greatest sacrifices was being deprived not only of daily Mass but also of the presence of Christ in the Eucharist. Sister Blanche Marie's holy death was a fitting ending to her life as a Victory Noll sister.

2. Excardination is the term used for the release of a cleric from a diocese to which he has belonged, and has been incardinated. The *exeat*, the release, is not effective unless the cleric has letters of affiliation with the diocese to which he is transferring.

3. Mr. Dougherty, a native of Huntington, headed the church envelope department at Our Sunday Visitor, Inc. In 1931 he married Muriel Noll, becoming the Bishop's brother-in-law.

4. The July 1925 issue of *The Missionary Catechist* carried a full and detailed account of the dedication day.

10

Expansion

N 1924 JOHN SIGSTEIN WROTE JULIA:

I feel confident that our Sweet Mother is going to answer our prayers for ideal perfect subjects and for funds. We certainly have had a great many applications, but unfortunately many among the first who applied were too old, and now many of those who apply are too young. I think the fault lies in the editorials written by good Monsignor Noll. The first editorial gave the impression that the age limit was one hundred years. In the second editorial he made reference to our Training Institute as a training *school* with the result that many young girls, sixteen and seventeen years of age, have gotten the impression that it is a school for a special course in this work. Since I have spoken to Monsignor, he has corrected the first impression regarding age limit. Now I must speak to him about correcting the false impression that young girls get about our Training Institute being a mere training school.[1]

John's prediction regarding vocations proved correct. The years that followed, especially during the thirties, forties, and into the fifties were years of tremendous growth, growth in the number of vocations and in the number of mission centers opened. By the end of 1929 the Society numbered 103 women. Many others had come and gone, but this was the actual number of Catechists at Victory Noll and in the missions. Yet it was not enough to satisfy John Sigstein. On October 23, 1929, he wrote his friend Francis Collins that only seventeen had entered this year. He had expected twenty-five or thirty.

Father Sigstein had reason to be concerned about vocations. He was receiving requests from missionary bishops and priests begging for

Catechists. When Bishop Noll returned home after attending the 1927 meeting of the American Board of Catholic Missions, he reported to John that every western bishop he met asked for Catechists. These missionaries needed the services of the Catechists, and besides, they came free! When Archbishop Gerken was appointed to the See of Sante Fe in 1933, he commended the work of the Missionary Catechists to Bishop Lucey, his successor in Amarillo, and added: "No other religious will work without salary."

Father's original plan was for the Catechists to establish a mission center, train lay catechists and then move on to another town. This was the aim in the beginning but it did not prove feasible. After working for a year in Watrous and its out-missions, the Catechists transferred their center to Ocate, New Mexico. It had six out-missions and two stations, all under Father Dumarest's jurisdiction.

Julia did not favor the move to Ocate. She felt that they had not nearly finished their work in Watrous. The foundation was not firm enough yet. The few young women who had helped the Catechists were not in a position to carry on alone. As early as November 1922 when Father Sigstein, Father Dumarest, and Mr. Frey suggested going to Ocate the following year, Julia pointed out the disadvantages. She wrote John:

> You would be making a mistake to extend the work to Ventanas or Ocate. Both are off the R.R. and living would be very high. One head of cabbage costs 70¢. Everything has to be hauled there by wagon. At Watrous all the children except four have made their First Communion but that does not mean that they know their religion.

Julia's practical advice did not prevail and Ocate was opened on the feast of the Assumption, August 15, 1923. Marie Benes had returned to Indiana, leaving Julia and Marie Bodin to carry on.

Julia refers to the Ocate convent as an "ex-saloon." Much work had to be done on it to make it habitable, but the inconveniences faded when Father Dumarest told the Catechists he would leave the Blessed Sacrament in the little mission chapel provided they furnished the oil for the sanctuary lamp. Father Sigstein assured Julia that he would find the money so that they could have this great privilege.

Ocate remained open until 1925, but by this time John was convinced that foundations should have a more permanent basis. Chaperito was opened in 1924, closed two years later, opened again in 1928, and was closed permanently in 1930. Anton Chico, Holman, Las Vegas, Cerrillos, Grants, and Santa Rosa — all in New Mexico — were opened between 1925 and 1929.

In all of these missions the people were extremely poor. The Catechists were kept busy visiting the sick and providing food and clothing. From the very beginning John Sigstein was very insistent on this aspect of the work of the Society. The Catechists were not only to instruct the children in their religion, but they were to be servants of the poor, especially the sick poor. Even in the first month the Catechists were in Watrous John wrote Julia that she had not reported any visits to the sick the previous week.

Father Sigstein need not have been concerned. The Catechists made their visits at great sacrifice. Winters were rugged. Time after time Julia wrote that they were unable to drive because of the heavy snow that made the roads impassable. When the snow melted, there was mud. Neither snow nor mud kept the Catechists from visiting the sick. Sometimes they walked almost two hours, battling the drifting snow. It was exhausting but they were compelled to answer sick calls out of their great love and compassion for the poor.

The missionary priests were no less zealous, and Michael Dumarest was outstanding in his dedication to his people. Julia confessed that at first she had been afraid of him but her awe was not long-lasting. She wrote, early in 1923, that he was not always practical "but we love him."

Father Dumarest was a big-hearted, big-bodied Frenchman who was loved by all who knew him. He did not spare himself for the poor people of his difficult parish with its many out-missions. Like so many missionaries at that time and for years to come, he suffered much from the long trips he undertook in order to offer Mass at his various stations. Sometimes it was a whole day before a priest could break his fast.[2] Nearly all the priests suffered greatly from severe headaches and stomach disorders. When they did break their fast, it was to eat hurriedly what they themselves prepared or to eat the highly seasoned foods that the people ate as regular fare.

The only fault the Catechists found with Father Dumarest was that the poor man never remembered to prepare for emergencies on his mission trips. These emergencies were a fact of life in New Mexico in those days. Invariably Father Dumarest would forget to take along the shovel that was so necessary to dig the car out of the sand or the snow, depending on the season. He would leave at home the inner tubes needed to replace the frequent blowouts. On a forty-five-mile trip one day Father Dumarest had three blowouts. Each one meant an hour's wait in the grueling hot sun for the two Catechists who were with him, while he repaired the damaged tube.

The Catechists matched Michael Dumarest and the other padres in enduring hardships. Though the priests lived in very simple rectories, they were not nearly so primitive as the early "convents" of the Catechists. Their homes had few conveniences. There were no bath rooms. Water had to be carried into the house from a well or pump outside. They used to joke about the running water, water sometimes running right through the roof and down onto the beds. They cooked with wood just as the people in the villages cooked. Their light was from kerosene lamps.

In the hardships they endured, New Mexico's missionaries, priests and Missionary Catechists, had as an example their saintly Archbishop, Albert

Daeger.[3] The humble Franciscan, known as Padre Alberto by his flock, was the personal choice of Archbishop Pitaval who resigned as head of the Archdiocese of Santa Fe in 1918. Fortunately for New Mexico, the Holy See confirmed Pitaval's recommendation.

It is said that Albert Daeger at first did not believe that the news was true. One of the most humble and most saintly of men, he was a fervent lover of Lady Poverty. The stories told of his thirty years as a missionary in the most difficult areas of the Southwest read as if they were taken from the *Fioretti*.[4] His untimely death December 2, 1932, shocked and saddened everyone, especially Father Sigstein and the Catechists. For John, Archbishop Daeger was a kindred spirit, simple, self-effacing, unassuming, passionately devoted to the poor.

As a missionary Father Albert made trips on horseback, by wagon, and on foot — mostly on foot, carrying his valise in one hand, saddle-bag in the other, for sometimes he was loaned a horse for a day. With him were what he needed to offer Mass. On at least one occasion, it was said, he stayed up part of the night copying Mass texts because the altar missal was too heavy to carry.[5] He pushed himself to the limit and his superiors feared for his life.

Archbishop Daeger was only sixty when he died, worn out in body but not in spirit. His death, like his life, was humble and obscure. He was found bleeding and unconscious on the floor of a dark basement, having fallen ten feet through an opening on the street. He died three hours later as a result of a fractured skull and other injuries. Santa Fe was stunned. Exactly how the accident happened no one was able to explain clearly. The Archbishop was on his way to inquire about bus schedules for a confirmation trip. *The Santa Fe New Mexican* editorialized:

> Probably no part of his life so became the Archbishop of Santa Fe as his manner of leaving it. Modest and inconspicuous, he was on foot and alone going about his Father's business; and bemused with the welfare of his people, he stumbled, rapt, into eternity.[6]

In 1925 John Sigstein foresaw that with the opening of more missions in New Mexico there would be a need for a center large enough for the Catechists to come together for retreats and community gatherings. He heard that the old Santa Fe Railroad Hospital, just outside of Las Vegas, was for sale and immediately he asked for prayers that the Society might be able to obtain it.

The hospital had been used for many years for employees of the Atchison, Topeka, and Santa Fe Railroad. Many of these patients were victims of tuberculosis and this was in the day that persons suffering from the disease were advised to go West.

The location was ideal. Las Vegas (The Meadows) was on the Sante Fe line and the Catechists' missions were within reasonable distance though over very poor roads. It was Peter O'Donnell who bought the building for the Society for

$4,500 cash December 11, 1925. It was a magnificent Christmas gift.

For some reason Mr. O'Donnell could not complete transactions until April of the following year. The hospital had not been used for a number of years and was badly in need of repair. Nothing could be done, however, until the title was cleared.

Catechist Sophie Renier was appointed to take charge of Victory Mount, as the new center was named. She left Chicago May 17, 1926, and arrived in Las Vegas two days later. Will Frey met her and they picked up Ida Keller and Marie Bodin who were waiting at St. Anthony's Hospital in town. Will had already taken up residence at Victory Mount and was staying in a room on the second floor of an old barn that was on the grounds. An elderly man, Mr. Daley, who had been acting as caretaker since the hospital had ceased operation, was living in a one-room cottage nearby.

Before they ate their supper Mr. Frey took the Catechists on a tour of the building. Sophie, in relating the story, said that supper was very meager — cheese, bread, milk, and pickles. They probably would not have had an appetite for much more after seeing the condition of the place. The Catechists described it as being "dreadfully dirty." They hardly knew where to begin to make it habitable. They had Mr. Daley wash the walls three times. The Catechists from Holman and from Chaperito missions joined the others and they spent the greater part of the summer cleaning the place. They literally shoveled out the debris. The closets were littered with cans, bottles, crutches, canes, braces, and artificial limbs.

Father Sigstein regretted that Mr. Frey had not informed him of the condition of the building. He would have delayed occupancy until it was livable. More and more he was insisting that the priests provide better living quarters for the Catechists. He wrote to Julia agreeing with her that "we should have good houses for our mission centers. This is all we ask of the missionaries and surely this is not asking too much."

On the first of June Father Sigstein arrived in Las Vegas to see the place for himself. He offered the first Mass at Victory Mount on the following day, the feast of Corpus Christi. Father Balland, pastor of Our Lady of Sorrows in Las Vegas, and the Christian Brothers who had a school in town, loaned the Catechists vestments and altar furnishings. Mass was offered on a small kitchen table. Several days later Father bought an altar from the Brothers.

The Catechists were to have the privilege of having the Blessed Sacrament but there was as yet no tabernacle. They found a small medicine cabinet in the former drug room, removed the shelves, painted it white, and used it temporarily for a tabernacle.

The Society had been in New Mexico almost four years and a number of native young women had expressed the desire to become Catechists. In one small village, Dilia, New Mexico, an out-mission of Anton Chico, four young women presented themselves as candidates: Monica Ulibarri, Margarita Aragon, and Anna and Mercedes Gutierrez, blood sisters. Father Sigstein decided to establish a preliminary training school at Las Vegas, a kind of aspirancy where the New Mexico women would stay a year or more before going to Victory Noll in Huntington.

The aspirancy turned out to be short-lived. Six or seven young women did enter at Victory Mount, but John and the Catechists soon realized that it was a duplication of effort. Besides, the Spanish American girls had the advantage of being bi-lingual. They might just as well go immediately to Indiana and attend the classes there with the other candidates.

Las Vegas has served the Society well. In 1933 a house was opened in town, in the building that had been the Christian Brothers' school. The seventeen out-missions where the Catechists worked were divided now, some being taken from Victory Mount, the others from Blessed de Montfort Mission as the house in town was named. Two years later the work was consolidated and Victory Mount discontinued. The building had deteriorated and there was no money for repairs. This was during the worst part of the depression and there was hardly money for food.

A buyer was found for the Victory Mount site but after making a down payment of $600, the man was unable to pay more. Another person agreed to buy it for $3,500 but again there was trouble meeting the payments. Money was scarce. The transaction was not finally settled until 1944.

Meanwhile, the old school building where the Catechists lived in Las Vegas became more and more unsafe for occupancy and there was another move. Through the years the Catechists lived at several different locations. Recently when Our Lady of Sorrows school was discontinued, the Victory Noll Sisters were invited to live in the convent that had been occupied by the Loretto Sisters.

By the year 1928 the Catechists numbered fifty-five professed members with twenty-five or more in training. The Society had been in New Mexico for six years. John Sigstein decided it was time to move into other areas. He accepted the invitations of the Bishop of Amarillo in West Texas, Rudolph Gerken; and the Bishop of Monterey-Fresno, California, John B. MacGinley. The Diocese of Amarillo had been erected only in 1927 and Bishop Gerken was its first ordinary. Monterey-Fresno was separated from Los Angeles and given to Bishop MacGinley in 1924.

Typically, Father Sigstein accepted invitations to work in Lubbock, Texas, and in Dos Palos, California, because of the poverty of these missions. Over and over he would tell the Catechists that in making foundations they were to be guided by the poverty of the people, not by the personality of the pastor.

Dos Palos was transferred to Los Banos in 1931 but it was the same area and the work did not change. Lubbock has the distinction of being the only mission in which the convent is on the same site as it was when the Catechists began work there in 1928. It is not the same convent. A new one was built in 1964 to replace the house that was becoming more inadequate, to say the least. It was fortunate that the new convent was built. If it had not been, the house would probably have collapsed and the Sisters' lives have been endangered in the disastrous tornado of 1970. As it was, the convent was one of the few structures in the neighborhood that withstood the force of the tornado. It was the focal point for rescue operations. The Sisters housed as many of the homeless as they could, and dispensed food, clothing, and other necessities to the victims of the disaster.

When the Catechists first went to Lubbock it was a town of only 5,000. There was but one Catholic church with a congregation predominantly Mexican.[7] During the cotton picking season — from September to December — the little church was filled to overflowing. One of the first things the pastor asked the Catechists to do was to take a complete census of the whole town. He knew that there were many so-called "Anglo" Catholics who were not practicing their religion. This was just before the election of 1928 when Al Smith ran for President. Catholics were far from popular in many parts of the United States. Especially was this true in the Texas plains. The Catechists were often met with rudeness. On one of their first mornings of census taking, seventeen doors were slammed in their faces. But they were not discouraged. Their superior, Catechist Genevieve Sullivan (Sister Mary Genrose), exhorted them to pray especially hard for these people and to offer the insults for their conversion.

A year later a man asked the pastor to have the Catechists call at his home. When they did, he met them with tears in his eyes and apologized for treating them as he had when they called on him the year before. He told them that he had been a fallen-away Catholic but now he had come back to the Church.

The Catechists were welcomed and loved by the poor. The doctors, too, appreciated their coming. They cooperated with them wholeheartedly and gave their services gratis to the sick poor.

To the citizens of Lubbock the Catechists were a curiosity. Most of them had never met Sisters before. None of them had ever seen Sisters drive cars. The Catechists said that the people would stand on the curb open-mouthed, watching them. Only the car driven by the Catechists moved with the green light. Other drivers just stared.

Dos Palos, California, in the San Joaquin Valley, forty miles inland from the Pacific was also, like Lubbock, cotton country. The picking season lasted longer, however. Besides Mexican workers there were also many Italians and Portuguese. Some of the people were permanent residents. Most of them, however, came from Mexico and from other parts of California. The seventy cotton camps were dotted with one-room shacks that served as miserable living quarters for these poor, exploited people.

In each camp was a school, but the children were dismissed shortly before noon so that they could pick cotton all afternoon. The Catechists gathered the children together for religion classes from 11:30 a.m. to 1:30 p.m. They spent the rest of the time visiting the homes.

In the beginning the Catechists taught in seven different camps, each camp having at least sixty children. They ran into difficulty finding teaching centers. In New Mexico they had been permitted to teach in the public school buildings before classes in the morning, during the noon hour, and after school. In California this could not be done. The Catechists had to teach their classes on the highways and byways. As we will see, this was only the beginning of a long struggle for centers where religion could be taught in a way that befitted it.

The move out of New Mexico in 1928 was followed by a long line of foundations in California and Texas. Brawley and Santa Paula in the Diocese of Los Angeles-San Diego were opened in 1930. The Catechists went to Tulare in the Monterey-Fresno Diocese in 1931 and the following year began work in Redlands. In 1934 Carmel became a mission. This convent was moved later to Monterey. San Pedro, the harbor of Los Angeles, was opened the following year.

The tremendous increase in population in southern California called for another diocese. In 1936 San Diego became the new see with Bishop Charles Buddy as ordinary. Redlands and Brawley were under his jurisdiction.

Requests for Catechists came from California pastors everywhere. Father Nunez, pastor of Our Lady of Guadalupe Church in Ontario, followed up his original inquiry with a short but urgent message. "Are you sending me the Catechists in September?" he wrote Father Sigstein. "Please answer that you are. And do it promptly to relieve my mind of this great worry about my children."

Priests in the Coachella Valley and in the Imperial Valley had special reason to be worried about the religious education of the children. Thousands of Mexicans were moving into these parts of California seeking work. The miracle of irrigation made it possible to grow crops nearly every season of the year.

The Mexican American population in Los Angeles and its environs was growing rapidly also. Bishop Cantwell begged for Catechists for Azusa and for East Los Angeles. Every mission staffed by the Catechists had numerous outmissions. Their work was not confined to one parish.

Texas missions expanded more slowly because there were not enough Catechists to supply the need. Centers were opened in San Angelo and in El Paso. Like Lubbock, San Angelo was then in the Diocese of Amarillo. El Paso was under Bishop Anthony Schuler, a Jesuit. His diocese comprised 68,000 square miles. It included eight counties in New Mexico. Bishop Schuler used to say, "Babies baptized by one of my priests today may ask him to perform their marriage ceremony when he is able to complete his rounds again."

Priests and bishops who had the Catechists were almost extravagant in their appreciation. Some even claimed that the whole area was transformed after the

Catechists came. Father Oliver, the Franciscan pastor of Cerrillos in New Mexico, wrote Father Sigstein in 1929: "We have had a wonderful year at Cerrillos, thanks to Almighty God and Our Blessed Lady of Victory. The people were never so united as they are now. There has actually been no murder or knifing or shooting scrapes for two years, due to the wonderful influence of the Catechists. This formerly was a common occurrence."

An opportunity for a number of bishops to express to Bishop Noll and Father Sigstein in person their gratitude for the ministry of the Catechists came when the National Council of Catholic Women chose Fort Wayne as the site of their annual convention in November 1935. It was probably Bishop Noll's idea to have the delegates visit *Our Sunday Visitor* building and Victory Noll on one of the days of their meeting. He was always anxious for visitors to meet the Catechists and become acquainted with their work.

On Sunday afternoon a large crowd — ten bishops, eight hundred delegates and guests, including some priests — drove the twenty-five miles from Fort Wayne to Huntington. It was a long caravan. Among the bishops were some who already had Catechists in their missions and others who were hopefully waiting for them. Several bishops were interested in the Society because young women from their dioceses were members. Besides Bishop Noll there were: Archbishop Drossaerts of San Antonio; Bishop Cantwell who was to be installed as *Archbishop* of Los Angeles in a few weeks; Schuler of El Paso; Gorman, Reno; Morris, Little Rock; Busch, St. Cloud; Kelly, Boise; Gerow, Natchez; and Ritter of Indianapolis.

Archbishop Drossaerts had asked for Catechists before the Society was actually founded. Bishop Gerow and Bishop Gorman had put their applications in writing some years before also. They hoped to make their plea today in person. But the bishops were to be disappointed. John Sigstein was not there. He had left for Chicago the day before.

This was characteristic of John. Whenever there was a possibility of his being honored in any way, he disappeared. He was quite content to let people think (as most of them did then and many still do today) that Bishop Noll was the Founder of the Society of Missionary Catechists. Father confided to more than one of his "children" that he was altogether unworthy of being the Founder of the Society.

And yet Father Sigstein never hesitated to appear before an audience when it was a question of making a plea for his beloved poor, for begging for funds so that the Catechists might minister to the sick and provide for the needs of all who were under their care.

But face ten bishops Father could not do. He asked Father Clement Neubauer, novice master at nearby St. Felix Capuchin Friary, to act as host in his stead. Father Clement acquiesced, for he knew John Sigstein as few others knew him. For many years he was his spiritual director.[8]

Victory Noll had been growing by leaps and bounds. What were intended to be single bedrooms had long since become double bedrooms. Even that did not take care of all the Catechists. They had to use also the rooms that were once guest rooms. This was the wing on the west side that extended out toward the front of the building. Today the administration offices are there. To insure privacy for those who were sleeping in the wing, a door had been installed to close off the whole section.

The problem of taking care of eight hundred guests was a big one. It was decided to serve a buffet supper in the large basement room. This was referred to as the auditorium because there was a stage with a movie screen there, but it was put to many uses, even being used for hanging the wash on a rainy day.

The bishops and priests would be served dinner in the Catechists' dining room. A room was still needed where the guests could be received and also become acquainted with the work of the Society. The large classroom was fitted up for this purpose. Desks, chairs, and other classroom furniture were moved out and put in the west wing, the wing now used as sleeping quarters. This required quite a bit of stacking of furniture but it did not matter. The hall could be closed off and no one would be any the wiser.

In the converted classroom were displays of various kinds. There was a large map showing the location of the eighteen mission centers where the Catechists were instructing 14,000 children. A catechetical display included textbooks, slides, charts, and a miniature altar. The altar was the gift of Father Gales, at that time director of the Catechetical Guild in St. Paul, Minnesota. A special attraction was a small scale replica of the Old Mission at Carmel, California.

When all the guests had arrived, they went to chapel for Benediction of the Blessed Sacrament. Of course the chapel was much too small even with the benches and aisles filled. There was a huge overflow in the hall outside. The people moved from the chapel to the classroom where the Catechists answered their many questions about the Society.

Father Clement was to take the bishops and priests to the reception room at the end of the *east* wing. Ordinarily this would have been very simple but today the halls were jammed with women. However, Father Clement knew Victory Noll well. He figured that the best way to carry out the march would be to go down the west corridor, across the patio, and into the reception room from the outside. The door leading into the corridor was only a couple of yards from the classroom. But alas, the Capuchin had no idea that the west corridor was also jammed, not with women but with furniture piled high. It was an unexpected sight that met his eye when he opened the door. Nevertheless, he gamely led his charges through the obstacle course.

It was indeed the strangest ecclesiastical procession Victory Noll had ever seen. Arrived at their destination, the bishops sat down and lighted cigars passed to them by the Catechists. The bishops who had come, hoping to talk to

Father Sigstein, begged their hostesses to put in a good word for them with their Founder when he returned home. The Catechists readily promised, for they were fired with the desire to help the bishops in their missionary fields.

Notes to Chapter X

1. Letter of October 4, 1924.
2. Eating and drinking of any liquids except water are prohibited for one hour before the reception of Holy Communion. But it was not always so. From about the fifth century to 1953 the fast was very strict; nothing to eat or drink — not even water — after midnight. Some missionaries celebrated three Masses on Sunday, often at great distances apart. If they wished to drink coffee or another liquid between Masses, they could do so only with special permission of the Apostolic Delegate. In 1953 Pope Pius XII, prompted by the changed conditions of the times, mitigated the Communion fast. Abstinence from solid food was required but water and other liquids (except alcohol) were permitted until one hour before Communion. Four years later Pius XII made a further change. Abstinence from solid food and all drink except water was required to three hours before Communion. The present ruling came into effect under Paul VI in 1964.
3. Archbishop Daeger (1872-1932) was a friar of the Province of St. John Baptist, Cincinnati. He was ordained in 1896 and assigned to the New Mexico missions in 1902.
4. *The Little Flowers of St. Francis* (referred to also as the *Fioretti* from the Italian) was written, not by St. Francis of Assisi, but by Brother Ugolino di Monte Santa Maria who lived a century after the death of Francis. The work is a collection of delightful stories of St. Francis and his first followers. It has become a Christian classic.
5. This story, together with others like it, was published in the Cincinnati archdiocesan paper, *Catholic Telegraph,* at the time of the Archbishop's death.
6. *The Santa Fe New Mexican,* December 2, 1932.
7. At this time Lubbock was a mission from Plainview, having been cared for before that from Slaton. In October 1928 Father Luis Gonzales was appointed assistant to Father Krukker, pastor of Plainview. To minister to the growing congregation of Mexican Americans Father Gonzales took up residence at St. Joseph's Church, Lubbock. It was not until July 1929, however, that the parish was canonically erected with Father Gregory Boeckman as pastor.
8. Clement Neubauer, O.F.M. Cap., was Master of Novices and later, Guardian at St. Felix Friary during the twenties and thirties. From 1946 to 1952 and again from 1958 to 1964 he was Minister General of the Capuchin Friars throughout the world. Father Clement died in Milwaukee in 1969.

11

Public Relations

THE IMPORTANCE OF PUBLIC RELATIONS was realized by John Sigstein and his co-workers in their Lodging House Mission days. John himself had a flair for writing and speaking. He had an unerring instinct for the right story told at the right time.

Long before the Society of Missionary Catechists was actually established, John began making plans to publicize the work. He was somewhat handicapped in Chicago because of Archbishop Mundelein's attitude. He could not publish any articles in *The New World,* Chicago's archdiocesan paper, so he turned to *Our Sunday Visitor* in Huntington, Indiana. Besides, the *Visitor* had a much larger circulation than any of the diocesan papers. Its editor, John F. Noll, was always anxious to promote any movement or organization intended to propagate the faith.

As soon as the Society was incorporated in Santa Fe, New Mexico, and the Archbishop, Albert T. Daeger, had accepted the title of Honorary President, Father Sigstein launched his publicity campaign in earnest. A long article sent to *Our Sunday Visitor* in the summer of 1921 was published in its entirety. He sent the same article to the National Catholic News Service in Washington.[1] Many newspapers and magazines that subscribed to the service published the account, some complete versions, some abbreviated.

From the time that Monsignor Noll definitely decided to sponsor the Society in May 1923, hardly an issue of *Our Sunday Visitor* was published without some mention of the Catechists. At first it was in the "Readers Speak to Readers" section that various letters appeared. Only later did the paper run stories and articles.

There were letters to Father Sigstein from Julia, from Archbishop Daeger, Michael Dumarest, Sophie Renier, and Blanche Richardson. The Catechists wrote of their experiences and of the abject poverty of the people. The Archbishop and the priest extolled the work of the Catechists and their love and compassion for the poor.

There were letters to the editor from people all over the United States and Canada with donations for the building fund for the Training Institute being erected in Huntington for the Missionary Catechists. As the building progressed pictures of it appeared. In the November 9 issue in 1924 there was a large picture with this caption: "Above is a closeup front view of our new Catechists' Training Institute. The camera man was too close to get anything but the front whose portico encloses a beautiful patio, characteristic of Spanish architecture. This beautiful Training School which will be in operation by December 1, is located a quarter of a mile north of the world-famous banks of the Wabash and one mile west of Huntington, also world-famous as the home of *Our Sunday Visitor*."

Letters began to come now to Monsignor Noll from women who were interested in joining the Catechists. Letters came also from women who wished there had been a Society like this in existence when they were young. Now it was too late. They were married or they were too old.

Not a week went by without the "Catechists' Column" in *Our Sunday Visitor*. Very often Bishop Noll himself would write an editorial calling attention to the work of the Catechists. He would usually conclude by inviting young women to join the Society. The replies he turned over to Father Sigstein. More than once John confided to Julia that he was "swamped with inquiries."

This publicity was all the more valuable because it was at that time the only means of making Victory Noll known. Most religious communities depended for recruits on young women who were students in their schools and colleges. In some ways the weekly column in *Our Sunday Visitor* was more effective than advertisements are today. The articles for the most part were human interest stories that attracted young women. The life of a Catechist sounded adventuresome and what young woman does not dream of adventure?

This type of publicity continued for several decades until in the forties and fifties it was replaced by ads. By that time about eighty percent of the membership in the Congregation first heard of the work through the pages of *Our Sunday Visitor*. John Sigstein and the Catechists realized the tremendous debt they owed to Bishop Noll and the *Visitor*.

Besides the written word Father Sigstein was convinced of the power of the spoken word and especially the word illustrated by slides. In the spring of 1924 a seminarian from St. Meinrad, Indiana, wrote to *OSV* on behalf of their unit of the Catholic Students Mission Crusade.[2] They had "had the pleasure of hearing Ronald Fahey lecture on March 18 about the newly founded Society of Missionary Catechists." The writer recommended the lecture to other seminaries and to parishes.

Ronald Fahey, a Chicago man, was the Society's first public relations person. John had known Fahey during his years at St. Pius parish. He hired him because of his ability and also because he knew the young man needed work and the money it would bring him. He remained in the position in an off again, on again way for several years. His illustrated lecture which was referred to by the St. Meinrad seminarian was entitled "The Rediscovered Country."

The lecture was given in Chicago, Fort Wayne, Huntington, and a few other cities in the Midwest. According to news articles that appeared in various newspapers, there were 227 "artistically colored slides." This was in the days when slides were usually four by five inches in size and were extremely heavy, the hand painted pictures being enclosed in glass. Fahey's picture appeared with each news story. He was a handsome young man, smooth faced, wearing a wing collar.

The news release had the byline S. Cyril Hettich. Hettich was now referred to as public relations director and Fahey as lecturer. Father Sigstein never did anything except in a big way. Evidently he decided that one man was not enough. He needed two to make known the work of the Society. And even though money was almost non-existent, he rented and furnished an office for the men in downtown Chicago.

"The Rediscovered Country" lecture was condensed into an attractive booklet with the sub-head "An Unusual Treatise on the Romantic Southwest of Our Own Country." Its publication was made possible through the generosity of J.G. Steinbach, architect of Victory Noll, and of G.J. Gaul of Deprato Statuary Company. Both men were from Chicago. Mr. Steinbach had designed the Training Institute and the Deprato Company had been responsible for the chapel and its furnishings. The chapel was the personal gift of Bishop Noll himself.

The first page of the booklet contained pictures of Archbishop Daeger, Monsignor Noll, and Anthony Blaufuss. No mention of John Sigstein. Then there were the architect's drawing of Victory Noll and a photograph of the chapel. Father Sigstein's name does appear on the following page where he is listed as the President and Spiritual Director of the Society. Father Dumarest is identified here as the Vice President and Financial Secretary. Then are listed Charles J. Eckert, Acting Secretary, Santa Fe, New Mexico; S. Cyril Hettich, Publicity Director, Huntington, Indiana; Ronald P. Fahey, Lecturer, Chicago, Illinois. Besides, the names of Sophie Renier, Caroline Meister, Blanche Richardson, and Julia Doyle are there with various titles. It was an imposing list. On the title page, in large type, was the information that the Publicity Bureau of the Society of Missionary Catechists of Our Blessed Lady of Victory, Victory Noll, Huntington, Indiana, was the publisher of the booklet. And again, Hettich is identified as the Publicity Director.

In a small note "Mr. Ronald P. Fahey gratefully acknowledges the use of valuable material for this lecture taken from the Historical Works of Mr. Benjamin Read, the Historian of New Mexico, and Mr. Charles F. Lummis, author of *The Land of Poco Tiempo.*" Fahey probably put the lecture together but without a doubt, it was mostly the work of John Sigstein, as those who knew him well can attest.

On each page of the book is a picture, first of scenes in New Mexico, then of the Catechists with the children, with the poor, and finally in a predicament that was to happen again and again in New Mexico — the Catechists' Model T Ford bogged down in the middle of an arroyo. In the last picture the Catechists are being pulled out by a wagon hitched to two horses. The legend under the picture reads simply "The Finish," The thirty-six-page booklet is bound in imitation leather paper. On the cover, besides the title, is a line sketch of a typical adobe mission chapel. On the back is a map of the States of the Southwest. At the end of the book is a plug for *The Missionary Catechist,* "a monthly magazine at only fifty cents a year."

The magazine had just been published, the first issue dated December 1924. It was to continue for forty years and was dropped only because of the difficulty of finding enough personnel to work on it. The decision to discontinue the magazine proved providential. A few years later it became more and more apparent that mission magazines like *The Missionary Catechist* had, for the most part, served their purpose. Many of them were discontinued.

Until 1938 the magazine was printed on *Our Sunday Visitor* presses. After that time the printing was done by the Sisters on a second hand Kelly press, later on a Miehle. Father Sigstein, in 1928, thought it would be well to have a small job press for printing stationery and promotion material. Catechist Effie McConnell was the printer. The Kelly press which John obtained in the thirties was more efficient. One of the men from *Our Sunday Visitor* promised to demonstrate how to run it. The man was delayed so Catechist McConnell figured out from a book how to operate the press. Many years later she taught Agnes Ganse to run the large press, the folder, stapler, cutter, and all the other equipment needed to produce the magazine. Among the other Catechists involved in printing were Catherine Ganse and Bernadette Doiron.

A small but efficient Heidelberg press takes care of Victory Noll's needs today. Sister Agnes still prints letterheads, envelopes, and Christmas cards for the Motherhouse personnel.

Even in 1921 John Sigstein was making plans for a monthly magazine. He probably had it in mind before that date, but in 1921 there is the first evidence of it. In a talk he gave at the Incorporation meeting of the Society in Santa Fe, July 1921, John outlined his plans for *The Missionary Catechist.* A month later he was writing to Eula Lee and telling her that he had her in mind for editor. Characteristically he asked her to keep the plans secret.

The following year John was telling Julia he hoped to launch the magazine as soon as he had the funds. Money was not forthcoming, however, and the magazine did not appear until December 1924. Meanwhile Father Sigstein was soliciting articles to be published in *The Missionary Catechist*. Through the years many bishops, priests, and others wrote for the magazine at Father's request. Many of these articles were extremely well written and interesting, but what appealed most to subscribers were mission stories, actual experiences of the Catechists.

The busy missionaries had little time for writing articles for publication. The source of mission stories was what were called community letters. The idea of each mission center writing a monthly letter and sending it to Victory Noll and to the missions was the brainchild of Sophie Renier when she became Head Catechist in 1924. Father Sigstein quickly endorsed the idea.

Sophie was community-minded and was certain that the letters would be a means of binding the Catechists together and making them aware of what was going on in places other than their own centers.

Each Catechist took her turn writing the letter each month. These community letters proved to be a wonderful inspiration for the young women at Victory Noll who were preparing themselves for the missions. Also, they were an invaluable source of information for *The Missionary Catechist*. Most of the Catechists would probably have panicked at the thought of writing for publication, but they were not at all adverse to writing to their companions about what had happened in their mission.

The stories were illustrated with appealing pictures of Catechists and children and of the poor who depended so much on the services of the Catechists. Funds were always low and yet John Sigstein saw to it that each mission had a good camera. If the films did not come in regularly to Victory Noll, he would remind the Catechists that they must take pictures and send them to him.

Here is a typical story that came from New Mexico and was written by Catechist Susanna Michels. It was entitled "The Shepherd and His Flock."

Last week we took a different road to one of our little out-missions. We are glad we did, for now we have five more children enrolled in our catechism class. They live in a little shack up in the mountains. We visited the family and found the mother and her little ones in a pitiful condition. The father was away in search of work and the family was living on a few beans and the milk of several goats. None of the children have made their First Communion. We asked them if they would like to come to our religion classes, for they do not live very far from the mission. At first the oldest boy did not think he could attend because he had to take care of the goats. Before we left, however, he promised to come and bring his little brothers and sisters. Imagine how surprised we were when he brought not only his brothers and sisters, but the goats also! Several times during class he left his seat to look out and see if his goats were still there.

Early copies of *The Missionary Catechist,* as well as early descriptive literature complained about the proselytizing that was being carried out by Protestant organizations working among the Spanish-speaking people. Some of it makes rather embarrassing reading now but the truth is that anti-Catholicism had had a long and ugly history in our country. Sad to say it still exists on some levels. Conditions have changed and will continue to change, but missionaries among the Hispanic people in the earlier part of this century had reason to fear for the faith of their flock.

Not content with an illustrated lecture, a magazine, weekly articles sent out by N.C.W.C. news service, John Sigstein conceived the idea of having a movie to propagate the work of the Society. In 1926 an eight-reel motion picture, "In the Service of the Queen," was filmed in New Mexico, in Chicago, and at Victory Noll.

The Chicago-based Joyce Kilmer Players produced the film. The premiere took place in Chicago Sunday, December 5, 1926, at the Athenaeum Theater, Southport and Lincoln Avenues. The front cover of the program has the information that "Ronald P. Fahey presents The Joyce Kilmer Players, Chicago's Foremost Catholic Dramatic Guild, in 'In the Service of the Queen' for the benefit of the Society of Missionary Catechists."

Inside the front cover it was stated: "Scenario and Direction by William Roeder, Photography by 'Red' Felbinger, Edited by Orlando Lippert, Titles by Ronald P. Fahey, Laboratory Technician Frank Bauer, Production Advisers 'Red' Felbinger and Orlando P. Lippert." Lippert and Roeder are in the cast of characters, and surprisingly, the Rev. J.J. Sigstein is listed among the players as the Spiritual Director.

The music was by the Alvernia Symphony Orchestra, Sister Bonaventure and Miss Kathryn Mundstock being responsible for the special musical score for the production. The program contained a long list of patrons and patronesses. Special thanks were extended to "Goldenberg Furniture Company who let the producers use their store and fine furniture for filming various scenes. Special gratitude also to the Management of the Ridge View Hotel, Evanston, and to Mr. August Ott and Mrs. Charles Hollenbach for their kindness in extending the use of their wonderful summer home and estate on Pistakee Bay for various scenes in this production." The last page of the program was devoted to the purpose of the Society of Missionary Catechists. It was explained that the Catechists receive no salary or remuneration for their services, and depend entirely upon the generosity of charitably disposed Catholics for support. Correspondence was invited; communications were to be directed to the Rev. Spiritual Director. His address followed.

The story on which the film was based was written by Constance Edgerton, a popular author of the time, and Catechist Blanche Richardson. It was the story of a vocation. The Santa Fe train carrying a young woman from the East on her way to California for a vacation, was forced to remain in Las Vegas, New Mexico, twenty-four hours for repairs. To while away the time, Mary Garvey, the young woman, accompanies a missionary priest to one of his missions. There she meets the Catechists and becomes acquainted with their ministry. As a result she decides to join the Society. Her parents, not to mention her fiance, are indignant and create all sorts of difficulties, but in the end Mary enters Victory Noll. The Catechists themselves take part in the film though they are not mentioned in the cast of characters.

The whole thing was extremely well done and was received everywhere with enthusiasm. Reviews and descriptive folders sound somewhat lavish when we read them today. "In the Service of the Queen" was described as the most unusual picture ever filmed. "The Dramatic Story of a Modern American Girl — Society Offers Her Wealth and Position — Then She Hears a Great Call — And She Chooses a Life of Poverty — From the Glittering Palaces of Pleasure to the Humble Huts of the Poor — Never a Greater Sacrifice — Never a More Tender Tale of the Greater Love. Projector and Operator Furnished. Are you in line for a booking? Reels of Thrills, Pathos, Humor, and Romance!"

Inside this particular folder are recommendations from Bishop Noll; also from St. Francis Academy, Joliet, Illinois. There is a quote from *The Tower*, from Mt. Calvary, Wisconsin, and a comment from a Franciscan priest in Chicago. Further description declares: "An Epic in Feature Motion Pictures — pronounced by the Press and Critics as a picture worthy of a high rank among super screen productions. Clergy, press, large audiences recently confirmed this general approval at showings in Chicago, Denver, St. Louis, Boston, New Orleans . . . compares favorably with the famous film, 'The White Sister.'" Lucille Wolfe, who takes the part of Mary Garvey, is extolled as another Lillian Gish.

The film itself, good as it was, would not have been so successful had Father Sigstein not been careful in his choice of the people who represented the Society in showing it. In the beginning a young woman, Rose Donahue from Chicago, traveled ahead to book the movie. Walter Zieverink, also from Chicago, a former naval officer, showed the picture. Neither Rose nor Walter was in the best of health. They were personal friends of John's and took the work because they were interested in the Society. However, the traveling proved more strenuous than they thought it would, and Father was forced to look for others to replace them.[3]

Again, he was very discerning; and again, he found two excellent replacements. Mae C. Smith did the booking and Robert McCann operated the projector. Both were from Chicago. Miss Smith (only Father Sigstein called her Mae) had worked for a church goods company and knew the right approach in dealing with priests and religious superiors. She was dedicated to the Society and realized that the film was an excellent way to make known its work. It would have been hard to find a better representative.

John used to protest to Miss Smith that her expense accounts were lower than he expected them to be. He used to say that "Mae would rather drink tea in a first class dining room than eat a real meal in an ordinary restaurant." Miss Smith knew that the movie brought in very little money-wise and that the Society was hard pressed for funds. She purposely cut her own expenses.

Robert McCann was an excellent representative also. A former seminarian, he had been recommended to Father by his good friend Girard Picard, then Spiritual Director at St. Mary of the Lake Seminary in Mundelein, Illinois.

How the film was financed is not clear from the records. It can be reasonably certain that the Joyce Kilmer Players gave their services gratis. No doubt other expenses were met by donations from John Sigstein's friends, for he would have to pay for the transportation of the cast to New Mexico and to other locations. Some of the older Sisters recall their being in Las Vegas, but they do not remember where they stayed. It was not at Victory Mount which had barely been opened at that time and was in no condition to house guests.

Will Roeder who headed the Joyce Kilmer Players remained a friend of Father Sigstein and the Society through the years. It was he who donated the beautiful statue of Our Lady of Grace which is now in front of Archbishop Noll Memorial Chapel. Before it was moved to this location it was at the top of the hill leading to Victory Noll.

"In the Service of the Queen" would have had a longer life-span than it did had it not been that it was a silent movie and the so-called "talkies" came into being at this time. Good as it was, however, it did not produce such tangible results vocation-wise as did the illustrated lectures the Catechists themselves gave, especially during the thirties.

By this time the Society had a good collection of colored slides. They were still the heavy kind and the projector also weighed many pounds. Two Sisters went out "on the road" with the slides. One ran the projector and followed the script for guide. The other stood on the stage by the screen and gave the talk. There was no need for a podium; the talk was given from memory. More than one member of the Congregation traces her vocation to the slide-lectures.

In those days it was comparatively easy to go into schools, even high schools and colleges, at any time of year and on short notice. The Catechists first called on the Propagation of the Faith Director for permission to visit the schools of the diocese. After that it was up to the pastor or sister principal. Almost without exception these priests and sisters were most gracious to the Catechists. Sodalities, also, were enthusiastic about the slides.

The slide-lecture was more effective than the motion picture because the Catechists were there in person. Young women could see what they were like. They could speak with them and ask them questions. The stories the Catechists told were appealing. There were stories of adventure, sad stories, humorous stories. The audiences liked the one about the little girl whom the late Bishop Buddy of San Diego questioned on confirmation day. The Bishop had been asking about the sacraments that can be received but once and then he queried, "How many times can you receive the sacrament of matrimony?" Eight-year-old Lupe waved her hand and the Bishop called on her. "As often as my husband dies," she answered correctly.

It is always risky to name names lest some who should be included are left out. A number of Catechists were responsible for publicizing the Society in its earlier days. Besides those who spoke to various groups there were those who edited the magazine, were in charge of Associate Catechists of Mary bands and of Mary's Loyal Helpers (children who helped the missions), designed promotion literature, and served as contact persons for "In the Service of the Queen." Those who guided these projects and whose names appear most frequently in the records include: Blanche Richardson, Caroline Meister, Helen Srill, Margaret Campbell, Madelon LoRang, Dorothy Schneider, Viola Wopperer, Regina Torzewski, Mary Louise Perl, Elizabeth Clifford, and Mary Karl. Still longer would be the list were we to include those who went along on publicity trips as companions, a most important role, for they helped to answer questions, to give out literature, and make friends with audiences.

John Sigstein thought it well to have the Catechists attend conventions. He had Marie Benes come from New Mexico in the summer of 1923 to represent the Society at the national meeting of the Catholic Students Mission Crusade at the University of Notre Dame. Bishop Noll, host bishop and principal speaker, called attention to the newly founded Society and to Catechist Benes, one of the first members.

When two Catechists went to Cincinnati for the Catholic Press convention in May 1929, they were the only religious there. Perhaps they were the only women also. The Catechists attended meetings of the National Conference of Catholic Charities and of the Catholic Rural Life Conference. Their interest in the latter was its CCD aspect. The Confraternity of Christian Doctrine in this country grew out, as it were, of the Rural Life Conference founded in 1923 by Bishop Edwin V. O'Hara. Vacation schools were sponsored by Rural Life.

All of these activities were helpful for public relations for the Society, but if Father Sigstein had been asked at this time what he considered the best source of vocations and of funds also, he would undoubtedly have answered, "Priests." Ultimately it was priests who sent young women to Victory Noll; it was priests who helped to organize Associate Catechists of Mary bands. Father liked to have priests visit Victory Noll. Always hospitable to everyone who came, he was especially so to priests.

Two good Chicago priests should be mentioned here even at the risk of not naming others who helped the Society during its first two decades. They are George Lescher and Eugene Luke. Father Lescher, a professor at Quigley Preparatory Seminary, used to bring a carload of his student seminarians with him whenever he visited Huntington. Many of these young men were ordained to the priesthood and remained staunch friends of the Catechists. Both Father Lescher and Father Luke organized ACM bands that continue to this day.

It happened frequently that a priest from another part of the country, traveling by on U.S. 24, would come up the hill to find out what the mission-style building was. Nothing pleased Father Sigstein better than to show the priest visitor every part of Victory Noll. Usually he asked a Catechist to accompany them on the tour. If the visitor could not stay for a meal, at least he must have a light lunch. There was only one thing to watch out for on these occasions; for the Catechists to look out for, that is. If a fresh batch of bread had been baked this morning, it might be a good thing to stash it away. Father always gave away a loaf or two if the bread was cooling when visitors came to the kitchen. He literally cast his bread on the waters and it was returned to him four-fold in the good will he brought about.

Notes To Chapter XI

1. NC News Service was established in 1920. It is a division of the United States Catholic Conference. Father Sigstein was a personal friend of its director, Frank Hall, during the early years of the Society of Missionary Catechists.

2. The Catholic Students Mission Crusade was founded in 1918 by Father Clifford King, S.V.D. Its purpose was to acquaint students of Catholic schools with the Church's missionary activities. The National Center was in Cincinnati, Ohio. The annual convention held at the University of Notre Dame was always well attended by missionaries and students alike. The CSMC ceased activity in recent years.

3. Walter Zieverink suffered a heart attack and died while he was "on the road" with the film April 13, 1932.

12

Depression

T HAT'S THE NEW SUPERIOR," announced Margarita in a loud stage whisper to the little girl with her.

"Superior? What's that?" inquired her companion.

"The Catechist who buys the groceries," explained Margarita.

Margarita and her friend were referring to Josephine Penning, newly appointed Senior Catechist in Las Vegas, New Mexico. There was a certain irony in the description, Catechist Penning thought, overhearing the conversation. There was scarcely enough money to *buy* groceries. Many times the Catechists suffered from hunger as severely as did the poor whom they ministered to.

The Society of Missionary Catechists grew up during the depression years. There was hardly a year when the Catechists experienced anything but hard times. The community's beginnings were in poverty and obscurity. By the time the Society was becoming known — toward the end of the twenties — the crash came. The next decade was a struggle for survival.

John Sigstein's instructions to Julia were clear: "Go to the *poorest* first. Always have preference for them." John was determined that the Catechists would never accept any remuneration for their services. Moreover, it was doubtful whether the poor people for whom the Catechists worked could at that time have provided the smallest subsidy for them.

Not even his friend Anthony Blaufuss could dissuade Father Sigstein in this point. In a letter dated October 23, 1917, when the two men were corresponding on various aspects of plans for the Society, Anthony wrote: "I think gratuitous help should not be refused." A year later he was writing: "All missionary priests will want to have these Sisters because they will be free."

How true that prediction turned out to be. But it would not change John Sigstein's determination to take no money from the people nor from the missionaries. He refused to budge an inch from this stand. He would beg from Catholics in the East and Midwest. It was their duty and their privilege to come to the assistance of their less favored brothers and sisters in Christ.

Three months before Julia and Marie left Chicago for New Mexico John launched a direct mail drive for funds. The letter of appeal was addressed to 6,000 priests whose names were taken from the Catholic Directory. That it was a failure was partly, maybe mostly, due to the fact that the only address given was P.O. Box 334, Santa Fe, New Mexico. The letter was signed by Rev. Michael Dumarest, Treasurer, Society of Missionary Catechists of Our Blessed Lady of Victory. Since Archbishop Daeger's name was mentioned in the appeal, a few, but very few, priests sent donations to him. Father Sigstein had sent the bundle of letters out to Will Frey to mail from Santa Fe.

It is significant that one priest, a Father Trend of Elkton, Maryland, who sent a check to Archbishop Daeger for the Catechists, wrote that it was his opinion that such a Society could save the faith in Maryland. He lamented the fact that lay people were not permitted to teach religion.He also pointed out that not many priests would answer an appeal like that with only a post office box for address. And he could not find the Society of Missionary Catechists in the Catholic Directory. Hardly! Julia and Marie had not yet left for New Mexico.

Anthony Blaufuss consoled his friend when he heard that the drive for funds had failed. He reminded John that priests seldom answer appeals. They get too many of them. Anthony himself sent $1,000.

John's other priest friends were not in a position to help very much. Jim Douglas, who had kept in touch with John from Kenrick days, also chided his friend for being so anonymous. "I received your banks [mite boxes] and literature but I have nowhere found your name mentioned in any connection. Why shouldn't you let the world, the priests especially, know how all this came about, who the instigator is?"

Though the appeal to priests was abortive, Father Sigstein bounced right back. By September he was writing Anthony of his plans to mail 120,000 letters. These were sent under Julia's name: "Julia Anne Doyle, Missionary Catechist," the signature in Ronald Fahey's beautiful handwriting.

This campaign was also a failure but two months later John was writing to Anthony about a new plan he had. This was an advertisement in *Our Sunday Visitor*. Then in December Anthony received a copy of a Christmas appeal. Perhaps this yielded some returns, for there was an acknowledgment signed by the Rev. J.J. Sigstein and written on a letterhead of the Society with the post office Santa Fe address.[1]

Christmas appeals became an annual event. In 1932 when things were very bleak, Father sent out an appeal during Lent also. The answers to these appeals came, for the most part, from the poor and the middle class. Though the Congregation long ago discontinued sending appeals — because most Catholics receive so many — a number of good friends continue to send donations. The letters accompanying these gifts are often touching, for it would seem that in many cases, the money is sent at a great sacrifice.

In December 1922 John wrote Julia:

> Let us always be truly grateful to our benefactors and never forget every day to thank our dear Lord and our sweet Mother for sending such noble souls to assist us in the days of our greatest need and in the hours of our severest trials. May Jesus and Mary bless and reward not merely a hundredfold but a million times a hundredfold now and forever these truly Christian souls who have been inspired by our loving Mother to render us such valued assistance during the dark hours of the past month and in the days when the Cross seemed so heavy. Set this standard of gratitude, my dear spiritual daughter, so high that all those who come after you will be inspired to obey the rules of the Society which insist so strongly and so persistently on the cultivation of the spirit of unselfishness and the virtue of gratitude.

George Wolf from Chicago and his sisters Amelia and Helen were, from earliest days, benefactors of the Society. Though not exactly affluent, they were in a position to give more than others who sent their gifts to Father Sigstein. When Peter O'Donnell suffered financial reverses and could not help with the repairs on the old Santa Fe hospital building in Las Vegas, it was George Wolf who provided the money.

If it had not been for Peter O'Donnell and his wife Julia, Victory Noll would not have been built when it was. Peter paid almost half the cost of erecting the building. Bishop Noll put it this way in his *History of the Diocese of Fort Wayne* written in 1941: "Monsignor Noll built Victory Noll in 1923 at an outlay of $240,000. A California gentleman contributed $100,000 to this project."[2] Peter made the payment in two different installments.

There were months and years, however, when Peter's investments yielded little or nothing. Once, when they had no steady income, Mrs. O'Donnell sold her engagement ring to provide train fare for a young woman who entered the Society from California.

No one knew better than Julia and Marie that they were entering on a life of poverty when they became Missionary Catechists. Articles that are looked on as necessities by most persons, they considered luxuries. In a note to Marie written in the spring of 1922 Julia lists some clothing she is getting — gloves, kimona, apron, handkerchiefs, etc. Then she adds: "I may get some money donations that I will share with you and we can get a few *luxuries,* a dictionary for instance, dishes, etc." The emphasis is hers.

Though Father Sigstein was always struggling to pay bills, he was solicitous about the welfare of the Catechists. In May 1923 he commended Marie for managing to keep household expenses at nine dollars a week but he insisted that they practice no false economy. He wrote:

> When I wrote you that we must economize till it hurts, there was no thought in my mind at all that this should apply to your expenditures for groceries, meats, and other food. You know that the rules of our dear Society provide that you are at all times to have good, nourishing food, and plenty of it . . . So away with the skim milk. Mary [as he usually referred to Marie Benes] can use this skim milk for baking purposes but by all means get good milk to drink and to use for your coffee . . . It is false economy, and besides, it is not God's Holy Will, nor the good pleasure of our Blessed Mother, that you should be deprived of wholesome, nourishing food, in the midst of your laborious work in your missionary trips.

In this same letter John answered a question Julia had asked, about whether they might accept money for services rendered or for medicine and other things given to the people. His reply is emphatic:

> You know the rule, Julia. We may never ask for anything in return for our services. If someone who has been benefited by you in any way, wishes to show his or her appreciation, then you may accept whatever they offer if you think they can afford such an offering, but only on this one condition, clearly laid down and understood: THAT IT IS A DONATION TOWARD A BURSE OR A WORK OF THE SOCIETY, AND NOT AS PAYMENT FOR SERVICES RENDERED, OR A GIFT TO ANY INDIVIDUAL MEMBER OF THE SOCIETY. It is true, as you say, it is hard with so much money going out and so little coming in. But let us not forget that the period of struggle in getting sufficient funds for carrying on our work, will in the future history of the Society, be reckoned as ONE OF THE MOST FRUITFUL AND BLESSED PERIODS IN THE EXISTENCE OF OUR DEAR SOCIETY. As it is with an individual, so it is with any work of our Dear Lord or His Blessed Mother. These must be proved by trials, crosses and tribulations before they can receive the stamp and seal of a work of God. And so it must be with our own dear Society. The past eight months have indeed been in many respects a Calvary, but we felt that after our Calvary there would be a Tabor . . . And so at last we are coming to the dawn of a glorious day for the work of our dear Society.[3]

The "glorious new day" was being ushered in by Monsignor Noll's promise that *Our Sunday Visitor* would establish a burse. This would be paid in six annual installments of $1,000 each. Still more, Monsignor Noll told Father Sigstein that the *Visitor* was desirous of erecting a permanent monument of its missionary zeal by building a Training Institute for the Society of Missionary Catechists in Huntington. And that was not all. *Our Sunday Visitor,* according to its editor, would have no difficulty in raising $25,000 a year for the maintenance of the Catechists in training. Well could John Sigstein believe he was now on Mount Tabor.

Lack of money was always a great trial for Julia. Borrowing did not seem to bother John as it did Julia. He was always optimistic about getting funds. One of the money campaigns in the fall of 1922 cost $1,300 and returns amounted only to $500. John had borrowed $700 from the bank and now he had lost $800 on the appeal. Yet in March of the following year he was writing Julia that since they left Chicago in August, he had spent $700 on material for uniforms, coats, etc. He had to buy a lot of material, he explained, in order to get a wholesale price but he considered this a good investment. And at the time there were two Catechists in the missions and two more at Longwood in Chicago!

Even though Father Sigstein wished the Catechists to work without pay, he insisted that they *not* contribute candles, sacred vessels, etc. for the Church. He believed that the people, even the children, should be taught to support the Church. "Stole fees," he would always declare, "were a curse to the Church."[4]

Things began to look up considerably after the move to Victory Noll at the end of 1924. The Catechists who lived in Huntington were being provided for by the generosity of Bishop Noll and *Our Sunday Visitor*. The Catechists in the missions, however, continued to live sparingly, with scarcely enough money to pay for their needs. A letter from Cerrillos, New Mexico, written by Catechist Martinez a few days before Christmas reported that they would have a chicken dinner for the feast. "Father Oliver, the pastor, brought two roosters from Pena Blanca. Mr. Williams promised to bring us a bottle of milk for our Christmas present. Each one of us will have a glass if there is enough."[5]

John Sigstein concentrated all his efforts on ways to insure ongoing support for the Catechists in the missions. It was to the Associate Catechists of Mary that he turned for help. The idea of the organization was to have a group of persons raise at least $150 a year toward a burse which, when completed, would amount to $6,000. The money, when invested, would yield an income that would support a Catechist for life.

The bands of Associate Catechists were made up of ten people headed by a man or woman promoter. Each individual person paid $1.00 a year dues. All helped with fund raising events. Father Sigstein always stressed the spiritual benefits of the ACM, as it was called. The members would share in the prayers and good works of the Catechist laboring under the title of the burse chosen by the band. The Catechist was expected to keep in touch with the members, pray for them, and send an account of her work and needs.

Sister Blanche Marie Richardson, for many years, was contact person at Victory Noll for the Associate Catechists of Mary. Previously Sister Viola Wopperer and Sister Mary Karl had the position. Besides keeping in touch with the bands, these Sisters edited pages in *The Missionary Catechist* dealing with activities of the Associate Catechists of Mary. The same Sisters directed Mary's

Loyal Helpers. These were children who made sacrifices for the missions and sent their contributions to Victory Noll. For a time it was almost a cradle for vocations. A number of former Loyal Helpers are now Victory Noll Sisters.

In 1926 John Sigstein added annuities to his fund raising efforts. Most of the amounts invested were small, but it was a time when every little bit was a great help.

John did not spare himself but continued his begging trips, talked to various organizations, and wrote letters to persons who might be able to support the growing Society. In May 1929, even before the depression set in, John was writing to Anthony about financial difficulties. The worry, the travel, the constant pressures were taking their toll on Father Sigstein. He suffered from nervous exhaustion over long periods of time. Yet he always seemed to recuperate and begin again with new energy. Anthony told him he reminded him of jack-in-the-box, bouncing right back again.

Conditions were bad indeed in 1931. *Our Sunday Visitor's* funds were tied up in a Huntington bank and Bishop Noll was unable to provide the usual monthly subsidy for Victory Noll. The Bishop, however, made another magnanimous gesture, offering to sell *Our Sunday Visitor's* 160-acre farm to Father Sigstein and the Catechists for the sum of $20,000. This would be payable in yearly installments with the privilege of crediting on the purchase price of the farm, the monthly allowance that *OSV* had been providing (and hoped to provide again as soon as funds were available).

Two years later the Bishop made still another generous offer to Father Sigstein. Having given the Society title to the farm, he now wished to hand over the title to Victory Noll building itself. Again, the Society would apply the monthly $1,000 allowance as payment on the building. "Although the Bishop and *OSV* spent $200,000," John wrote to Anthony, "he is willing to let us have it for $75,000. Thus by applying our monthly allowance from *OSV* for six years, we will have title to our building. Isn't it wonderful when you consider that our good Bishop has practically given us the money to buy this building? No one knows better than you, dear Father, what a struggle it has been for us to make ends meet, but now, thanks to the unspeakable goodness of our dear Lord we are facing the dawn of a better day."

The dairy farm owned by *Our Sunday Visitor* originally occupied much of the space where the Archbishop Noll Memorial Chapel and Holy Family Building now stand. The large barn was located quite close to the road. Besides, there were some small sheds and, a little farther down the hill, a residence for the man who managed the farm. Father Robert Kelly, Bishop Noll's successor as pastor of St. Mary's Church in Huntington, was responsible for the farm and took a personal interest in it, driving out nearly every evening to see how things were going. .

At nine o'clock on the morning of December 23, 1930, a fire of undetermined

121

origin broke out in the barn. A strong wind not only made it difficult to extinguish the flames, but caused large sparks to fall in the direction of the Training Institute. The chronicler (Sister Mary Louise Perl at the time) reported that the Catechists gathered in chapel and Father Sigstein opened the tabernacle. All remained in prayer and the winds died.

The barn was a total loss, however, and so it was necessary to replace it when the farm was given to the Society. Ownership of the farm brought other responsibilities also. John looked around for a knowledgeable dairy farmer. Through his cousin, Father Peter Biegel, he brought to Huntington from Lafayette, a newly married couple, Bernard and Mildred Rethlake.

It was decided to move the farm operations over to what is now Flaxmill road where Schenkel's dairy is located. At that time it was part of the property Bishop Noll had given to the Catechists. Besides building the barn it would be necessary to provide living quarters for the Rethlakes. Rather than build a completely new house, a residence on another part of the Noll property was moved. Father Sigstein's mother died January 9, 1931. With $10,000 that she left him, he was able to build the barn, move the house, and make some necessary repairs on it.

The barn was completed; the house was moved and covered with brick that matched the Victory Noll building. But before the inside repairs were finished, money ran out. The floors sagged but there seemed to be nothing further that Father Sigstein could do. As he would say, Our Blessed Mother never failed him, and she did not fail him now. George Hesting was the carpenter on the job, working along with Howard Schilling, the contractor. Mr. Hesting will be remembered in the Huntington community as a fine Christian gentleman. He finished the job on his own, replacing the poor flooring and making other repairs that needed to be done. In 1932 Mr. and Mrs. Rethlake were able to take up residence.

The dairy products, especially the milk and butter, helped the Victory Noll budget but expenses kept on piling up. There seemed to be no end to the tight money situation of the thirties. John Sigstein was like a man in a boat, rowing with one hand and bailing water with the other. He tried everything. What money came in — donations, annuities — he invested in bonds and in farm property. He wrote Anthony and also the Catechists that farms were a wonderful investment, but his expectations were too sanguine. Only a 320-acre wheat farm in Montana survived. The others were a loss.

It is true that many of Father Sigstein's projects fell through, but it was not that he was more gullible than most people. Rather, he was more charitable, more compassionate, ready to give others the benefit of the doubt, to trust everyone. But even though he suffered so many business reverses, he was always able to bounce back, to recover, and plunge optimistically into what he judged a better way of doing things.

122

He worried about the Catechists in the missions and about the poor under their care. The Catechists knew what it meant to be hungry. In some cases the poor shared with them the little they had. In Grants, New Mexico, the Catechists lived for a long time only on potatoes. These potatoes had been given to them by one of the families in the parish.

Some of the experiences the Catechists had during these trying times border almost on the supernatural. They show the complete dependence they had on Jesus and his Mother. Sister Sophia Renkey relates what happened in Redlands, California, in February 1933. Eight Catechists occupied the convent, six of them newly professed on their first mission. The cupboard was bare. The Catechist whose turn it was to cook for the week attached the last bit of food, a piece of bread, to the hand of the statue of Our Lady of Victory in chapel. The whole community knelt in prayer. Ten minutes later there was a knock at the door. Two Knights of Columbus were there with what they called left-overs from the banquet they had had the night before. It was enough to last a week. Another time when the food ran out, one of the Catechists found a dollar bill as she swept the pavement in front of the convent. At that time a dollar would buy enough pinto beans to last for a number of servings.

Other Sisters have similar stories. Sister Mary Bernadette Wade tells of a day when there was no bread and no money to buy any. Again, the community prayed. At noon two of the Catechists who had spent the morning visiting homes came in with three loaves of bread. A woman on the street stopped them and asked whether they could use some bread.

Catechists were busy with bread lines and soup kitchens. The largest and longest-lasting were at Indiana Harbor, Indiana, and in Las Vegas, New Mexico. To this day people will tell the Sisters in Vegas and its environs how much they helped them or their parents during the depression, that if it had not been for them, they would have starved.

It was at this time that the Las Vegas Catechists were living in the old building that was formerly the Christian Brothers' school. Classrooms were converted into dining room, kitchen, community room, and chapel. Upstairs was a dormitory with fourteen beds. It was not exactly ideal for living.

It was the dream of the Catechists — and of Father Sigstein — to open a clinic in part of the one-time school. Catechist Genevieve Sullivan (Sister Mary Genrose) was elected to canvass the business men of the town for needed funds. She went to the office of Louis Ilfeld, a lawyer, to ask for a donation. At first he was very cold and distant but eventually he not only helped the Catechists but asked them to take charge of his works of charity.

Mr. Ilfeld was a Jew, a shrewd business man and very charitable to the poor. He became a devoted friend of Father Sigstein and the Catechists, especially Catechist Sullivan whose great love for the poor impressed him. He gave the Catechists $250 a month for the poor and persuaded his brother who was in the wholesale grocery business to contribute $100 worth of groceries for the Catechists to distribute.

As the depression years wore on, much more needed to be done. The Catechists begged leftovers from the town restaurants and opened a soup kitchen. Louis Ilfeld owned several ranches. Whenever the Catechists were getting low on meat, they could depend on him to have killed and dressed a dozen sheep. He influenced others to donate apples and whatever other fruit was available. The women helped the Catechists prepare the food.

The Red Cross contributed 100,000 pounds of flour, bolts of material, and some garments. The Catechists rented machines and invited the women to come in and make clothes for their families. The men, to show their appreciation, cleaned the building and the streets around the area. The daily paper took note of this and wrote: "We have to take off our hats to the Catechists. Even the dumps are cleaned up." The people declared that the Catechists actually saved the lives of their children.

Mr. Ilfeld's benefactions continue to this day, long after his death in 1950. He established the *Auxilio de Don Carlos,* a fund to be administered by the Catechists in Las Vegas. It was named in memory of his father, a man whom all of northern New Mexico loved. It was Charles Ilfeld who had given his three sons their love and compassion for the poor. Today Sister Carmelita Vigil sees that the charitable bequest of the Ilfeld family is carried out.

The steel mills of northern Indiana closed down during the depression and many of the Mexicans from Indiana Harbor, Gary, East Chicago, and other towns were deported to Mexico. There was neither work nor food for them in Indiana. The lot of these deportees was sad indeed, but that of those who stayed was not much better. They were in desperate straits and the Catechists did everything in their power to alleviate their condition. Through the efforts of Father Eugene Luke and a number of business men in Chicago, the Indiana Harbor Catechists were able to set up a bread line each week.

Joseph Dister, R.J. Mirzek, Martin Schell, and Joseph Kanthack are the only names on record, but there were others also. The men themselves visited the area and were appalled by the poverty and destitution they saw. Mr. Dister and Mr. Mirzek were in the baking business. Every week they sent out an average of 2,500 loaves of bread and several barrels of cakes and pastries. Besides, whenever possible they collected clothing and other necessities and took these to Indiana Harbor. Without this help the Catechists would have had to turn away many of these poor people who had nowhere else to go for help.

In the early days there were very few bequests. Those who remembered the Victory Noll Congregation in more recent years have been, for the most part, benefactors of long ago, persons who knew Father Sigstein and the first Catechists. An exception was John F. O'Dea, an industrialist from Canton, Ohio, who retired after the death of his wife and went to Hollywood, California, to live.

On a visit to Palm Springs Mr. O'Dea met the Catechists and observed their work among the poor in the Coachella Valley. In the next ten years or so he gave generous help to the missions in Los Angeles, Coachella, and Brawley. When Mr. O'Dea died in 1956 at the age of eighty-four he left $100,000 in bank stock to the Congregation. From the O'Dea Fund which was then established, the Sisters have been able to supply needed help for the poor.

Mr. O'Dea's estate benefited many religious institutes. He and his wife are buried on the grounds of the Monastery of the Poor Clares of Perpetual Adoration in Canton, Ohio. The O'Deas had given their home to the Sisters and had built the shrine of Perpetual Adoration adjoining the monastery.

Two other bequests might be mentioned here because of their uniqueness. Mrs. Nancy Cheney, a widow living in Redlands, California, where the Catechists had a mission, remembered them generously in her will. The will, however, was contested by relatives of Mrs. Cheney's deceased husband. It was further complicated by the accidental death of Mr. Cheney's sister and her daughter, the actress Carole Lombard. The details were too involved to repeat here and it is not necessary. Eventually there was a settlement. The Catechists did not receive nearly so much as Mrs. Cheney intended for them. They were given a check for $3100.74 from the estate and a Pontiac car which they referred to as "Nancy."

Litigation had dragged on so long that by the time the Catechists received "Nancy," she was beginning to show her age. However, her motor was good and no one cared how old fashioned she looked. It was war time and gas was scarce. The Catechists worked in more than thirty mission centers in the San Bernardino Valley. It took a bit of juggling of cars and schedules to reach every place once and some twice a week. "Nancy" arrived at just the right time and gave many years of service.

The other bequest was odd, to say the least. A priest left a stereopticon and slides to be used between St. Benedict's College, Atchison, Kansas, and the Missionary Catechists in Huntington, Indiana. The outlay was valued at $4,000. No one at Victory Noll has any recollection of the slides so it is safe to presume that Father Sigstein relinquished his share of the bequest.

The Church in America has prospered principally because of the generosity of middle-income contributors. Donations are more frequently made dollar by dollar than in large sums. The history of the Congregation of Our Lady of Victory Missionary Sisters is marked by this pattern.

Several times a year the Sisters receive a donation from a man in Pennsylvania who writes only a line or two but packs much meaning into what he says: For example: "You can light your pipe with this dollar bill. It is hardly good for anything else." When he increased the amount to a two-dollar bill, he explained that he was switching from George Washington to Thomas Jefferson. His handwriting grows shakier each time he writes. It is not hard to imagine that the gift is taken from his meager social security check.

Some of the good people who send donations to the Victory Noll Sisters are friends from long ago. They or their parents probably sent a gift to Bishop Noll for the building fund and were put on the subscription list for *The Missionary Catechist*. Through the years they have remembered the Catechists and sent their offerings. It has been a pleasant duty for the Sisters to pray for these generous friends daily. They have not forgotten Father Sigstein's repeated admonition to remember with gratitude all who help them and their poor.

Notes to Chapter XII

1. This form letter of acknowledgment is in the Victory Noll Archives.
2. John F. Noll, *History of the Diocese of Fort Wayne,* Vol. II (1941), p. 153. The first volume was written in 1907 by Bishop Noll's predecessor, Herman Joseph Alerding. No publisher's name is in either book. Evidently each one was published by the Diocese.
3. The capital letters are Father Sigstein's own.
4. The term "stole fees" was often used at that time in the sense that "stipend" is used now.
5. The letter from Cerrillos, New Mexico, is dated December 23, 1927.

13

Crisis

VERY RELIGIOUS INSTITUTE has suffered a crisis. For some it meant suppression. Others split over differences of various kinds and each faction went its way, forming separate communities. The crisis for the Victory Noll Congregation occurred in 1938, brought about by a combination of circumstances which resulted in the first canonical election of a Superior General. Father Sigstein was no longer the head of the institute.

The event should not have provoked a crisis, and yet because of misunderstandings, it did. John Sigstein knew better than anyone else that he could not continue in his role as superior. A religious community of women must be autonomous. He himself initiated the move that would bring about the change.

One of John Sigstein's boyhood friends, James Donahue, had entered the Congregation of the Holy Cross at Notre Dame, Indiana; eventually he became the first American Superior General of the Congregation. In 1928 Father Sigstein wrote his friend that it was his wish that the Society he had begun would attain canonical status and be approved by Rome.

Father Donahue not only outlined broadly the steps to be taken, but he offered his friend the services of a French priest, George Sauvage, C.S.C., a secretary of the Sacred Congregation of Religious and procurator general for the Holy Cross Congregation. Father Sauvage, who resided at the Holy Cross Generalate in Rome, made frequent trips to the United States. The next time he came to Notre Dame Father Donahue would have him visit Father Sigstein at Victory Noll.

Father Sauvage's help proved invaluable; moreover, he took a personal interest in the assignment his Superior General gave him. He admired the work of the Society and assured Father Sigstein that there would be no problem getting approval. He pointed out to him that until the Society was erected as a diocesan institute, it was merely a pious association of women with no canonical standing as a religious organization. Dr. Sauvage explained the procedure to follow and offered to make the petition to the Sacred Congregation for Bishop Noll and Father Sigstein.

Father Donahue also helped John assemble the needed information and on March 25, 1930, Father Sigstein sent the documents to Rome. Included were a resume of the present Constitutions together with letters from missionary bishops approving them (the Constitutions) and recommending that the Society be erected as a religious institute. These letters, dated in the fall of 1929, were from the bishops in whose dioceses the Society had houses. Besides letters from Bishop Noll; Archbishop Daeger, Santa Fe; Bishop MacGinley, Monterey-Fresno; and Bishop Gerken, Amarillo, there was also in the packet a letter addressed not to John Sigstein as the others were, but directed to the Holy Father. It was from Archbishop Valencia of Durango, Mexico. The Archbishop had visited Indiana Harbor and Gary and was so touched by the Catechists' apostolate among the poor Mexican people there that he added his request that the Society be given Rome's approval.

According to the statistics given there were at the time sixty-four professed Catechists at work in twelve mission centers. Forty-eight were in various stages of training. It was explained that the Catechists receive no remuneration from the poor to whom they minister but are supported by burses made up of contributions from generous Catholics. At the time of writing it seemed assured that funds would continue to be available for the support of the Catechists. Bishop Noll, through *Our Sunday Visitor,* provided for the Catechists in training at the motherhouse.

John Sigstein was eager to receive canonical approval. He wrote in his cover letter to Father Sauvage: "May I respectfully call your attention to the fact, dear Doctor, that you recommend that we should specifically come under the Congregation of Religious Orders as a regular Religious Congregation?"

The Holy Cross priest carefully explained that the first step to receive approval from the Sacred Congregation was for Bishop Noll to petition Rome for permission to erect the Society of Missionary Catechists as a Diocesan Congregation. This permission was not long in coming. As we have seen, Father Sigstein sent Dr. Sauvage the data required of him on March 25, 1930. Bishop Noll made his own formal petition on July 31, 1930. The Sacred Congregation granted the request December 29 of that year, 1930, and Father Sauvage wrote to both Bishop Noll and Father Sigstein informing them of the good news.

Father Sauvage gave further proof of his concern and friendship by offering to bring the Constitutions of the Society in line with the Code of Canon Law. He advised both Bishop Noll and John Sigstein not to make formal petition for canonical erection until the work on the Constitutions was "completely finished and approved by the members of the Society. "You see," he wrote February 14, 1931, "as long as you remain in your present state — not being a real religious Congregation — you have all freedom to discuss and arrange things."

In the same letter Father Sauvage admits that he is having great difficulty in writing the Constitutions, especially the section on the government of the Society. It would be much easier for him if he could talk things over with John Sigstein. This he would do if he should go to America the next summer. If he should not go, Father would have to do the best he could without him.

Dr. Sauvage did come to Notre Dame the summer of 1931. He made his retreat there, attended summer school, and before returning to Rome, visited Victory Noll. The following summer he again returned to the United States. By that time he felt that there should be no further delay in applying for the Decree of Erection even though the Constitutions were not finalized. He suggested that Bishop Noll proceed with the matter. This the Bishop did under date of October 31, 1932. Two months later he received the Decree and duly issued it December 31, 1932, "with legal public effect." The Society of Missionary Catechists was now a Diocesan Institute.

During the next six years very little progress was made on the Constitutions. Under the old plan of government John Sigstein was Spiritual Director and Superior of the Society. A Head Catechist, Secretary-Treasurer, and three members of a Board of Governors were to be elected yearly by the professed Catechists. Three other board members were appointed by Father Sigstein. The position of Head Catechist did not equate the role of a Superior General. In 1923 John wrote Julia that he was appointing her "Head Catechist under me." Others who held the position through the years were: Sophie Renier, Catherine Olberding, Mary McConville, and Clara Leutenegger.

Mary McConville (Sister M. Frances Therese) was elected Head Catechist in 1929. In the following years elections were deferred. Catechist McConville resigned in 1935. Finally, in 1936, elections were held (but still under the old regulation) and Clara Leutenegger (Sister Mary Clare) became Head Catechist. Mary Dickebohm (Sister Mary Angela) was elected Secretary-Treasurer. Serving with them on the Board of Governors were Caroline Meister, Catherine Olberding, Mary McConville, and Cecilia Schmitt.

At this distance it is easy to see the many factors that added up to Father Sigstein's delay in turning over the government of the Society to the Catechists themselves. He had suffered intensely in bringing the Society to where it was and he was reluctant to entrust it to others. He often talked about St. Vincent de Paul's wisdom, as he called it, in setting a priest over his Daughters of Charity. Perhaps he hoped that some such arrangement could be made in his case.

Meanwhile, membership was growing and more space was needed at Victory Noll. Rooms intended for other purposes had long since given way to bedrooms for the Catechists. Bedrooms originally meant for one person were used by two. John Sigstein decided to build. St. Joseph's Building, costing $61,000, was completed in 1937. Since it was to be used mainly for a print shop, supply rooms, and offices for various departments *(The Missionary Catechist,* Associate Catechists of Mary, Mary's Loyal Helpers, etc.), John called it St. Joseph's Workshop. The late Daniel A. Lord, S.J., visited Victory Noll just after the building was completed. The name amused him. "People usually give a place some fancy name to cover up the fact that it is a place to work," he commented, "I admire your courage in calling your new building a workshop."

At this time — 1936 — the community owned one car and a small truck. Yet Father Sigstein built a large garage extending out from the other part of the building. There is space for five cars and a truck. Remarkable too it is that the doors of the garage were made wide enough that through the years they have easily accommodated ever-widening cars.

In all this activity the canonical elections were postponed. For weeks and months John was ill, unable to attend to his duties. His nervous exhaustion was brought on by the feverish pace he sometimes kept and it was aggravated by worries over finances. No doubt he hoped to see the Society solvent before he stepped out as superior.

More than anything else, Father Sigstein feared that changes over which he would have no control would be made when he was no longer in authority. Over and over in his correspondence with George Sauvage he emphasized that there be no deviation from the original purpose of the Society — to minister to the poor, to choose as field of labor those places where no other religious community was working. He insisted too that it be kept in the Constitutions that the Society would not conduct schools, hospitals, nor other institutions, and would never engage in any remunerative works. In the resume describing the foundation, work, purpose, etc, of the Society, John Sigstein underlined the sentence: *The work of our Society is international and not diocesan in its character and scope.*

Until the sixties it was generally not the custom in most religious institutes to consult the members of the community when changes were contemplated. In most cases they were not even informed until the decision had been made by the superiors and announced as something to be carried out without question.

We need not wonder, then, why the Catechists in general were not aware of all that was leading up to the summer of 1938. Father Sigstein did mention in his letters to the community that he was working on new Constitutions and that he had received invaluable help from Father Sauvage. But the full impact of what the changeover to the new Constitutions would mean was lost on most of the Catechists.

They were deeply devoted to their Founder and revered him greatly. They accepted without complaint the regulations he made. For example, they knew there was no money for vacations so they did not ask for them. According to the earliest Society literature the Catechists were permitted to spend a month each year with their families. Also, they might go home to care for an ailing father or mother. Because of lack of funds these privileges proved to be unrealistic. After 1927 very few Catechists visited their parents and other members of their families.

When Monsignor Noll in 1923 offered to build a motherhouse for the Society of Missionary Catechists at Huntington, John Sigstein accepted the offer with the proviso that there would be no interference in the internal affairs of the institute. Two years later John F. Noll became Bishop of Fort Wayne. He continued his benefactions to the Society, frequently visited Victory Noll, but made no actual visitation required at that time by Canon Law. Bishop Noll later acknowledged this. He said that he went to the other motherhouses under his jurisdiction but he felt that all was well at Victory Noll and it did not occur to him to make a formal visitation.

Everything was well in a spiritual sense and the Bishop always gave Father Sigstein high marks for the direction he had given the Catechists. All was not so well financially. Besides, the Bishop realized that time was running out on the matter of the Constitutions and subsequent canonical elections. After consulting with Father Sauvage who was at Notre Dame during the summer of 1938, he wrote to the Sacred Congregation of Religious.

In a letter to Rome dated July 6, 1938, Bishop Noll outlined what had happened up to this point. Though the Society of Missionary Catechists had been properly erected as a Diocesan Congregation six years ago, the members were not yet living according to revised Constitutions. He then mentioned several things that would have to be brought into line with the Code. He asked specifically what norms the Sacred Congregation wished to lay down "for the reception of vows, the constituting of a General Council, and the designating of other General Officers, for the Congregation has been living without Constitutions, and has performed its work just as it did before its erection into a Religious Congregation, though that work has been to the great advantage of souls." The Bishop concluded his request:

> The members of the Society have labored these thirteen [sic] years and still work with admirable zeal and great fruit always for the greatest glory of God and the salvation of souls, as the Ordinaries in whose dioceses they work amply testify, working among inhabitants and families of different and distant places, among people with whom priest missionaries hardly come in touch.

The Sacred Congregation answered almost immediately. The letter is dated July 23, 1938. A generous *sanatio* was granted for any irregularity that might have occurred.[1] The Bishop was told he might "select a Superior General among those who have made profession of perpetual vows, a Sister who is outstanding in her religious life, dispensing if necessary in any defect as to age; and having consulted with this Superior General, you may also appoint four Councillors General, and a Secretary and Procurator General . . . Three years from now a General Chapter must be convoked and celebrated according to the norms of Canon Law and the Constitutions of the Institute."

Bishop Noll felt that he did not know the Catechists well enough to appoint officers and so he wisely chose to hold an election. Instructions were sent out immediately providing for the election of delegates to the Chapter.

The Catechists from New Mexico and Texas were gathered together at Las Vegas, New Mexico, for their retreat. The California Catechists were at Redlands, California. Bishop Noll wrote to Archbishop Gerken of Santa Fe and asked him to preside at the election of delegates for Texas and New Mexico. He made the same request of Bishop Buddy of San Diego. He would take every precaution to see that everything was carried out in proper order, though it was not necessary to have the ordinary preside at election of delegates.

Two "superior delegates" and two "subject delegates" were to be elected from the Texas area and likewise from the group of Catechists working in New Mexico and from those in Indiana. At Bishop Buddy's suggestion a division was made between the Archdiocese of Los Angeles and the Diocese of Monterey, numbering altogether twenty-eight Catechists, and the Diocese of San Diego where twenty-four Catechists were working. The Bishops, at Bishop Noll's request, secured railroad passes for the delegates, evidently a simple thing to do in the late thirties.

With Bishop Noll presiding, the first General Chapter was held at Victory Noll August 25, 1938. When three rounds of voting for Superior General gave no candidate an absolute majority, a fourth and last ballot was required. Only the two Catechists receiving the highest number of votes were eligible, Catherine Olberding and Clara Leutenegger. The vote resulted in a tie and according to the Canons, the older in profession was declared Superior General, Catherine Olberding.[2] Bishop Noll commented: "This was a close race. The Catechists have equal confidence in these two persons. I trust you will accept this as the Will of God."

As might be expected, Clara Leutenegger was elected first assistant or vicar. The other three chosen for the General Council were, in order of election: Helen Srill, Caroline Meister, and Josephine Penning. Helen Srill was elected General Secretary. The Treasurer, Margaret Dunsmore, was appointed.

Catherine Olberding was born in Baileyville, Kansas, and became acquainted with the Society of Missionary Catechists through her pastor, Father Anthony Blaufuss. She entered the Society at Gary in 1924. John Sigstein recognized her leadership qualities and entrusted her with a number of special assignments. He had sent her to Notre Dame to confer with Father Sauvage early in the summer before the election. She was then superior of the convent at Indiana Harbor. Though she had not yet reached the age of forty when she was elected the first Superior General (the age required at that time for major superiors), Bishop Noll exercised the privilege of a dispensation that had been given him by Rome.

This first election was for three years. In 1941 and again in 1947 Catherine Olberding was chosen to lead the Victory Noll community. In 1950 she relinquished the office, having served the maximum number of years permitted by the Holy See. She was succeeded by Cecilia Schmitt.

Father Sigstein was not present for the 1938 election. On June 28 he left Victory Noll for Sacred Heart Sanitorium in Milwaukee where he spent most of the summer. At his own request and with the consent of Bishop Noll, he then went to Monterey, California, where the Catechists had a mission center. Though both the Bishop and Father Sauvage told him he could remain at Victory Noll, he knew he could never adjust to a new role. Since he could no longer govern the Society, he preferred to live elsewhere. It was not until twenty-two years later, in 1960, that he returned.

Unfortunately there were some, both inside and outside the community, who did not understand the situation. They wrongly surmised that Father Sigstein had been forced to leave.

Bishop Noll did everything he could to reassure the Catechists. He did not spare himself but spent almost a whole month at Victory Noll after the Chapter, meeting with the Council and answering the questions of the Catechists. One question asked the Bishop was whether it was necessary to have a change of habit in order to receive approval of the Holy See. This question arose because a change had been contemplated by the members of the Board of Governors immediately before the Chapter. These Catechists designed a habit and veil that they thought would make the members of the Society "look more like Sisters." The veil would completely cover the hair, a short cape would be added, the cincture narrowed, the skirt lengthened.

Not all the Catechists were in agreement; in fact, very few were. When word reached the Catechists in New Mexico and California in July 1938, there was a strong protest. Telegrams were sent to Bishop Noll and upon his advice, the whole thing was dropped. When questioned then about a change of habit the Bishop explained that any decision along those lines did not rest with him, and that Rome would readily approve of the simple uniform the Catechists always wore.

Much of the Bishop's attention was directed toward the finances of the Society. It can be said without any qualification that if the Bishop had not stepped in when he did, the Society would have had to disband.

Annuities had to be investigated and adjusted. An annuity is an investment that yields interest during the holder's lifetime and at death becomes the possession of the organization issuing the annuity. The annuities of the Society were not correctly drawn up. Contracts contained a withdrawal clause which meant that the Society might have to return the entire amount at the request of the annuitant. Interest should be paid according to the age of the annuitant, but there was no record of ages at Victory Noll and everyone was receiving the same amount of interest.

133

Bishop Noll personally wrote to each annuitant and explained the situation. It was necessary to determine the age of each one, regulate the interest rates accordingly, and write new contracts. Some persons with small sums invested donated the money to the Society. Others preferred to withdraw the whole amount. A few accepted the new conditions, which, the Bishop explained, were necessary because "the Holy See requires us to add up annuities as liabilities against the Society and requires the funds to be invested safely and profitably during the entire lifetime of the annuitant."

There was no money to pay interest on annuities much less make refunds to those who asked to have their principal returned. The farm was auctioned, some small pieces of property that had been given to the Society were sold, and every effort was made to raise money to meet obligations. Bishop Noll wrote off a large amount the Society owed *Our Sunday Visitor* for printing *The Missionary Catechist*. Other debts were paid little by little until eventually the picture began to change.

This was due in large measure to the expertise of Catechist Margaret Dunsmore (Sister Margaret Mary) whom the Council appointed General Treasurer at one of their first meetings after the election. She managed the affairs of the Congregation in an admirable way, continuing in office for the next thirty years.

Before mission work was resumed in the fall of 1938 Bishop Noll wrote to every bishop in whose diocese the Catechists had centers and explained to them that subsidies would have to be provided for them. They could not continue as before. The Bishop assured the Catechists that the money would not be taken from the poor people to whom they ministered, but would come from funds available to the diocese. This is how he explained the situation in a letter to one of the Catechists who feared that the money would come from the poor:

> I had very positive word from Father Sauvage who is a member of the Sacred Congregation of Religious in Rome, that the approval of the Holy See for the Society of Missionary Catechists would depend largely on the ability of the Society to maintain itself. Rome does not approve of missionary workers in the field receiving all their support from the motherhouse unless through some endowment, the motherhouse is able to do it. In every other organization the motherhouse is supported from the field.[3]

By assessing the parishes staffed by the Catechists (that is, those parishes that were able to contribute) and supplementing the amount from other sources where necessary, the bishops had been taking care of convents, utilities, cars, and their upkeep. Other funds had come from Victory Noll. Now Bishop Noll was asking the bishops to provide enough for the living expenses of the Catechists. He suggested they contribute fifteen dollars a month for each Catechist. If they could not give that amount, then let them give at least something.

Better than anyone else Bishop Noll knew that these missionary bishops could appeal to the American Board of Catholic Missions for needed funds. In 1925 when the Board was set up by the bishops of the United States, Bishop Noll became treasurer, a position he held until his death in 1956. He knew exactly how every bishop spent the money he applied for.

Bishop Noll discovered that it was more difficult to get his message across to the bishops who had had the Catechists working for them for a number of years than it was for those who were getting the Catechists for the first time. Bishop Gorman of Reno, Nevada, and Bishop Hunt, Salt Lake City, Utah, had for a long time been on Victory Noll's waiting list. Bishop Noll thought it well for the Catechists to begin work in what the Congregation refers to today as the Mountain Area. Winnemucca, Nevada, was opened in the fall of 1938; Elko, Nevada; and Salt Lake City, the following year. These two bishops provided the fifteen dollars monthly subsidy for each Catechist.

One of the bishops who had had the Catechists for a number of years, told Bishop Noll it was impossible for him to provide fifteen dollars for each Catechist. He might be able to give fifteen or twenty dollars for each *house*. He had seventeen Catechists working for him in three different mission centers.

This same bishop actually wrote the Catechists that the pastor had reported that they were receiving "a small monthly donation from the Knights of Columbus, some small amount from the children in the centers, and probably something from other sources." The superior of the mission replied that the Knights were giving them five dollars a month and that they had once received fifty dollars from one of the organizations in the parish. This was used for the poor fund. Then she added, "We have not been meeting any personal or Society bills with these donations, and we will be glad to turn them over to the pastor or use them in any manner you may suggest." They were instructed to give the money to the pastor.

It is only within the past ten years that the Victory Noll Sisters receive the same subsidy that school Sisters receive, and then not all. One-third of the Sisters who minister to the poor are being subsidized from Victory Noll.

In the fall of 1946 Bishop Noll was again writing a personal letter to each bishop who had the Missionary Catechists in his diocese. There were more bishops this time, for the Society was represented in fifteen dioceses. In 1947, he informed the bishops, the Society of Missionary Catechists would celebrate the silver jubilee of its foundation. He felt it would be an opportune time to send the Constitutions to Rome for approval. The Catechists had been living according to these Constitutions since 1938. Since 1940 they had had perpetual vows. Approval of the Constitutions would be the first step toward petitioning the Holy See for pontifical status with the granting of the Decree of Praise.

Bishop Noll also told the bishops he wished to ask the Sacred Congregation of Religious to change the name of the Society and replace the title "Catechist" with "Sister." He would appreciate it if the bishops would write him of their opinion of this change. Most of the bishops were enthusiastic about the change. Some simply wrote that they were in agreement. Archbishop Vehr of Denver was the only one who said it made no difference to him, that it should be up to the Catechists themselves to decide. Most of the bishops seemed to equate the change of title with the status of what they called "Sisterhood."

The title "Catechist" had long been a stumbling block for many, especially for Bishop Noll. He told Father Sigstein that it was a title given to lay persons who instructed pagans. For John Sigstein it was an honorable title. In a letter to Anthony Blaufuss dated February 28, 1922, John wrote:

> I hope that you received the copy of the very beautiful little work by the learned and pious Gerson. In this little work, "On Bringing Children to Jesus Christ," you will find one of the best expositions of the catechetical office to be found in any work. In this little treatise Gerson refutes certain objections made by some of his critics among the regular clergy of his time. He said: "You accuse me of starting a new work. I answer: 'Granted that it is a new work, what of it? Must we not have new works in the Church? And if we did not have new works, what would become of the future of religion; what would become of the future of society?'" Then he goes on to show that teaching catechism is by no means a new work. Our Divine Lord was the first Catechist. St. Paul and the other Apostles were Catechists. The great Saints of the Church regarded this as their highest office. St. Augustine, St. Cyril of Jerusalem and other saints of both the Eastern and Western Church were Catechists *par excellence.* Now the same objection urged against Gerson because he undertook the catechetical office in behalf of the poor neglected children of his time, these same objections are urged against our Society today by some members of religious orders.[4]

Catechist Olberding and her Council sent out a letter to the Congregation November 30, 1946, with the Bishop's proposal regarding change of title and change of name for the Society. Various names were proposed: Society of Missionary Sisters of Our Lady of Victory, Missionary Sisters of Our Lady of Victory, Sisters of Our Lady of Victory for Home Missions, Our Lady of Victory Missionary Sisters, Congregation of Our Lady of Victory, Society of Our Lady of Victory, Victory Noll Sisters. It was noted that this last suggestion might be used with any title that would be chosen, a kind of "popular name" for the community.

Bishop Noll's own choice was Our Lady of Victory Missionary Sisters. On January 1, 1947, the changes went into effect. The community was now known as Our Lady of Victory Missionary Sisters. Most of the Sisters preferred to keep their baptismal names, but to prevent duplication, Mary, Marie, Ann were added to some. In 1968 almost everyone reverted to the name she had received in baptism, and family names were used once more as they had been in the first twenty-five years of the Society. Also, the titles "Mother" and "Superior General" were dropped in favor of "Sister" and "President."

In February 1947, Father Sauvage, acknowledging the receipt of the Constitutions, proposed, but did not insist, that the Congregation become of Roman Right for a period of seven years. He listed for the Bishop the documents to be forwarded to him if this should be the choice of the Sisters. He would need the story of the progress of the community during the past five years and also letters of the commendation from each bishop in whose diocese the Sisters worked.

George Sauvage died in March 1951. Work on the pontifical approval of Our Lady of Victory Missionary Sisters was carried on to completion by Edward L. Heston, C.S.C., who had worked under Father Sauvage's tutelage for many years.[5] In March 1956, Mother Cecilia Schmitt and her Council made formal petition for the Decree of Praise. It was granted June 16 of the same year. The Constitutions were approved *ad septennium;* that is, to be used experimentally for seven years. Finally, on December 30, 1965, Father Heston sent a Happy New Year cable to Victory Noll with the news of the Congregation's definitive approval by the Holy See.

James Donahue, George Sauvage, and Edward Heston are buried side by side in the Holy Cross Congregation's cemetery at Notre Dame, Indiana. Our Lady of Victory Missionary Sisters are deeply grateful to these three men and to Archbishop Heston's successor as the Sisters' "agent" in Rome, Father Bernard Ransing, C.S.C., all of whom worked unselfishly for the Victory Noll Congregation.

Notes to Chapter XIII

1. *Sanatio in Radice* — from the Latin meaning literally "healing at the root." This is a canonical term used principally in marriage cases. Applied here, it meant that any irregularities were rectified by the Holy See. It was not necessary, for example, for any member of the Congregation to make a "canonical novitiate." The novitiate under the old Constitutions was sufficient.

2. Canon 101.

3. Letter to a Catechist in the Archdiocese of Los Angeles dated October 26, 1938.

4. Jean Gerson (1363-1429) is usually referred to by historians as the "pious Gerson." He held the position of Chancellor of the University of Paris for most of his life. His writings on the spiritual life and on theology appealed to Father Sigstein for their practical common sense and lucidity.

5. Edward L. Heston was born in Ravenna, Ohio, September 9, 1907. He was ordained a Holy Cross priest in Rome in 1924 and spent most of his life there in various administrative positions for his own congregation and for the Church. In 1969 Father Heston's work in the Sacred Congregation for Religious and Secular Institutes culminated in his being named its Secretary. Two years later Paul VI named him President of the Pontifical Commission for Social Communications. During the Vatican Council it was Father Heston's communications activities that helped much to improve relations between the working press and the Vatican. In 1972 he was ordained Titular Archbishop of Numedia. Archbishop Heston died May 2, 1973, of a heart attack as he stepped from a plane at Denver's Stapleton International Airport.

14

Ministry: Catechesis

AFTER THE CANONICAL ELECTION in theVictory Noll Congregation in 1938, many changes took place. And yet the Victory Noll apostolate did not change. Only the manner of fulfilling it changed. The apostolate itself remained three-fold: religious education, health care, social service. Because the times had changed, these works would be carried out in a way that differed from former years.

By the mid-thirties the Confraternity of Christian Doctrine in this country had come of age. Though it had taken a long time to gain official recognition in the United States, it had been active in some dioceses, among them Pittsburgh, Great Falls, Brooklyn, Monterey-Fresno, Santa Fe, Boise, Leavenworth, and Sioux City.[1]

In 1917 the Confraternity was not so visible, as John Sigstein discovered. When he learned of the activities in the Diocese of Pittsburgh, he wrote to the director, the Rev. T.F. O'Shea, telling him of his plans to found a Society of Catechists who would, besides teaching religion themselves, train young women "Sunday School Teachers" to conduct classes in out-of-the-way places.

Father O'Shea wrote a lengthy letter outlining their diocesan program and telling how the teachers went out into the mining camps every Sunday to instruct children and adults. He encouraged Father Sigstein and offered to help him in any way he could. Six years later John was writing again to Pittsburgh to O'Shea's successor, the Rev. E.A. Lawless. This time he wanted to know how to go about enrolling his Catechists in the Archconfraternity of Christian Doctrine in Rome.

The two men corresponded off and on during the next few years and in October 1926, Father sent Blanche Richardson (Sister Blanche Marie) to Pittsburgh to learn all she could so that she might organize lay teachers in the little villages of New Mexico. Caroline Meister accompanied her. A year later Catechist Richardson, with the approval of Archbishop Daeger, was appointed supervisor of Confraternity work. She was an excellent choice for the assignment. She spoke Spanish fluently and had had several years' experience in New Mexico. John Sigstein outlined the details to the Archbishop and emphasized that nothing would be done without consultation with the pastors. The Confraternity would be the answer to the requests for catechetical work in out-of-the-way places.

When the Catechists first went to New Mexico, Father Sigstein, as we have seen, thought that they would open a mission center; then, after working there for a year or more, move on to another place, leaving the first center in the competent hands of lay teachers who would not only catechize the children but take care of the sacristy, train acolytes, act as organists, and do all the things the Catechists had been doing. It was soon realized that this was not practical. More time was needed to establish the work on a firm basis.

This was the assignment given to Catechist Richardson — to organize Confraternity schools and train lay teachers. Her first companion and co-worker was Catechist Genevieve Vasquez (Sister Guadalupe), a native of Mexico. She was replaced later by Catechist Elvira Vigil (Sister Carmelita). Both these women, being Hispanic, were invaluable in the work.

The Confraternity schools were well planned and well carried out. An average of fifteen young women were enrolled in each institute. They came from almost as many different villages. Because some were school teachers, it was necessary to have the sessions during the summer. Besides, at other times of year, travel was difficult because of rain or snow. The women lived together and formed a real community, sharing in household chores and other projects.

The Catechists used to refer to the schools as summer camps because camp furniture was used: folding cots, folding card tables, etc. Sister Blanche Marie describes their kitchen cabinet as consisting of coffin-like boxes holding dishes, kitchen utensils, and other culinary necessities. These were transported to the site of the school by truck. The boxes were then placed one on top of the other and hooked together, doubling for shelves. When Raphael Weisenbach, a Franciscan friar in charge of Jemez, New Mexico, and its missions, learned how the school would be run, he designed a folding washstand. Like most missionaries, Father Raphael was a handyman. Using his stand as a sample, the Catechists had more of them made.

The cots were covered with only thin pads. After the first two summers the Catechists decided to see what they could do to provide better mattresses. They bought raw wool from Ilfelds in Las Vegas. After washing it four or five times until it was clean, they then engaged the help of Dona Marianita, maiden aunt of Catechist Marcelina Montoya (Sister Celine). First she fluffed up the wool; then, as the native New Mexicans did, she knelt on the floor and beat the wool with two broomsticks in rhythmic motion. The Catechists stuffed the wool into the original mattresses. They were comfortable to sleep on, a vast improvement over the others.

After being invited by a pastor to hold the catechetical school, the Catechists visited the villages to acquaint the young women with the program and to observe the recruits as well as they could in order to judge whether they would profit from the experience. The next step was to find a suitable house. Usually this was a four-room building. One room served as classroom, two as dormitories, and the fourth was a combination kitchen and dining room. There was no bathroom nor was there water indoors. Sometimes, but not always, the Catechists were able to locate a house close to the village school and conduct classes in the one or two rooms available.

The first two schools lasted eight weeks. By rearranging their schedule the Catechists discovered that six weeks would be sufficient. This would decrease the cost of the institutes. This was not charged to the parish, much less to the students themselves. Generous benefactors contributed to the expense. The young women brought food: flour, beans, dried meat, eggs, canned milk, chili peppers, garden products. Sometimes they brought a live chicken or two.

Each day opened with morning prayer and "Spiritual Mass and Communion" in church. Except in one place, Chaperito, there was no resident priest. In some of the villages the priest came once a week for Mass while the schools were in session, but not on Sunday. Puerto de Luna was only twelve miles from Santa Rosa, the parish church, so while the school was being held there, the Catechists found transportation for the students and themselves and attended Mass every Sunday.

The daily schedule was a tight one, ending with rosary and night prayer in the church. Subjects covered were: Christian doctrine, Bible study, Church history, liturgy, principles of Christian pedagogy, singing, sewing (making of small altar linens), and organ lessons. Four organs were brought in from mission chapels fifteen or twenty miles distant! The girls learned to sing Gregorian Mass VIII *(Missa de Angelis)* and simple hymns for Mass and Benediction. Some learned to play also.[2] Explanations of the catechism were given with colored charts. A list of texts is interesting: *Theory and Practice of the Catechism* by Gatterer, Krus, and Culeman; Bishop Dupanloup's *Ministry of Catechizing;* Benziger's *Bible History; Stopping the Leak* by Josephine Brownson; and Sloan's *Sunday School Teacher's Guide to Success.* For liturgy class there were listed *Sacristan's Hand Book,* and Mass Prayers from Vandermaessen's *Spanish Catechism.* The charts were French charts from Bonne Presse. The Catechists used these for years. Nothing else was available in this country at the time except charts from Protestant publishing houses which the Catechists also put to good use.

The summer sessions ended with a religious ceremony presided over by the pastor. Each lay teacher who had fulfilled all the requirements was received into the Confraternity of Christian Doctrine, given a certificate and badge of membership together with a rule book. But that was not the end. The Catechists visited every teacher yearly, traveling thousands of miles over poor roads to reach tiny villages up in the mountains.

Catechist Richardson also sent out a monthly newsletter to the young women. It was written in both Spanish and English. Besides helpful ideas for the lay catechists to use in their teaching, the bulletin contained items of interest concerning the young women themselves. An issue of February 1931 reported that Leona Jeuschke of Hayden had written that their village had Mass Christmas and that for her it was the first time in her life. However, the missionary had car trouble on the way and Mass did not begin until after twelve o'clock noon. Some people had already gone home. Leona taught those who stayed, children and adults. "If she went to Holy Communion as she usually does," Catechist Richardson added, "You can imagine how hard it was to teach during such a long fast. But Leona didn't mention that part of it!"[3]

Once a year the Catechists provided a closed retreat for the lay teachers. The women welcomed not only the spiritual refreshment, but also the opportunity of a reunion with the Catechists and with those they had lived with during their training.

When the lay women were enrolled in the catechetical schools, it was with the understanding that they would give at least three years of service to their parish. Most of them continued to teach long beyond the years of their commitment.

Unfortunately the summer catechetical institutes were discontinued. The last one was held in 1934. In a letter dated February 7, 1936, addressed to "the Brothers, Sisters, and Religious Catechists of the Archdiocese of Santa Fe," Archbishop Gerken solicited their "generous and wholehearted cooperation in the organizing and work of the Confraternity of Christian Doctrine." He enclosed a copy of the Constitution for the Confraternity in the Archdiocese.

The Archbishop explained in his letter that because it was impossible for the pastor to give weekly instructions to the children "who have been drilled in their Catechism Lesson by the teachers, I would love to draft the Brothers, Sisters and Religious Catechists to supply for the Pastor. The children would be brought together by the teachers and the only work you would have to do would be to explain the Lesson, which the children had studied during the week."

Evidently the Archbishop, like so many others in his time, was not convinced that lay teachers could explain doctrine. They were only to drill the children in memory work. Such a directive defeated the purpose of the Catechists' summer schools and they were discontinued. If the role of the "teachers" was simply to help the children memorize their prayers and catechism answers, it would not be worth the effort in time and cost to hold the catechetical institutes. Yet Monsignor Garcia, then vicar general in the Archdiocese of Santa Fe, told Sister Blanche Marie that the schools "were the finest work you ever did in New Mexico." In a letter to Bishop Noll, Archbishop Gerken himself extolled the work that Sister Blanche Marie had done.[4]

As a result of the new direction taken by the Archdiocese, the small mission centers of the Catechists were closed. Santa Fe, Albuquerque, and Las Vegas became Confraternity Centers. From here the Catechists went out into the parishes to organize and supervise the work of the Confraternity. As traveling missionaries they had to take with them all their supplies. Besides personal belongings, charts, books, chalk boards, etc., they also had to carry their bedding, cots, food, kerosene lamps, kerosene stoves. Since their "convent" was usually the sacristy of the little church, living conditions were primitive — no water inside, no bathroom. They tried to return to home base every week or ten days to wash their clothes, stock up with groceries, and literally refuel: fill the kerosene cans.

Edwin V. Byrne became Archbishop of Santa Fe in July 1943. Two years later the Catechists "settled down," at least to a certain extent. When a pastor requested it, some Catechists went out on Confraternity trips and trained lay workers to teach. For the most part, however, the Catechists in Las Vegas and in Santa Fe resumed their usual work of religious instruction in the area, undertook sodality and choir activities, and visited the homes of the poor.

Despite the many inconveniences the Catechists experienced in living conditions in those earlier days in New Mexico, they were not troubled with finding a place to teach. They were permitted to teach in the village schools. They would have a class first period in the morning, then move on to another school fifteen or twenty miles distant, and so on through the day.

Far different were circumstances outside New Mexico. Only very recently have parishes provided catechetical centers. Even when there was a parish school, the pastor did not always permit the public school children to use it for their religion classes. These after-school classes were relegated to a hall, basement, or other area.

Before school opened in the fall the Victory Noll Sisters were busy house-hunting, garage-hunting, or even back-yard-hunting. Through the years they taught in some strange places: motels, American Legion halls, abandoned stores and restaurants, private homes, porches, front and back yards in places where the weather is mild. *The Southern Cross,* diocesan paper for San Diego, in its issue of June 7, 1946, reported that the Catechists were teaching once a week in Leo Turner's seed mill at Imperial, California.

In one center the Sisters taught in two different fire stations, one of them with the delightful name Possumtown Fire Department. By coincidence one of the Sisters who taught at an engine house was the daughter of a fire chief, Sister Ruth Banet of Fort Wayne.

From their mission in Winnemucca, Nevada, Sister Isabelle Kestler and Sister Irene DeMeulenaere drove seventy miles every week to the little town of McDermitt on the Oregon border. There they taught in a hall. When the cold weather came it was impossible to use the hall because it could not be heated. The man who owned the hall also owned a bar. He suggested the Sisters use it for class. When he saw that they hesitated to accept his invitation, he assured them that he would lock the doors as soon as the children arrived, and not admit customers. Since he had two children of his own in the class, the Sisters knew he would keep his word. However, the school principal, a Quaker from the East, when he heard of the arrangement, thought that religion classes deserved more fitting surroundings. He and his wife offered their own apartment to the Sisters and they gladly accepted the gracious invitation.

The Sisters of Azusa, California, had a unique classroom for their use. It was a trailer that once was used as a hot dog stand. The men of the parish renovated it and it served as an ideal classroom. Its home base was on the grounds of the Sisters' convent. Every morning one of the men of the parish stopped by the convent, hooked the trailer to his car, and on his way to work dropped it off at a Catholic home near a public school. It was used all day long for released time classes. On the way home the same man returned the trailer to the convent. The men who belonged to the Confraternity of Christian Doctrine took turns hauling the trailer-classroom.

This was not the first classroom on wheels. At Dos Palos, California, in the late twenties, the Catechists had a large bus that not only served as a means of transportation for the children who lived in the cotton camps but also as a classroom for them. *Extension* magazine in its issue of December 1929 told its readers about the bus and commented:

> There is a touch of sardonic humor in a Missionary Catechist waiting outside a public school at which she has been refused the privilege of teaching catechism even after school hours and receiving the children into a classroom on wheels parked beside the building in question. It is daring and ingenious, but it works. The children are thus gathered before they scatter to their homes, and after class can be carried to their respective dwellings.

Released time was in its heyday during the forties. It had its merits and yet it also had its drawbacks, especially when there were hundreds of children and they were all released at the last hour of school. This was usually the case in large parishes in California; in San Bernardino, Colton, Los Angeles, Brawley, among others. The children had to be met at the school and walked to the church or other place where classes were held. Marching hundreds of boys and girls for several blocks can be a draining experience. Then in the evening came the paperwork. Every child had to be accounted for and his/her presence reported to the school.

This was also the decade in which more and more Catholic schools were built. The Victory Noll Sisters rejoiced when they worked themselves out of a job, and the children they had been teaching entered a Catholic school. In one place where a school was about to open, a little boy asked one of the Sisters, "Are you gonna teach us next year?" She replied, "No, the Notre Dame Sisters are going to teach you, Tom." Tom thought about that for a little while and then he asked eagerly, "Gee, Sister, are they gonna teach us football?"

First Communion days were special for every Sister, no matter how frequently they occurred. There were always First Communicants from six to sixty and beyond, many of them with unusual stories. The Sisters encouraged having the parents receive Communion with their children. The pages of *The Missionary Catechist* magazine abounded with touching stories and appealing pictures. One picture, published in the October 1950 issue was especially interesting. Two young children, a boy and a girl, dressed in traditional First Communion clothes, were putting their hosts into the outstretched ciborium of the priest. The caption explained that this was a revival of the ancient practice of bringing up the gifts to be offered in the Mass. Priest and town were identified, and it was reported that the practice had a very positive effect on both children and parents. For them it was a moving experience. A short time later the picture and comment elicited a *monitum* from the Apostolic Delegate in Washington, D.C.[5] He might have been on the mailing list, but it can be doubted that he faithfully read the little missionary monthly unless his attention was called to something in it.

More than one parish traces its origin to the activities of the Victory Noll Sisters. They would start out with a religion class of a few dozen children in a neighborhood, usually teaching them in a private home or a store front. The number increased, a census of the area revealed the presence of many baptized Catholics, and a parish was born. Typical was the beginning of Our Lady of Victory parish in East Los Angeles in 1942.

Sisters Florentine Lohr and Loretto Hall taught the children who attended a public school in one section of Resurrection parish. It was too far to expect the students to attend class at the church and hall where the other children gathered, and so two women living near the school offered their homes to the Sisters. In the beginning there were only a few children, so few that it seemed it would be better to get transportation for them and teach them with the larger group. But after a few weeks boys and girls began to come from every direction. Sister Florentine was delighted to report to the other Sisters at the convent that she had triplets in her class: Raquel, Rebecca, and Rosalva. By the end of the year the attendance had climbed to 150. The next fall Father Daniel Sweeney, the pastor, rented an abandoned commercial garage. Two classes were taught simultaneously all afternoon two days a week, but alas, there was no partition between them. By the end of that year the enrollment had doubled. The following September the garage was painted and refurbished so that it could be used for Sunday Mass. The mission, named for Our Lady of Victory, soon attained parish status.

For a long time the slogan had been "Every child in a Catholic School," but at the mid-century it was heard less frequently. Instead, the trend was toward training lay teachers to instruct public school students who were not being reached.

Victory Noll Sisters were asked by bishops and priests to conduct these courses for the laity. It meant a change of lifestyle because most of the classes could only be given in the evening. Not only were the Sisters doing this work in the parishes; they were also being asked by other religious Congregations how to go about training lay teachers.

As early as 1939 Catechist Margaret Campbell was serving on a national CCD committee that was revising the Confraternity Manual. In New Mexico during the forties the Catechists were asked to draw up the CCD curriculum. Then in 1963 Sister Margaret was again involved in texts. She spent a year at the national CCD headquarters in Washington working with other religious in revising and expanding Confraternity courses. Other Victory Noll Sisters were also concerned with writing texts, among them Alma Bill and Helen Burch who co-authored the first edition of Book VII of Sadlier's *On Our Way* series.

At the present time many Victory Noll Sisters serve as religious education co-ordinators in parishes in all parts of the country. The Sisters who have been serving in diocesan offices have had a great impact on the catechetical apostolate. They have played — and continue to play — a significant role in developing adult education and family-centered religious education programs. Parents are primary educators, and the importance of involving them in their children's religious training cannot be over-emphasized. The Sisters have been instrumental in effecting the transition from child-centered to family-centered programs.

A look through copies of *The Missionary Catechist* for the late fifties and early sixties indicates that *TMC* (as it was referred to) had definitely gone CCD. Beginning with the January 1959 issue, there was a page named "Your CCD Question." Books reviewed were nearly all of a catechetical nature. Religion classes taught by lay people were becoming so common now that only the unusual stories were published; for example, a story contributed by Sister Josephine Konrad. Vatican II was not yet underway when, in the spring of 1962, the parish in Reed City, Michigan, where the Victory Noll Sisters worked, had a "Ceremony for First Communion." The occasion was the children's First Confession. The parents, most of whom had been involved in preparing their children for the sacraments, took part, together with their youngsters. It was an altogether moving ceremony concluding with both children and parents receiving the sacrament of reconciliation.

An article from a prison chaplain near El Paso, Texas, the Rev. Bernard Bianco, appeared in the *Catechist* magazine in June 1963 entitled "CCD Goes to Prison." He had asked the Victory Noll Sisters in El Paso to set up a course in the Federal Correctional Institution, La Tuna, Texas, his "parish" of almost four hundred men. From the many men who volunteered for the thirty-hour course in methods of teaching religion, eighteen whose record of achievement and past participation in things religious warranted it, were selected. Sister Kathleen Leven was the instructor. One of the men themselves wrote the story in *The Border Sentinel,* La Tuna's own publication. He entitled it "When a Sister Goes to Prison," and gave his opinion that the classes "scored another first in the field of rehabilitation through Christianity."

The Victory Noll Sisters had (and still have) religion classes for deaf children, the blind and the retarded. In mountainous areas where it was sometimes difficult to travel during the winter, children were reached by correspondence courses.

In places as far apart as Texas and Massachusetts there were TV religion classes in the sixties. In the summer of 1963 the Missionary Sisters in Midland, Texas, were being greeted on the street and in the stores by children whom they had never seen before. They were puzzled at first, but the children identified themselves by explaining, "You are my teacher on TV!" To the children who sat before their television sets every afternoon from four to four-thirty, Monday through Friday, from June 10 to July 5, the Sisters were real indeed. It was estimated that the program reached eight to ten thousand viewers a day in fifteen towns in the area. So successful was it that the TV School of Religion continued for three more years. The Knights of Columbus from Midland, Odessa, and Big Spring sponsored the West Texas project.

The Massachusetts program, presented as a public service by a New Bedford station, was geared to pre-schoolers and their parents. The Sisters were responsible for writing, producing, and appearing in the series. Titled "Little Flock," it also continued for three years.

Well might the Sisters use every conceivable means to reach Catholic children who attend public schools, for the number of students was constantly increasing, and is today. In a pastoral letter issued at the beginning of 1963, the late Bishop Buddy of San Diego called attention to the gravity of the situation. At that time 61,433 Catholic children in the diocese were in public grade schools and only 38,000 were being reached. Of 19,000 in public high schools, 12,400 were under instruction. He appealed to the laity to present themselves for training, for it was impossible for the catechetical Sisters to continue to carry the burden by themselves.

That the situation has improved in recent years is due in great part to the laity who give unselfishly of themselves in programs of religious education on national, diocesan, and local levels.

Because their catechetical work always took the Victory Noll Sisters far afield, they were dependent from the beginning on various means of transportation. Mr. Frey was chauffeur of the Model T Ford the first few years in New Mexico, but there were many times when a horse and buggy were more practical. In the fall of 1923 Julia was writing to John Sigstein about the car problem. The roads were so bad that Mr. Frey was reluctant to drive the Catechists to visit the sick. He was afraid they would break an axle. Julia admitted that her neck was still sore from the jolts she got on the last trip but, she continued, "These people are more deserving of care because they are so far from a doctor. Yet how can we take the risk of so much damage to the car?" It was indeed a dilemma.

Sometimes there was nothing to do but walk. Julia wrote that they had had their shoes mended again and again, but still they wore out quickly. Then, characteristically, she added that she hoped the Probationers knew what they were getting into. "This is no place for someone who expects to find convent life with clock-work routine or who thinks she will find salvation in prayer alone."[6]

After recounting a story to Father Sigstein about driving across a frozen river and having the ice break beneath them, Julia teasingly added, "We are waiting patiently until an Eastern Friend comes to Watrous so we can give him a ride. We have all the places picked out. Please come prepared."

Mishaps crossing streams were common, for bridges were almost non-existent. In the early summer of 1923 New Mexico had so much rain that even the old timers could not remember such a deluge. One Friday the car got stuck in the river and according to Julia, "It took an army to pull us out. Men, boys, horses, women, and children came to the water's edge to see the fun. It was a Roman holiday. Some came on horseback; four or five men came in an auto. All took off their shoes and socks and waded knee deep into the water to rescue us."[7]

In Chaperito, Anton Chico, and Holman (missions that began after Watrous and Ocate), the horse was the Catechists' means of transportation. Most of the horses were old. The Anton Chico Catechists named theirs *Despacio* and *Perezoso*. These were not nouns at all. *Despacio* is an adverb meaning slowly; *Perezoso,* an adjective meaning lazy. Their pace matched their names. Once when *Despacio* was sick and the other horse was already scheduled for a trip in another direction, two of the Catechists walked to Llano, one of their out-missions. A woman sent them home in her surrey with her daughter driving the horses. The Catechists remarked that it was "a treat to feel ourselves really moving. Our own poor old horse walks so leisurely we have to look at the telephone poles to make sure we are moving."[8]

Many of the Catechists were women from cities and had much to learn about horses. Rafaela Mendoza in Holman, New Mexico, was one of these. One Sunday she hitched their horse Dolly to the buggy and with another Catechist started out to a distant mission for Mass. The horse took to the road and raced so fast that it was all Rafaela could do to hang on to the reins. Dolly was foaming at the mouth but her passengers thought it was because she was running so fast. The left wheel rim disappeared and the buggy was running on spokes. Horse and buggy flew past Cassidy's General Store where the men of the village gathered to exchange the latest news. They saw that something was wrong so they jumped on their own horses and with great effort, stopped the runaway. Immediately they recognized the bad harness job and took off poor Dolly's collar which was literally choking her. They repaired the wheel while Dolly rested by a clear mountain stream, recuperating from the unintentional pain she suffered. There was no Mass that day. Two weary Catechists returned home in the late afternoon, hungry, and with splitting headaches.

One of the most unusual horse and buggy stories concerned Julia. Once when she and Marie Bodin were crossing an arroyo, they lost a wheel from their buggy. What could they do? They retrieved the wheel but the bolt was gone. The resourceful Julia took out her scissors, cut off some of the horse's tail and with it fastened the spokes to the hub. Then she stuffed the hub with more "horse hair."

By the year 1928 cars had replaced horses but even so, mission trips continued to be adventuresome. Frances Meyer and another Catechist whose name is not given in the story were returning to Anton Chico from Pintada. They were nineteen miles from home when the car refused to budge. After trying everything they could think of, they discovered that the auto would travel in reverse. So straddling what they referred to in New Mexico as "high centers" in the road, they moved slowly in reverse for eleven miles. They could not force themselves to go through the streets of Anton Chico traveling backwards, so they stopped several miles outside the town and experimented again with the shift. Much to their delight, the car went forward and they finally arrived home.

Trains have been modes of travel for the Victory Noll Sisters in their mission work. In 1926 the Catechists went twenty miles by train from Las Vegas to Watrous for their religion classes. Forty years later the Sisters were traveling every weekend by train from Salt Lake City to Cedar City, Utah, at the rim of the Grand Canyon.

Though they have had some close calls, the Victory Noll Sisters have been specially protected by Divine Providence in all their travels. A story Sister Blanche Marie Richardson tells is not only exciting but it involves a most unusual mode of transportation known as a speeder. Like a handcar it ran on tracks but it was motorized and was capable of going very fast. It was used as a means of transportation between a lumber mill at the base of the mountains to the camp at their summit where the logs were cut.

Raphael Weisenbach, the Franciscan missionary in Jemez, New Mexico, had permission from the lumber company to use the speeder when he went up to Eagle View on the fourth weekend of each month. Whenever Catechist Richardson and Catechist Vigil were working in the Jemez area, they accompanied the priest. By taking the speeder they could get to Eagle View in forty-five minutes. Otherwise the trip would be two hours or more over tortuous mountain roads. All Father Raphael had to do when he was ready was to call the camp and a man would come down with the speeder to pick up the

148

passengers.

It seemed that something was always happening to remind Father and the Catechists that they were traveling at their own risk. Once the gasoline tank began to leak and a fire broke out, kindled by sparks from the rails. The passengers had to jump off while Pete, their driver, repaired the break. Another time there was a horse on the track ahead. Pete blasted the horn and the horse cleared the tracks a split second before the speeder whizzed by.

The most exciting trip was the Saturday afternoon when Father and the Catechists feared they would have a head-on collision with another speeder. Father Raphael had phoned the camp for the speeder but it did not come and it did not come. He decided to call again. Ten minutes later the speeder appeared. Pete paled when the priest told him he had made another call. They all hoped and prayed that a second speeder had not been sent down. There were two tunnels to go through on the way up to the lumber camp. What if they met a speeder in one of the tunnels? Or at any point for that matter. They shuddered at the thought.

The story had a happy ending. They reached the camp without mishap.

Notes to Chapter XIV

1. In March 1976 many Catholic papers carried an excellent account of the origin of the Confraternity of Christian Doctrine and of its development in the United States. The article, syndicated by NC News Service, was written by Sister Mary Charles Bryce, O.S.B., a professor in the Department of Religion and Religious Education at the Catholic University of America. The copy in the Victory Noll Archives is from *The Catholic Post* (Peoria, Illinois), March 21, 1976.

2. Some of these details were given in an article in *The American Ecclesiastical Review* by Raymond J. Prindeville, C.S.P., in 1932. Entitled "The Confraternity of Christian Doctrine at Work," the story was run in the August and September issues. Prindeville quotes also from *The Missionary Catechist,* Vol. VII, April 1931.

3. See Chapter X, Note 2, regarding the Communion fast at that time.

4. Quoted in a letter from Bishop Noll to Catechist Olberding June 26, 1941.

5. A warning: Don't do it again!

6. October 14, 1923.

7. June 18, 1923; to Father Sigstein.

8. Community letter written from Anton Chico May 3, 1926.

15

Ministry: Health Care and Social Service

IN 1916 JOHN SIGSTEIN WAS WRITING to his friend, Anthony Blaufuss, about his dream of a Society of Catechists. The big obstacle was, as it was almost always to be, lack of funds. John seriously thought of taking his plan to Extension Society and yet he feared the whole project would be taken over by it. It was *his* idea, *his* undertaking, and he did not want to see it suffer the same fate as Our Lady of Victory Lodging House Mission which was taken over by the Archdiocese of Chicago and the work eventually terminated.

Father Blaufuss encouraged John to "get in touch with a number of missionary bishops and tell them about the Catechists for Poor Missions. Find out whether they would welcome such itinerant religious in their dioceses." Unless Father was armed with all the facts before going before the Extension Board, they might "consider the whole thing the beautiful mirage of a visionary."[1]

The following year, on July 6, 1917, Anthony assured John that he had kept the great plan in his mind and prayers. Recently he had had the opportunity to speak of it to two priests whose opinion he valued. One thought it fine theoretically but not workable in practice. The other expressed fear regarding the Catechists. "He considered the dangers to these young ladies too great. I have been thinking myself that I fear very much for the Catechists as a division apart from the regular school sisters. Young lady Catechists I am afraid would be looked upon with much doubt and suspicion even by priests."

Fortunately John was not influenced by the apprehension of others. He was certain, and often expressed it, that his Catechists would be prepared to go out among the people with no detriment to their religious life. It might seem strange today to think that a religious society such as John Sigstein envisioned

150

would not be readily accepted, but at that time most Sisters lived in large groups, and had little contact with the "world" outside of their schools and hospitals.

From the very beginning the Catechists not only taught religion but ministered to the physical needs of the poor. When the community celebrated its fifteenth anniversary in 1937, a news story gave this summary:

> The Society of Missionary Catechists is a religious community of women whose members engage in religious and social welfare work. Their ideal is the spiritual and corporal welfare of the poor. They accomplish this through the visitation of homes of the needy and the religious instruction of their children. They live in a convent provided for them in their mission district. From this center they go out to the surrounding towns and settlements, often reaching as many as twenty-seven districts from one center. They not only care for the needy poor in their homes and furnish them with the necessary medical care, but also make house to house visits providing food and clothing and thus relieving the necessities of the suffering poor. The Catechists also care for the humble mission chapels, train altar boys and choirs, and organize sodalities.[2]

Julia and Marie were always being reminded by Father Sigstein that they should not neglect their visits to the poor and the sick. At the end of their first year in Watrous an entry in the minutes of the meeting of the Corporation notes that 364 visits were made to the sick poor in their homes, and forty-two persons were taken to doctors and dentists. No matter what the weather, what the conditions of the road, the sick were not neglected. In November 1923 the Catechists walked a mile in two feet of drifting snow to reach a sick child.

In the earliest years of the Society, the Catechists supplied simple remedies and gave what aid they had been trained to give. There was no doctor in the villages, no drug store or pharmacy. Even if the people had means of transportation and could go to Las Vegas, they could not have paid for the doctor's services.

The Catechists suffered real anguish when they were unable to help their patients. Blanche Richardson had no sooner arrived in Ocate in 1924 when there was an epidemic of typhoid and several babies died. It was a sad beginning for her. She treated the babies as well as she could and had the consolation of being told later by a doctor that she had done the right thing. Nevertheless, she wrote pleadingly to the other Catechists: "Please pray for my babies that they live after my amateur doctoring."

Catechist Richardson had a very different experience some years later when she and Catechist Vigil were working in the Laguna Pueblo in San Fidel parish in 1934. An eight-year-old Indian girl and her younger sister were playing in a wagon near a cliff and fell over the edge. The younger child was killed and her sister had her thighbone broken. Blanche was summoned to come

151

quickly. She reached the home of the parents of the children at the same time the doctor and nurse from the local Indian agency arrived.

The doctor placed the injured girl on the kitchen table and asked Catechist to administer the anesthetic — laudanum sprinkled on cotton and contained in a small glass. The nurse's task was to keep the child's leg in position after the doctor had pulled it into place. The doctor warned Blanche not to tilt the glass too much because the laudanum would burn the girl's face. Yet it had to be held close enough for her to inhale the fumes.

"Perhaps I displayed too much anxiety," Sister Blanche Marie said in relating the incident. "After all, I had never administered an anesthetic before. Seeing how nervous I was, the doctor had me exchange places with the nurse. Finally the 'operation' was over and the doctor took the child to the government hospital. He was elated when the x-ray showed a perfect meeting of the bone, but he was not more elated than I, for I had a real part in it too."

In April 1930 the Catechists opened a clinic in two rooms of an old school building in Las Vegas. It was under the direction of Catechist Bridget Hynes who had long experience as a practical nurse. Doctors generously gave their services and although equipment was very primitive, fifty patients a week were treated. Later, as the number increased, the clinic was moved to a four-room adobe house. Salome Dorava, (Sister Mary Salome) a registered nurse from Wisconsin, joined the "staff." With the added space, the Catechists were able to initiate what they called hygiene classes for mothers. They taught them infant care with special emphasis on proper feeding.

In Grants, New Mexico, the Catechists were fortunate to have the services of an excellent woman physician, Dr. Emelyn Clark, a convert to the Catholic Faith. Dr. Clark lived in Albuquerque where she had her own practice. Once a month she had been going to the little town of San Mateo where she held a clinic under Protestant auspices. After she became a Catholic she continued her monthly visits, working now with the Catechists. She also held a clinic in Grants, a mission the Catechists had opened in 1929.

A more compassionate woman than Dr. Clark would be difficult to find. After her conversion she suffered much from the misunderstanding of her family and friends, but it did not embitter her. She gave herself completely to the poor people in the area. The Catechists treasured her friendship. She was solicitous for them and did everything she could to help them. When Catechist Marguerite Srill, the superior at Grants, was ill with pneumonia, Dr. Clark stayed at her bedside all night and would not leave until Marguerite was out of danger.

From these early, sometimes poorly equipped clinics, others evolved. Some of them were well baby clinics, though school-age children also received inoculations, and both adults and children were given chest x-rays. The Victory Noll Sisters were receptionists, kept records, helped with examinations, and acted as interpreters when necessary. Our Lady of Guadalupe Clinic in

San Bernardino, California, was especially successful during its operation in the forties. Sister Mary Eileen Masterson who was in charge, was assisted by Sister Pauline Wapiennik. This was a parish clinic serviced by public health nurses.

A clinic by the same name — Our Lady of Guadalupe — was opened in 1946 in Brawley, California, near the Mexican border. Sister Mary Camillus Spisak, a registered nurse, was in charge. There were the usual routines — vaccinations, tuberculin tests, physicial examinations — but the Sisters were handicapped because there was no means of making referrals for medical care and treatment. Much of the work was concerned with health teaching. This was valuable but under better circumstances much more could have been done.

The work did not go unnoticed, however. The late Bishop Buddy of San Diego observed the efforts of the Sisters in Brawley and wrote Mother Catherine Olberding, then Superior General, to ask for Sisters to staff a much larger clinic in San Diego. This had begun as a parish project but it needed to be built up and operated on a more professional basis. Mother Catherine and her Council weighed the request very seriously before making any promises to Bishop Buddy. They feared that if the Congregation were to take over the management of a diocesan clinic, it might lead to institution work. And this could not be. It was completely foreign to the Victory Noll spirit and purpose.

Bishop Buddy assured the Sisters that their fears were unfounded, and so, encouraged also by Bishop Noll and with his permission, they sent three Sisters to San Diego in August of 1948 to staff Our Lady of Guadalupe Clinic. It was located in the area known as Logan Heights where many poor Mexican Americans lived. Sister Aurelia Jane McMahon was chosen as director of the Clinic. She was accompanied by Sister Otilia Mendoza to serve as interpreter when necessary and Sister Marie Jane Chettle to be receptionist and bookkeeper. The work expanded so rapidly that another nurse, Sister Mary Camillus Spisak, joined the staff the following year. Each year another Sister was added until the Clinic reached its full complement of seven. There were, besides, a number of lay workers as well as volunteers.

Sister Aurelia Jane remained executive director until the Clinic closed in 1961. She was a remarkable woman, greatly admired by all who knew her. She entered Victory Noll, a thirty-nine-year-old widow, in 1928. She was a native of Marshfield, Wisconsin, and had received her nurse's training at Cook County Hospital in Chicago. Her nursing experience included public health work and supervisory positions in several different hospitals. Her frail appearance belied the strength of will that was hers. Sister Aurelia knew exactly what the Clinic needed and how it could reach its goals.

Guadalupe Clinic served outpatients in the low income bracket. It was open also to Mexican nationals, to transients, and to non-residents who were not eligible for service in other clinics. In its second year the Clinic was staffed by 152 physicians and dentists of the San Diego Medical and Dental Societies. The number was later to increase. These doctors volunteered their services on a rotating basis. Interns and resident physicians from Mercy Hospital practiced outpatient treatment at Guadalupe Clinic. Both Mercy and County Hospitals accepted patients referred to them by the Clinic.

The Clinic was a Community Chest Agency and also a member of the Community Welfare Council. In the 1957 United Fund campaign more contributions were designated for Guadalupe Clinic than for any other agency. Patients, when able, paid a small fee for services. However, if they were unable to pay, they received the same treatment as those who could pay. The Sisters managed to operate the Clinic without asking for funds from other outside sources. The greatest expense was for the necessary professional equipment and its upkeep.

In 1961 Guadalupe Clinic was a victim of what might be called San Diego's phenomenal growth. A freeway system would wipe out the Clinic's location on Kearney Street. Also, an enlarged outpatient department at Mercy Hospital would mean that Mercy's interns and resident doctors would no longer use Guadalupe Clinic for their training.

The doctors who gave their services to the Clinic as volunteers protested its closing. They were not convinced that the Mercy Clinic would be a replacement. A dentist expressed his opinion:

Guadalupe Clinic be satisfactorily replaced? This is strictly my personal opinion, but I don't think so. I question that people there would travel out of their area to get dental service.

A pediatrician was still more articulate:

I have worked at Guadalupe from the time it was taken over by the Missionary Sisters of Our Lady of Victory who are the heart and soul of the clinic. I have worked in big clinics in New York City and for the Navy. There has not been a clinic where I've worked that has the atmosphere this clinic has. The sisters are always interested in the social problems and are anxious to get the home stabilized. That's what makes the difference. The average big city clinic is a rather impersonal thing. At Guadalupe the medical problem relates to the total welfare. You feel that what you are doing is of some permanent good. I think that Guadalupe fills a real need where it is. Later, there absolutely will be need for more than just one clinic. I am convinced of that. But I would hate to see Guadalupe replaced. It fills a place that would not be taken care of by such a clinic at Mercy. The Logan Heights location is what makes it so valuable. There the clinic has become so well established; it has the confidence of people in the area. When a doctor is busy he tends to shy away from extra work unless he knows it is doing some real good. That is why Sister Aurelia has the support of so many doctors — and a great deal of them are not Catholic doctors.[3]

Largely responsible for working out the social problems that the doctor

154

referred to was Sister John Francis Radler who had joined the Guadalupe staff in 1952. Sister Aurelia had asked for Sister John Francis when the Clinic was opened, but she was then working at Bishop Noll's own Catholic Social Services in Fort Wayne and could not immediately be replaced. Sister Aurelia renewed her request, and Sister John Francis was replaced by Sister Mary Helen Rogers in 1952. She was then free to go to San Diego.

For a time it seemed as if those in authority had second thoughts about closing the Clinic rather than have it absorbed into the outpatient department of Mercy Hospital. However, by then the Victory Noll Congregation had promised Bishop Green of Tucson, Arizona, to staff a proposed Clinic in his diocese. A few days after Our Lady of Guadalupe Clinic was closed (February 28, 1961), a book of testimonials from mayor, civic officials, and every charitable and social service agency in San Diego was presented to Sister Aurelia Jane and her Sisters.

Several months later the Sisters took up residence in the city of Tucson where St. Elizabeth of Hungary Clinic was opened in November 1961. Here again the Sisters have gained the good will of physicians and dentists who serve the Clinic on a volunteer basis. The Clinic is a non-profit health facility of Catholic Community Services of Southern Arizona, Inc., operated by Our Lady of Victory Missionary Sisters. It is funded by United Way of Greater Tucson, the Bishop's Charity and Development Fund, donations from the civic community, and small fees for services from patients. Charges are based on a patient's ability to pay, but those unable to pay are treated without charge. Patients are disadvantaged persons regardless of race, creed, residence, or potential, provided they are: ambulatory, unable to pay for private care, and not qualified for free care elsewhere. It is significant that St. Elizabeth of Hungary Clinic gives preventive and remedial dental care to a part of that group (estimated as twelve percent of the population) who have never before been seen by a dentist.

As in San Diego, the Tucson Clinic is marked by personal service. The Sisters and their staff of lay workers see in every patient a person whom God made in his own image and likeness; and they seek to give to the patients a sense of their own worth, to help them achieve the purpose for which they were created.

From the earliest days of the Society John Sigstein set this ideal before the Catechists. He gave them a special prayer to say daily: "O Jesus, Father of the Poor; Mary, Mother of the afflicted and neglected, give us a great love for the poor, so dear to your Sacred Hearts."

When the Catechists began their work in New Mexico they had no county or state agency to turn to. Julia often lamented this. The Catechists rejoiced when welfare programs began to appear, Aid for Dependent Children being the first. They lost no time in helping the poor to apply for benefits.

In earlier years much of the Catechists' social work consisted in providing food and clothing for the many who were in need. In 1930 the Las Vegas Catechists established their own employment agency. The jobs available were small but they served to enhance the dignity of those who were fortunate enough to get them. As more and more welfare agencies were set up during the next decade, the Catechists became involved in programs for the poor. Not that emergency help was stopped. It is necessary even today. But now it was possible for the poor to receive help from the county, city, state, or federal government and the Catechists were happy to assist them in applying for aid.

Father Sigstein had the Catechists attend the conventions of the National Conference of Catholic Charities. On at least one occasion he himself went to the convention and agreed to serve on a national board set up to help alleviate the plight of Mexicans in the United States. The meeting was held in New Orleans in the fall of 1929. Archbishop Drossaerts of San Antonio became chairman of the special board. The secretary was Linna Bresette, at that time national secretary of the Catholic Conference on Industrial Relations. Father was later to bring Miss Bresette to Victory Noll to give lectures to the Catechists.

Because John Sigstein felt so strongly about helping the Mexican laborers, he agreed to serve on a board that had for its aim the betterment of Mexican people. According to the *Denver Register,* the purpose of the board was to make national the work begun by Thomas F. Mahony of Longmont, Colorado, and the Colorado State Knights of Columbus Mexican Welfare Committee. The special target of the Knights was the sugar beet industry. They sought means to correct the evils that existed. The *Register* predicted that the new board "with the backing of some of the most powerful forces in the American Church, is likely to put Colorado communities that are unfair to the Mexicans in a rather perilous predicament." [4]

Sadly, the sanguine prediction did not come true. Although some of the bad conditions were eradicated, Mexicans continued to be victims of unfair labor practices, not only in Colorado but in many other areas of the country, a condition that is only beginning to be changed today.

Home visiting, parish census taking and updating have always been an important part of the Victory Noll apostolate, but there are also hospital visits and visits to nursing homes. As early as 1927 the Catechists were visiting the jail in Gary, Indiana. *The Missionary Catechist* had many stories of these visits "behind bars" in Gary, Santa Fe, Denver, and other places. The Catechists visited the jails not just to console and comfort the inmates, but also to instruct them. A number of Sisters also are members of pastoral care teams in hospitals. They work with the dying and with their relatives, bring Holy Communion to the sick, and counsel and console those in need.

Social action in which the Victory Noll Sisters are engaged has, like many other things, changed through the years. That is, methods have changed, but the same love for the poor and concern for them are still evident. To help bring about more effective and lasting changes, some Victory Noll Sisters are in supervisory positions in a number of social service offices.

In Lubbock, Texas, Sister Regina Foppe is Diocesan Director of Social Action and Human Development (Diocese of Amarillo). Her program for justice, particularly for Mexican Americans, includes Head Start, food stamp awareness, housing, and other projects. Sister Regina uses every means to educate disadvantaged persons of West Texas in political awareness and is ever on the alert to foster community action and overturn prejudice. When it is a question of proposed legislation that might be helpful or detrimental to the poor, Sister Regina reacts accordingly, reaching to city hall, state capitol, and even the White House in Washington, D.C.

Other Sisters, too, are active in community organization, using every opportunity to obtain legislation to help the poor. In northern New Mexico, in the same area where Julia and Marie began their mission work, Sister Clarita Trujillo combines her ministry of training CCD teachers with programs to acquaint the people with the rights and privileges that are theirs as United States citizens.

Meeting the social problems of the elderly and the handicapped is another concern of the Victory Noll Sisters. Each year more and more Sisters are engaged in this apostolate. They visit senior citizens and shutins, prepare them to receive the Eucharist, and then bring them Holy Communion. They pray the rosary with them; provide them with reading material, tapes, and records; make transportation available and help them on shopping trips. The Sisters multiply themselves by enlisting volunteers to share in their ministry. This is the special aim of COR, a Community OutReach begun in North Miami, Florida, by Sister Marie Welter in 1971 under the auspices of Catholic Service Bureau in Miami.

Special emphasis is being given to outreach programs by Catholic Social Services and other agencies. Sister Francesca McGarry supervises such an office in Detroit and Sister Mary Alice Murphy in Denver. Another branch of Catholic Social Services in Denver is located in Holy Spirit Center with Sister Mary Helen Rogers in charge. Since 1947 the Victory Noll Sisters have lived and worked at the Center. Serving the needs of the neighborhood has always been a part of the apostolate of the Sisters there, but now it is more far-reaching and professional, though nonetheless warm and personal.

Victory Noll Sisters support the United Farm Workers in their struggle for justice. For many years Sister Mary Eileen Masterson has worked with Mexican American migrants, especially those who come to the Midwest to harvest the crops.

These are but a few of the ministries in which the Victory Noll Sisters are engaged. There are others and there always will be others. As new needs appear, there will be new ways of meeting them. The Congregation of Our Lady of Victory Missionary Sisters has committed itself to justice. The theme of the most recent General Chapter was *The Victory Noll expression of religious life: a life of justice for the sake of the kingdom.*

Religious congregations have become increasingly more aware of justice and peace efforts in the Church. More and more attention is being given to policies and actions of institutions or systems that limit human rights of individuals and create social, political, cultural, and economic injustices. Decisions are being made by multinational corporations that affect the lives of many people in our own country and abroad. The Church cannot ignore the human implications of many of these decisions and is calling upon its members to strike out against injustices. Religious congregations have taken up the challenge and are using their rights as stockholders in business corporations to monitor corporate social responsibility and bring about changes in practices that cause abuses.

In January 1978 the Victory Noll Congregation joined forces with eleven other religious communities to form CCRIM — Conference of Corporate Responsibility in Indiana and Michigan. This is the eighth regional Catholic group to combine resources in an effort to promote corporate social responsibility in companies in which funds are invested.

The Conference is assisted by the Interfaith Center on Corporate Responsibility in New York City. This Center coordinates research and information on specific matters. Each year stockholder resolutions on a wide variety of issues pertaining to social justice are submitted to companies, issues such as: energy and environment, equal employment opportunity, rights of women and minorities, land use, nutrition, racism, military production and sales, unfair labor practices, loans and sales to repressive governments, and the like.

Any religious group that owns stock in a company to whom a resolution is submitted may be a co-filer of the resolution or may exercise its right as a stockholder to vote in favor of a proposal submitted by another Church group. In many instances company managements are making efforts to comply with the requests of these groups. Slowly, but gradually, this striving for justice is making progress.

A decision of the Victory Noll 1974 Chapter was the adoption of a Resource Sharing Program, prepared by a task group on corporate and individual response to the needs of the Church and the world. The object of the program is to utilize more effectively the resources of the Congregation, both the personnel and finances, on behalf of the poor. A board of Victory Noll Sisters has the task of reviewing each proposal submitted by other Sisters and then monitoring the programs accepted for funding. The Resource Sharing Program is financed by fifteen percent of the Congregation's yearly net income.

So far a number of diverse and worthwhile programs have been submitted, approved, and carried out. Sister Virginia Schmitt received funds for Project New Hope, as it is called. The Mental Health Center that she serves as psychiatric counselor and coordinator for the daytime treatment program, was much in need of case workers to find the poor who needed help. The Center, located in southeastern Jackson County, Missouri, is responsible for providing and developing mental health services for 150,000 residents. The Victory Noll Resource Sharing Program made it possible to hire more workers who literally went into the highways and byways in search of the hidden poor. Very soon word spread that someone cared, and aid was at hand for many who were living almost in despair over their helplessness. The day treatment program at the Lee's Summit Center is preventive in that it seeks to help patients before they have a total breakdown. The patient can choose either counseling or group therapy.

Funds from the Victory Noll Congregation made it possible for Claretian Brother Modesto Leon to develop a youth program for boys and girls in East Los Angeles. Brother works closely with law enforcement agencies and with the office of the Catholic Community Center. He and his workers concentrate on the younger youth, endeavoring to prevent them from being influenced by older brothers and sisters who often are hard core gang members. He aims, he says, to "make youth free to walk through the turf of any gang; free not to join a gang; free to receive an education; free to worship freely without being laughed at."[5]

Sister Ann Shirley Kelly, religious education coordinator in Our Lady of Soledad parish on Los Angeles' East Side, realized the worth of Brother Modesto's street ministry and applied for funds to make it more effective. Since then, three other sources of revenue have been added, but Brother still stresses how important his first backing (received from Victory Noll) was for the development of his program.

When the Archdiocese of Denver initiated its Justice and Peace Commission, it asked Sister Jeanette Halbach to be Director. Sister Jeanette assumed the office at the time Denver and other dioceses were planning to act on the Bicentennial Program called for by the National Conference of Catholic Bishops. She became coordinator of the program, a discussion/listening process based on the Bishops' statement, "Liberty and Justice for All." Her work took her to every part of the Archdiocese of Denver and culminated in the momentous Call to Action meeting in Detroit. Sister Jeanette would have continued as Director of Denver's Justice and Peace Commission but she was called by her Congregation in 1977 to assume the office of President.

Long before there were social agencies in the Catechists' missions, efforts to help the poor were necessarily individual actions. Shortly after the Catechists began to work in Gary, they learned of the suffering of Mexican men who stoked the fiery blast furnaces in the steel mills and tried to protect themselves from the intense heat by wearing burlap bags over their heads. When Father

159

Sigstein heard of this, he had one of the Catechists go to an executive, point out the evil, and ask that something be done to protect the men. The request was honored and conditions improved.

Today's action is not always so direct. There is more involvement on the social scene, and sometimes the process takes longer; but the results give promise of being more permanent and long lasting. Being a part of the Conference of Corporate Responsibility, working in social agencies, trying to bring about better legislation for the poor, visiting the elderly and the handicapped — these and other like works are in the Victory Noll tradition. They are all instances of meeting modern needs with modern means.

Notes to Chapter XV

1. Letter dated December 29, 1916.
2. In the Victory Noll Archives there are a number of clippings from diocesan papers with this story. The one quoted here is from the *Denver Register,* August 11, 1937.
3. *San Diego Magazine,* May 1959. Used with permission.
4. *Denver Register,* November 1929.
5. Sister Ann Shirley Kelly, "Freedom for Youth Development," *The Challenge,* Vol. VII, No. 3, p. 3.

*Catechist Catherine Olberding,
first canonically elected
Superior General,
1938-1950.*

*First General Council, elected 1938. Seated:
Catechist Olberding and her first assistant,
Catechist Clara Leutenegger. Standing: Cate-
chists Caroline Meister, Helen Srill, Josephine
Penning.*

Bishop Noll at his desk at Victory Noll, 1944.

Mother Cecilia Schmitt,
Superior General
1950-1962.

Sister Florentine Lohr,
President
1962-1971.

Sister Gertrude Sullivan,
President 1971-1977.

Sister Jeanette Halbach,
elected President 1977;
re-elected 1980.

General Assembly 1971. Sister Florentine Lohr, outgoing President, receives roses
from Sister Madeleine Sophie Renier who is being aided by Sister Patricia Heaney.

Postulants and novices in Our Lady of Victory Chapel (original building), 1953.

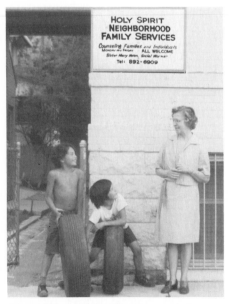

Sister Mary Helen Rogers, social worker at Holy Spirit Center, Denver, chats with some of her friends.

Sister Carmen Montoya conducts a sewing class for women in East Los Angeles.

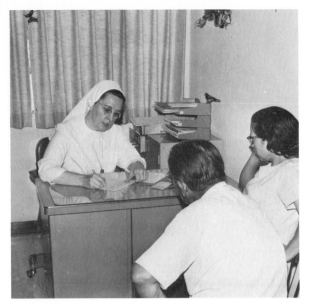

Sister John Francis Radler, administrator of
St. Elizabeth of Hungary Clinic, Tucson, Arizona.

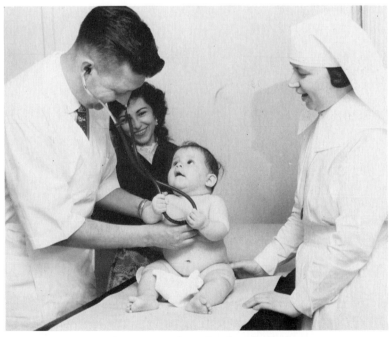

Sister Mary Camillus Spisak, R.N.,
and one of her favorite patients, 1961.

*Sister Carolyn Ortega, veteran of
mission in Oruro, Bolivia, S.A.*

*Sister Carolyn, lower left,
visits with campesinos in Oruro.*

Sister Mary Edna Butler with some of the prisoners she ministers to in Oruro.

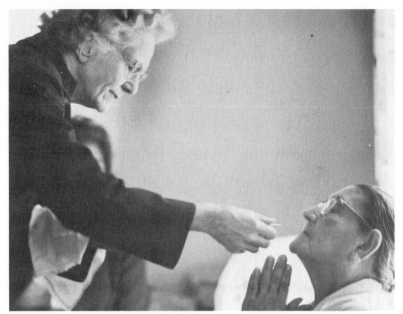

*Like many Victory Noll Sisters, Sister Margaret Ann Harrison
is a Minister of the Eucharist and brings Holy Communion to persons
in their homes, in nursing centers, and in hospitals.*

*Sister Otilia Mendoza directs the nutrition program for Senior Citizens
in Our Lady of Guadalupe parish, San Antonio, Texas.*

General Assembly 1971. Bishop Leo A. Pursley is giving the homily. With him are the Rev. Keith Clark, O.F.M.Cap. (left), and the Rev. Edward J. Stokes, S.J. Father Stokes was canonist at the Assembly.

Father Sigstein shortly before his death in 1963.

16

Outreach

THOUGH THE FORTIES AND FIFTIES were years of greatest expansion in the Victory Noll Congregation, even in the thirties there was a tremendous increase in personnel and in mission centers in California. The convent in Redlands had been opened in 1932 with ten Catechists. Four years later there were fourteen. Even by using the garage for a dormitory, the Catechists were crowded. Meanwhile, the number of Catechists in California had increased to sixty. It was necessary to find a place where they could come together in the summer for retreat, refresher courses, and relaxation.

For several years the Catechists were given accommodations during retreat in one of the mansions for which the city of Redlands was famous at that time. The Cheney residence was one. The Sterling family and the Stillmans also opened their homes to the Catechists. But they needed something permanent. Just west of the Sterling home was what was known as the Burrage mansion. It had been empty for twenty years, but the Catechists learned that they might live in it if it would serve their purpose. A group of Redlands business men who were the present owners of the house were happy to have the Catechists move in, for it was not only falling into disrepair, but it was being vandalized.

On May 24, 1937, feast of Our Lady of Victory, Catechist Mary McConville and her companions took up residence at 1205 West Crescent Avenue. They might have looked like millionaires on the outside, because the house was indeed beautiful, but appearances were deceiving. The inside was far from being in good condition. Vandals had destroyed electrical fixtures and much of the plumbing. The Catechists had to use candlelight on the second floor. Water for most purposes was reserved in two huge tanks and in large cisterns. To obtain drinking water a pipe was laid from the street to the top of the 103 steps leading to the house. From there the water had to be carried by a bucket brigade. Neither of the two furnaces worked; the thirteen fireplaces were used for warmth in winter.

The Burrage mansion, surrounded by twenty acres of orange groves, was in a section called Smiley Heights. The property occupied the highest spot in Redlands. It had been built in 1901 in the popular Moorish style (known later in California as mission style) prevalent at the time, but the owner copied the twin towers of Santa Barbara Mission and the cloisters of San Juan Capistrano.[1]

Albert C. Burrage was a native of Napa, California, who went to Harvard and worked his way through law school. Soon after he received his degree he discovered an important flaw in the charter of the Brookline Gas Company, allowing the company to sell gas to Boston. The information proved advantageous also to several oil companies. Burrage himself received a fee of $1,000,000. He invested his money in nitrite mines in Chile. This investment and others he made were very successful. Besides owning a mansion in Boston, he had property on the Atlantic shore. At the turn of the century he bought land in Redlands for a winter home.

Many are the stories the old timers told the Catechists about the house they were using as a convent, stories substantiated by clippings and pictures from the *Redlands Daily Facts*. Shortly after the building was begun in the summer of 1901, Mr. Burrage's Redlands agent, S.C. Haver, received a telegram from his employer saying that he and his family were planning to spend the holidays in Redlands and the building must be finished by Thanksgiving. D.M. Donald, the contractor, hired more men and pushed the work as fast as he could, though it seemed to him all but impossible to complete a building of that size in ninety days. There were thirty-six rooms. He purchased as many kerosene stoves as he could find in Redlands, San Bernardino, and elsewhere and burned them around the clock to dry out the plaster. After Christmas when the family had departed, the plaster had to be removed and replaced properly.

The Burrage family came out from the East in their own private railroad car and with two carloads of horses, polo ponies, and vehicles attached to a Santa Fe limited. For some reason they used their new home (winter "cottage" as they referred to it) for only a few years. When they did come to Redlands they entertained lavishly, making good use of the polo field and the heated, glass-enclosed swimming pool directly behind the house. They came to California off and on until 1907. Then they did not return until 1916. On March 28 of that year they gave one last elaborate party. Part of the account of the affair, taken from the *Redlands Daily Facts,* follows:

Mr. and Mrs. Albert Cameron Burrage of Boston, who with a party of relatives are now occupying their magnificent estate, "Monte Vista," on the Heights, hospitably opened its portals last evening to receive a large company of friends in honor of their return to this land of sunshine and flowers after an absence of about nine years.

Guests motored up the avenues, illuminated with Japanese lanterns, to the residence, itself aglow with many brilliant lights. The cloisters of Spanish type with their climbing vines and potted palms were strung with myriads of incandescent globes and later the sounds of joyful music, merry laughter and conversation were wafted from out the open doorways and windows into the open air, rife with perfume of orange blossoms and roses . . .

The host and hostess had planned a rare surprise for their guests by having their glass-enclosed natatorium (indoor swimming pool) which occupies the center of a court facing south, entirely covered with flooring for this occasion, and dancing thereon to music that "lifted one's feet" was the principal amusement of the evening . . .

Refreshments were served at small tables, placed throughout the patio, dining room and on the piazzas. Centering each exquisitely laid festive board was a basket of white lilacs and pink Killarney rose buds, daintily matched in tone by delicious items of each course. The ices were in the forms of pink-cheeked apples, pears and yellow bananas. The cakes were frosted in pink and white and were in dainty paper holders. Beautiful candy baskets were another novelty.

Concluding the affair there were confetti and serpentine dance numbers to create a Mardi Gras spirit and it was only at a wee small hour that regretful adieus were said and the guests departed at the close of one of the most radiant and successful social functions given in Redlands in many a season.[2]

Several more paragraphs described the gowns of the hostess and women guests. It was the last party given by the Burrage family. They returned to Boston soon afterward leaving the property up for sale. A pugilist from Hollywood bought it, intending to turn it into a gymnasium for millionaires, but without success. A group of Redlands business men acquired it, hoping to turn it into a first class hotel for winter tourists, but that project failed also.

The mansion was said to have cost $100,000 in 1901. (In reporting this in 1963, the *Daily Facts* reminded its readers that at this time steak cost twenty-five cents a pound.) Masonry work on the stone wall across the front of the property and along the winding driveway was done at an additional cost of $300,000. Still more money was spent on the caretaker's house and the two-story carriage building, used by the Catechists as a garage. What the business men paid for the estate is not known. When they permitted the Catechists to live there in 1937, it was with the understanding that they would have to leave if there should be a buyer for the property. Because of this condition the Catechists could not make any substantial repairs.

All this was changed in September 1940 when Bishop Noll purchased the

Burrage mansion for $13,000, made necessary repairs including a new roof and a furnace, and gave it to the Congregation. Dedicated to Mary under her title of Queen of the Missions, the Redlands convent served the community well. It was home for eighteen Sisters and summer home for many times that number when the Sisters came from their California missions for retreat and relaxation. From the center at Redlands the Sisters at one time served forty-six parishes in the area.

In the late sixties Redlands was no longer needed as a summer convent for the Victory Noll Sisters. Many of them now either had their degrees or were attending summer schools and living on campuses. Eventually seven, then only five Sisters staffed the large convent. Some of the parishes where they had worked were now being cared for by lay teachers whom the Sisters themselves had trained, or by Catholic schools. Besides, the house, though well built, was in need of almost constant repairs. Each year the financial burden increased. The few Sisters who worked in the area and were living in the convent could easily, and more economically, be housed elsewhere. All of these factors resulted in a decision by the President and the General Council to sell the property, a decision arrived at after taking a vote of the total Congregation. The Redlands convent was sold in 1974 to a professor at Loma Linda University Medical Center.

Much more could be written about Queen of the Missions, the beautiful convent that was home to so many Victory Noll Sisters for thirty-seven years. When in 1963 the city of Redlands observed the diamond jubilee of its founding, the convent was opened to the public together with other historic homes. The *Redlands Daily Facts* referred to the "plush Burrage mansion now being the Spartan home of the Missionary Sisters." The Redlands Historical Society, in one of its brochures, credited the Sisters with preserving both the house and grounds by their devoted care and their hard work.

This hard work was done by all the Sisters, but especially by Olivia Olivera, Elizabeth Hann, and Anna Hitzler. Sister Olivia went to Redlands in 1940 and continued in her role of gardener and mechanic until shortly before her death in 1962.[3] Sister Elizabeth joined her in 1944 and served in the same capacity until the convent was closed. Sister Anna went to Redlands in 1964 and worked on the grounds also. Their work was a labor of love that made the convent in Redlands a place where the Sisters could pray, relax, and enjoy one another in beautiful surroundings.

It is said that eighteen gardeners were employed by Burrage. When the Sisters began their work of restoration, the grounds had been neglected for almost thirty years. It was the wish of the owner to have planted on his property every kind of tree that would grow in southern California. And he succeeded in having this done. There were rare and exotic specimens, including especially a variety of palms and of evergreens. The dates and coconuts did not mature but were delicacies for the squirrels who tossed the date seeds all over the 103 steps leading up from the street. The Sisters did not use the steps but they did sweep them at least once a week. The five hundred fruit trees included naval, Valencia, and St. Michael oranges; lemons, tangerines, figs, avocados, plums, strawberry guavas, apricots, grapes, and olives.

When the Catechists were living as tenants, they hung their laundry in the glass-enclosed swimming pool. After 1940 when the property was theirs, they used the pool as it was intended to be used. Since there was no blueprint of the water line to be found, neither the Catechists nor anyone else could figure out how to turn the water into the pool. Through the years they used garden hoses connected to the nearest faucets. It took two and a half days to fill the pool by this method.

Though Bishop Noll made major repairs when he bought the building, through the years the Sisters themselves worked to make needed improvements. They laid vinyl tile, steamed off the old wall paper and painted the walls, even put in a 100-gallon water heater that was offered them at cost if they would do the installing. Much to the surprise of the appliance company, they accepted the offer.

Everything about the house and grounds lent itself to its being used as a convent. The library and adjoining billiard room became a devotional chapel. The caretaker's cottage was just right for the chaplain's home. The huge two-level stable and carriage house built into the hillside made a perfect garage for the many cars needed for the Sisters to do their work throughout the San Bernardino Valley.

During the forties when the California missions were expanding so rapidly, Victory Noll was getting crowded also. St. Joseph's Workshop that Father Sigstein had erected in 1937 had to be referred to now as St. Joseph's Building. The top floor had been converted into dorms and bedrooms for novices. Postulants were using cramped quarters in the original building. The chapel was becoming more and more crowded, especially in the summers when Sisters east of the Mississippi came to Victory Noll for retreat. Though two retreats were scheduled in 1949 to accommodate the crowd, the Sisters had to use not only the choir loft but an additional two rows of chairs in the hall on the second floor outside the choir. To help the situation, two Masses were scheduled every morning that summer. The older Sisters wondered why the novices and postulants should be the lucky ones to attend the later Mass.

Bishop Noll was aware of this crowded condition and as usual, did something about it. On May 24, 1948 (again, the feast of Our Lady of Victory), the Bishop bought what was described as a war assets building in Fort Wayne. It was a two-story structure, 136 feet in length. It was moved to Victory Noll from Baer Field and placed on a concrete basement on a site that had always been referred to as the sunken garden. John Sigstein had hoped to landscape this western end of the grounds but he never had the funds to do anything but plant grass and a tree or two.

165

Once the building was erected, the partitions in, and the flooring laid, Sister Effie McConnell, who had since 1938 served as Victory Noll's maintenance person, took charge of the interior work on the barracks. Besides supervising the work, she personally laid asphalt tile on all floors — 12,000 square feet — throughout the building. Sister Cecilia Schmitt (mistress of postulants at the time and later Superior General) painted the walls and ceilings in the entire building. Other Sisters helped with varnishing of doors, window frames, cupboards, and by doing various other jobs.

In December 1948, before the interior work had begun, it looked as if the whole thing might literally go up in smoke. The community was at supper on December 14 when the doorbell rang. A young man told the Sister who greeted him that the new building was on fire, that he had seen it from the highway below. On hearing the news several Sisters picked up the nearest fire extinguishers and hurried to the scene of the fire. By the time the Huntington Fire Department arrived, the fire was under control and little damage had been done.

Sacred Heart Building, as it was named, was faced with brick, and a breezeway built to connect it with the main structure. The ground floor became the dining room, kitchen, and storage area with a tunnel making it accessible to the main building. The second floor served as postulancy and the third as novitiate.

By providing living quarters for the Sisters in formation, the new building eased crowded conditions at Victory Noll. But Bishop Noll knew that still another need would soon be felt, a place for the sick and retired Sisters. When the Congregation celebrated its twenty-fifth anniversary in August 1947, there were only three Sisters buried in the cemetery. Julia Doyle died in October 1947, and Rose Ann McBride the following month. In May 1948 Marie Benes died. There were no more deaths for eight years. The Bishop knew, however, and the Sisters knew that it would soon be different; that death would strike more frequently as the community grew older. So again the Bishop made generous provision for that time.

On November 19, 1953, Bishop Noll informed the Sisters that for a long time he had been setting aside funds to build a chapel and infirmary. In 1955 he turned over to the Congregation the money he had accumulated. It would not cover the entire cost of building, but it was a substantial beginning. However, construction costs continued to rise even before the project began. The Sisters launched a building fund and publicized it through *The Missionary Catechist* magazine. There were no outstanding donations, but many good friends responded and helped to increase the amount on hand. Generous relatives and friends also contributed the furnishings of the chapel and infirmary. Though Bishop Noll died in 1956 and did not see the plans brought to completion, he knew that they would soon be a reality.

It was in 1958 that the surveyors laid out the plot for the new building (the chapel and infirmary were to be one unit) and ground was broken October 11 of that same year. In March of the following year the workers poured the first slab of concrete. On July 23, 1960, the infirmary was completed enough for some of the Sisters to move in and make more rooms available in Our Lady of Victory Building. The beds did not arrive for another ten days so the Sisters slept on mattresses and springs laid on the floor. Such a sleeping arrangement was comfortable, though making the bed entailed some gymnastics. The rest of the bedroom furniture did not arrive until many weeks later. Boxes served as improvised night stands and reminded the Sisters of mission stories of some of their predecessors who used wardrobe trunks for dressers. Since most of the Sisters were used to living out of suitcases, the arrangement caused little inconvenience, especially since it was only temporary.

On July 2, 1960, Bishop Leo A. Pursley consecrated the altar. Two weeks later, July 22, Monsignor James P. Conroy, chaplain at Victory Noll, celebrated the first Mass. Because more work needed to be done in both the chapel and infirmary, the Sisters deferred the solemn dedication until May 24 of the following year.

Bishop Pursley and Bishop Grutka (of the Diocese of Gary) blessed the building. Over two hundred special guests, mostly priests and others from the area, attended the celebration. On two Sundays in June the Sisters held open house for the public. More than four hundred came the first Sunday. The next week the number doubled. By naming the chapel the Archbishop Noll Memorial Chapel, the Victory Noll Sisters honored their friend and patron. The infirmary is known as Holy Family Building.

In the mid-forties there was a different kind of expansion, different in that it was not a material one involving only buildings. As the Congregation grew and became better known, requests for Sisters increased. Bishops and priests around the world begged for foundations for their dioceses, their parishes. Letters came from as far away as Australia, Japan, India, Thailand, Guam, and New Guinea; from the Philippines, Hawaii, Puerto Rico, Canada, and other countries. Father Sigstein himself once wrote that he "longed for the day when we can send Catechists to the Philippines and to Puerto Rico." He never intended that the Catechists confine their ministry to the United States.

In 1945 the Most Rev. Francis Beckmann, Archbishop of Panama, visited Victory Noll and asked for Catechists. Archbishop Beckmann was a Vincentian from the Netherlands, and for a long time had been a missionary in the Central American Republic. There were no parochial schools in the area, he told Catherine Olberding and her Council, and he was especially anxious for the Catechists to train the laity to teach both children and adults. It was exactly the work for which Victory Noll was founded.

The Superior General and her Council favored the request. Bishop Noll, however, felt that it was not yet time to make a foundation outside the States. Archbishop Beckmann accepted this decision of the Bishop but at the same time he was convinced that the Republic of Panama needed Missionary Catechists like those in the United States. He selected a small group of Panamanian women with the intention of forming a new community and in 1947 he wrote again to Mother Catherine Olberding at Victory Noll. This time he asked for two Sisters who would help in the formation and practical training of his Sisters. To this request Bishop Noll acquiesced.

The Sisters chosen for this important work were Monica Ulibarri and Mary Bernarda Marquez. They left Victory Noll January 10, 1948, and spent the next two and a half years helping the group of women Archbishop Beckmann had brought together, *Las Misioneras Catequistas de la Medalla Milagrosa* — Missionary Catechists of the Miraculous Medal. January 25, 1948, was the founding date of this Religious Congregation, the first to be established in Panama.

Archbishop Beckmann personally directed these Sisters until his death October 30, 1964. He was succeeded by Archbishop Tomas A. Clavel Mendez who resigned the See in 1968. The following February Bishop Marcos G. McGrath, C.S.C., of the Diocese of Santiago de Veraguas, was named Archbishop of Panama.[4] He had been Archbishop Beckmann's Auxiliary from 1961 to 1964. No group could have been happier over Bishop McGrath's appointment than the *Misioneras Catequistas*. They had known and loved him when he was their Auxiliary Bishop, and they staffed a mission center in his Diocese of Santiago de Veraguas. As Archbishop of Panama he has continued his personal interest in the Congregation.

A request similar to Archbishop Beckmann's came to Mother Catherine in 1949. It was from Monsignor John C. Ryan of Detroit and he was writing with the approval of his Archbishop, Cardinal Mooney. Monsignor Ryan saw the need of a religious community of women to work with Detroit's Black population. He had two young women who were called to this work. He would be responsible for their spiritual direction but he would like to have two Victory Noll Sisters live with them and guide them. In the terminology of the day, he was asking for a mistress of novices and another Sister as her assistant.

Mother Catherine and her Council, though pressed from all sides for more and more personnel for rapidly expanding mission work, were happy to accede to Monsignor Ryan's request. Six years earlier it was Monsignor Ryan who had welcomed the Missionary Catechists to Detroit and he had been their friend and counselor through the years. The Monsignor was head of the religious education department of the Archdiocese, and the Catechists worked directly under him. Now, when seeking help for his new community, he turned to Victory Noll.

Mary Louise Perl and Helen Flaspohler were the Sisters appointed by Mother Catherine to assist Monsignor Ryan in establishing the Congregation he envisioned, a Congregation to be known as Sisters, Home Visitors of Mary. Mary Schutz, a librarian, and Agnes McGinnis, a nurse, were the first two candidates. The two women, together with Sisters Mary Louise and Helen, took up residence on Cardoni Street in Detroit, in what was then St. George's parish. On November 21, 1949, feast of the Presentation of Mary, the two pioneer Sisters formally began their religious life. They were received as novices the following May.

At the General Chapter of the Victory Noll Sisters in August of that year Sister Mary Louise was elected Councilor and General Secretary. She was replaced in Detroit by Sister Benigna Furst. In 1951 the little community — Mary and Agnes, Benigna and Helen — moved to a convent provided for them on Arden Park, only a few doors from the Victory Noll Sisters. This was ideal for both communities and there was much interchange on every level. Although by the following year the first two Home Visitors had professed their vows and were "on their own," Monsignor Ryan asked for a Victory Noll Sister to live with them for another year. Sister Julia Marie Schmitt, a former novice mistress at Victory Noll, was given the assignment.[5]

The Victory Noll Sisters feel very close to the Home Visitors of Mary and to the *Misioneras Catequistas*. They know it was a privilege for them to share with these Sisters their beginnings and their own spirit. Proximity between Indiana and Michigan makes interchange easier than between Indiana and Panama. However, Panama City has become a stopping off place for the Victory Noll Sisters going to and from their missions in Bolivia. And at the Collegial Assembly held at Victory Noll in 1971 Madre Maria Margarita Moreno, Superior General of the Panamanian Sisters at that time, was a special guest.

During the decade of the fifties a large number — thirty-four — of mission centers were opened by the Victory Noll Sisters, but all of them were in the United States. A number of requests for Sisters came from various places in Latin America. In reply to the Apostolic Nuncio who had written from LaPaz, Bolivia, in 1956, Mother Cecilia Schmitt, then Superior General, wrote that she seriously considered sending Sisters to Bolivia but that it might be several years before they would be ready.

In August 1961 Mother Cecilia was present at a joint meeting of the Conference of Major Superiors of Men and of Women Religious at the University of Notre Dame when Monsignor (now Cardinal) Casaroli in the name of the Holy See, asked every Congregation to pledge ten percent of its personnel for Latin America. Even if no such request had come from the Holy See, it was but natural that Our Lady of Victory Missionary Sisters would favor Latin America for its first venture outside the United States. There were many Hispanic Sisters in the Congregation. Besides, many other Sisters were "at home" in the Spanish language and were trained in pastoral work.

According to the minutes of the General Chapter of 1962 several topics, after being discussed, were entrusted to the Superior General to be carried out. Among them was the mission in Latin America. In the elections that took place at this time Mother Cecilia Schmitt was succeeded by Mother Florentine Lohr.

It was her task to make definite plans for Victory Noll's first foreign mission. There were many volunteers, but among other things it had to be decided not just who would go but where they would go.

Providentially a way was opened to discover the "where." At one of the annual meetings of Major Superiors of Women (now Leadership Conference of Women Religious — LCWR), Mother Coleman, Superior General of the Maryknoll Sisters at this time, made a generous offer. For a religious community trying to decide where to locate in Latin America, it would be wise to make an exploration trip, she said. The Sisters could live and work with the Maryknoll Sisters and then make a decision. This sounded like a good thing to Mother Florentine and her Council, for the Maryknoll Sisters had had much experience in the foreign field and they staffed a number of missions in Latin America. Mother Coleman's offer was gratefully accepted, and Muriel Balch and Carolyn Ortega were asked to do the "scouting."

The Sisters left New York on a freighter, the *Santa Margarita,* September 8, 1966. The ship was scheduled to leave the day before, but the longshoremen did not finish loading the cargo until four o'clock the morning of the eighth. The Sisters were happy that the sailing date was the Nativity of Mary to whom they had dedicated their mission. They arrived in Panama a week later and were warmly welcomed by the *Misioneras Catequistas* there. During the month they spent with these Sisters, they visited other parts of the Republic — Santiago, Atalya, and Chitre. On October 13 Muriel and Carolyn went to Puerto Armuelles where they lived with the Maryknoll Sisters. They taught religion in the schools, worked with youth groups, and gave marriage instructions to couples in the *fincas,* the banana plantations. It was with reluctance that they left the Sisters and the people of Puerto Armuelles in January and flew south to Santiago de Chile.

But it was not to Chile that they felt the Spirit was calling the Congregation. Mother Florentine meanwhile had received a request from the St. James Fathers in Oruro, Bolivia. One of them, David G. Sevigny, had known the Victory Noll Sisters in Vermont and asked that they consider coming to the Altiplano. Sister Muriel and Sister Carolyn took the train north from Chile to Bolivia where they remained six months working with the St. James priests in the *parroquia de San Pio Decimo* in Oruro. They would have liked to stay longer but they were to enroll in the *Instituto Catequistico Latino Americano* in Manizales, Colombia. The Institute, which was in session from March to October, accepted the Sisters on the recommendation of Bishop McGrath of Panama.

Even while the Sisters were attending classes, translating, taking exams, they were privileged to do apostolic work, though they had not planned it that way. The apostolate sought them out, as it were. One afternoon when Carolyn Ortega went to the bus she was horrified to see a young woman under the wheel, bleeding profusely. Carolyn went with her to the hospital and when she was released, she and Muriel took care of her at home. Petronilla had no one but a sister Teresa who was dying of cancer. The Sisters visited them every day and looked after them. One of their priest classmates from the Institute came every other day with Holy Communion. Teresa, after receiving the sacrament of the sick, died on the feast of her patroness, Therese of Lisieux. Sister Carolyn ended her story: "Teresa must have lived a very holy life to have had such a beautiful death . . . We had to make the down payment on the little wooden coffin because it would not be provided unless there was an advance payment. The poor are wrapped in a sheet here and buried the same day they die. Teresa looked like Lazarus in her white wrappings."[6]

After another stop, at the invitation of a bishop in Central America, the Sisters returned to Victory Noll. They were convinced that Oruro, Bolivia, was the place where the Spirit was calling. They believed that it was what the Congregation expected a Victory Noll Latin American mission to be. The people are desperately poor, for next to Haiti, Bolivia is the poorest country in the Western Hemisphere. At that time there were no other North American Sisters in Oruro. The Altiplano is too high and too bleak for many missionaries. A foundation in Oruro, then, was recommended to Mother Florentine and her Council.

Much as the Congregation would have liked to open the mission immediately, there was a delay. A General Chapter was scheduled for the summer of 1968 and both Muriel and Carolyn were elected delegates. Had this been an ordinary General Chapter, it might have been different, but this was the Special Chapter called for by Vatican II and it was important that the Sisters take part in it and postpone going to Bolivia until fall.

For Muriel Balch it meant not just postponing the trip to Bolivia, but giving the opportunity to someone else. She received another call, having been elected a member of the General Council and Area Coordinator of the Southwest. Those who were accepted for Oruro were: Carolyn Ortega, Ruth Banet, Mamie Garcia, and Rose Anita Salas. The founding date was the feast of the Immaculate Conception, December 8, 1968. Mary Edna Butler joined the others in 1970 and subsequently other Sisters went to Bolivia: Lorraine Masters, Margaret Gutierrez, Mary Ellen Descourouez, Evelyn Mourey, Alberta Walter, Melanie Persche, and Diana Gutierrez.

Meanwhile native young women expressed interest in joining the Victory Noll Congregation. The first to do so was Maria Adela Amoroso of Oruro. Adela, the daughter of a miner, had been a catechist at San Jose mine for six or seven years and after the Sisters went to Bolivia, worked closely with Ruth Banet. In January 1973 Adela began a Live-in Program in Oruro, a first step toward the postulancy, novitiate, and profession. It was agreed that a house of formation was needed if the Congregation were to accept Bolivian women.

When Sister Gertrude Sullivan, President of the Congregation, and Sister Lucy Marie Vega, a member of the General Council, visited Bolivia in 1973,

Adela was accepted as a postulant. It was decided to open the house of formation in Buena Vista. There were several reasons for choosing this pueblo. The St. James priests had asked for the Sisters some time before. Buena Vista is in the *campo* in a part of Bolivia that is expanding, and the mission itself offers the type of ministry that can be adjusted to part-time work and part-time study, ideal for those in formation.

Buena Vista, in the Diocese of Santa Cruz, is in a tropical part of Bolivia and the Sisters from Oruro could go there for altitude leave.[7] For several years they had gone to convents of other Sisters who lived at a lower altitude, but by having a home in Buena Vista, they could be with their own. With the permission of the Bishop of Santa Cruz, the house of formation was officially established May 24, 1974. Ruth Banet pioneered the new foundation. That same year Margarita Quispe who, like Adela, is from Oruro, began a Live-in Program in Buena Vista. Both young women were professed but left the community at the expiration of temporary vows. This is not a unique situation. Other American congregations have experienced it. It would seem that at this time the call to formation work in Bolivia means that the Sisters prepare native women to minister to their own people as dedicated Christian lay women rather than as Our Lady of Victory Missionary Sisters.

From colonial days to the present time the people of Bolivia have suffered from oppression and from every kind of hardship. The country has long been in slavery from ignorance, hunger, poverty. Oruro, 12,500 feet above sea level, is in the Altiplano, the Andean high plateau. Its climate is harsh and vegetation is sparse. Llamas and sheep roam its stark plains.

The people of Boliva are sixty-five percent Indian, twenty to thirty percent mestizo, and five to fifteen percent, European background. The percentage of Indians is probably still higher in the Oruro area, for here are the tin mines and it is the Indians who labor in the mines. They work deep in the earth for long hours. The men chew coca leaves, a narcotic which gives them energy for the job and acts as a sedative against hunger and cold. The mines are filled with fumes which attack the men's lungs. In fifteen years or so the workers are forced to retire, broken-down men who look years older than their age. Most of them succumb to the dread lung disease, silicosis.[8]

Although Bolivia's minerals, especially silver, tin, zinc, and ore, are the backbone of its economy, only a small percent of the people are beneficiaries. Nearly all others live on the poverty level. In the mining districts infant mortality rate is extremely high, six hundred deaths to one thousand live births.[9]

Living in a stage of siege, not being able to travel without a permit, curfews at night — all these have become almost a way of life for the Sisters in Bolivia. Presidents come and go; few finish out their term of office. There is a never-ending succession of military takeovers, plots and counter plots, rumors of one coup after another. Missionaries long for the day when all Bolivians will enjoy their freedom as sons and daughters of God.

The national religion is Catholicism and there is a law requiring that one period each week be devoted to the teaching of religion. In some ways the Sisters' catechetical apostolate differs little from their work in the States. The Sisters teach high school students and adults. They train catechists and help to surpervise their work. To accommodate the young people of all ages who work during the day and go to school at night, the Sisters have night classes in a poor school near the convent.

Students on all levels have no text books and must copy everything into note-books. They are extremely handicapped when, and if, they are accepted at the university. It was evident to the Sisters that home study was difficult, for the young people needed lighting, desks, books, and other tools. Sister Carolyn opened a study center making use of an empty parish building next door to the convent. The next step was Honor Loans for students at the university, at the school of nursing, and at a technical school. Each student who applies is given a loan of about one hundred dollars a year — ten dollars a month for ten months. With this small amount a student can begin studies, pay room and board, and purchase clothing. After the students graduate they pay back the loan plus an additional ten percent. This money is put back into the Honor Loan fund with the idea that in the future it will be Bolivians helping Bolivians. Both Sisters and students feel that this arrangement is more in keeping with human dignity than outright gifts. Today mining engineers in various parts of Bolivia are paying back their loans.

Carolyn Ortega has a special gift for working with students and other young adults, a gift that was long recognized before she went to Bolivia. Her experiences in Latin America have been enriching. Very soon after her arrival in Oruro she was asked to be a member of a diocesan team concerned with the three cultures — Quechua, Aymara, and Spanish. The center sponsored workshops and lectures in order to form the social consciences of leaders and make the people aware of their human dignity. The apostolate reached out especially to leaders of labor unions, to pastoral agents, and others. With a Canadian Oblate priest fluent in both Quechua and Aymara, Sister Carolyn worked on a Quechua grammar designed to be used by agents of change who work among the Quechua-speaking *campesinos*.

Mary Edna Butler, another veteran of Victory Noll in Bolivia, is involved in many activities on the diocesan level: Sisters' Council, pro-life movement, catechetics, vocations, pre-baptismal catecheses, to name but a few.

The Sisters' work with handicapped children has been most rewarding. Sister Mary Edna has special classes for the mentally retarded and Sister Lorraine, for blind children. At First Communion time it was a group of older blind girls who sang the Mass. They laboriously copied the words of the hymns in Braille and then memorized them.

The apostolate in Bolivia extends to hospitals and prisons. Sister Ruth Banet, who began work in the prison in Oruro, was joined by Sister Mary Edna

Butler in this ministry. The Sisters not only conduct Bible classes in the prison but have been fearless defenders of the many victims of injustice. Some inmates have been imprisoned for years and never brought to trial. With the help of a dedicated young Bolivian lawyer Sister Mary Edna has been instrumental in obtaining the release of a number of prisoners.

Conditions in the prison are appalling. Over a hundred men and ten or more women are crowded into inadequate space. Small children are in jail with their mothers. Sister Ruth Banet was tireless in her work for prisoners in Oruro. She succeeded in setting up a shoe shop, a tailor shop, and a carpenter shop in order to provide work for the inmates. With the little income the work brings them, some have hired a lawyer and obtained their release. Others are able to support themselves and their families while serving their terms. Another much appreciated service is the circulating library of magazines and books that Sister Alberta helps to maintain. The prisoners are grateful for reading material, especially during the long evening hours when they have nothing at all to do.

Buena Vista, seventy miles northwest of Santa Cruz, is different from Oruro in every way. It is tropical, bordering on the jungle. Buena Vista, though a very small village of about two thousand, can boast of a long history. It was founded in 1624, one of the first of the famous Jesuit Reductions in South America.[10] Buena Vista and the surrounding settlements provide opportunities for catechetical activities, social work, and the nursing apostolate. Sister Evelyn Mourey uses her nursing skills not only to provide direct health care, but also to instruct mothers in the care of their children.

It was a happy coincidence that the Victory Noll Sisters opened their first mission in Latin American in 1968, the year of the bishops' conference in Medellin. It was a historic meeting, the Second General Assembly of Latin American Bishops. Pope Paul VI traveled to Bogata, Colombia, in the fall of that year to convoke the conference that would take place in the nearby town of Medellin. The Medellin documents, as they have come to be known, denounced the social and economic inequalities in Latin America. It was a turning point for the Catholic Church in Latin America, but the price has been high. Priests, religious, and laity have suffered, but they have suffered bravely, knowing that their cause is a just one. Though conditions have not improved politically, nor economically, the people have awakened to the injustices around them.

Medellin was followed by Puebla, the Third General Assembly opened by Pope John Paul II at the end of January 1979. The Pope told the assembled bishops that they must be concerned about the ways in which human dignity is infringed today. "Those who bear responsibility for the public life of the states and nations," he said in his opening address, "will have to understand that internal peace and international peace can only be insured if a social and economic system based on justice flourishes. Christ did not remain indifferent in the face of this vast and demanding imperative of social morality."[11]

The struggle will continue and religious will continue to be caught up in it. Cardinal Eduardo Pironio of Argentina who is head of the Vatican Congregation for Religious has said that religious who serve the Church and world today must live more radically the Gospel values they have accepted. Religious must seek new modes of presence in today's world, the Cardinal said. They must be involved in concrete challenges for justice and develop sensitivity in the problems of justice. The Church and its religious must be present in the workers' world.[12]

The Victory Noll Sisters in Bolivia are engaged in what might be called a witness of presence. They are the prophetic voices of the oppressed in socio-political affairs. They are *la voz de los sin voz* (the voice of those without voice). Because of their religious commitment the Sisters can do what mothers, wives, workers cannot do: denounce specific injustices, act as observers at union elections, at university elections, and other events. All of this involves risk because any one who works for human rights under a military dictatorship is accused of being involved in political activities.

The Sisters have no illusion that they themselves or their mission might be "God's gift to Bolivia." Rather, as Sister Carolyn Ortega points out: "Bolivia is God's gift to us, a sign that we are *missionary* and a constant reminder that Victory Noll Sisters are sealed with a special vocation: to live, to suffer, to work with the oppressed so that they themselves may become creators of their own destiny."[13]

Notes to Chapter XVI

1. The Burrage home and its surroundings were the locale for Harold Bell Wright's novel, *The Eyes of the World* (1914). Fairlands was Redlands; Fairlands Heights, Smiley Heights. The mansion was on the highest point in Fairlands. Wright describes the beautiful mountain peaks: San Gorgonio, San Bernardino, San Antonio, Cucamonga; and the San Timeteo Canyon close by. The Missionary Sisters can easily recognize the layout of their former convent: the patios, steps, glass-enclosed pool, the grounds. But there the similarity ends. Except for their wealth, the author's characters have nothing in common with the family that built the beautiful home.

2. *Redlands Daily Facts,* March 29, 1916.

3. Sister Olivia (Mary Olivera) was born in the Azores in 1909 and came to the United States with her family when she was eleven years old. She was taught by the Catechists in Los Banos, California, and joined the community in 1934. Sister Olivia died at Victory Noll in 1962.

4. Marcos McGrath was born February 10, 1924, in Ancon, Canal Zone, where his father, a native of Trenton, New Jersey, was employed; his mother was a Costa Rican. McGrath attended schools in Latin America and in the United States, graduating from the University of Notre Dame. He entered the Congregation of the Holy Cross and was ordained in Panama in 1949. After graduate studies in Paris and Rome, Father McGrath served as rector of Holy Cross Seminary in Santiago, Chile, and in 1959 became dean of the theology faculty of the Catholic University in Santiago. The Archbishop has been an active member of the Latin American Bishops' Conference (CELAM) and has served as its general secretary.

5. Monsignor Ryan died February 16, 1957. Sister Julia Marie Schmitt, a native of Dubuque, died August 1, 1961; and Sister Mary Louise Perl, Mansfield, Ohio, December 7, 1971.

6. Letter from Manizales, Colombia, October 17, 1967.

7. For reasons of health North Americans find it necessary from time to time (depending on the individual) to live at a lower elevation for certain periods. This is referred to as "altitude leave."

8. See *Maryknoll,* January 1978. The entire issue is on Bolivia.

9. See *National Catholic Reporter,* October 20, 1978.

10. See *New Catholic Encyclopedia,* Vol. 12, p. 166.

11. Quoted in *Origins,* February 8, 1979, Vol. 8, No. 34.

12. Cardinal Pironio's remarks were taken from a news release published in *Our Sunday Visitor,* May 14, 1978.

13. *Shaping Visions,* Proceedings of Our Lady of Victory Missionary Sisters' Tenth Chapter of Affairs, August 1978.

17

Education

W HAT ARE YOU DOING HERE?" the priest asked accusingly.

It was the summer of 1934 and two Victory Noll Catechists were on their way to the dining hall on the campus of the University of Notre Dame. They were somewhat taken aback by the question, to say the least. Surely, they thought, they had just as much right to attend summer school as the other Sisters all around them. From the expression on the face of their questioner, it would hardly seem so.

The Catechists explained that they were attending classes in the department of journalism. At that, the priest was a little more cordial and said, "Oh, that's all right. I thought you were coming here for education classes and would be teaching in parochial schools. Your Founder knows what he is doing. Don't let them make you teach school!"

With that admonition, the priest continued on his way. It was only later that the Catechists learned his identity. He was president of a well-known university in the West. Perhaps the priest also thought the Catechists, because they taught "only" religious subjects, did not need degrees. It would have been impossible for a woman at that time to major in theology. Most religion courses in college were in apologetics, though there were some instances of Bible studies. It was not until several decades later that college curricula included solid religious subjects.

Father Sigstein, knowing exactly what his Catechists would be doing in the missions, set up courses that would prepare them for their work. When the first few women were living at the Academy of Our Lady in Chicago, they had classes in Spanish and in methods of teaching. Mother Aquinata invited them

177

to attend her class in apologetics that she gave to the academy students. John arranged for a social worker to come out to Longwood to conduct a course in her field. He also engaged a dietitian to give the Catechists a short course in dietetics. He reserved for himself the all-important instructions in Christian doctrine and in the spiritual life.

In the summer of 1923 when Marie Benes returned from Watrous to attend the meeting of the Catholic Students Mission Crusade at Notre Dame, she was replaced there by Marie Bodin. In the fall Sophie Renier joined Marie Bodin and Julia Doyle in New Mexico. Father Sigstein intended to put Catechist Benes in charge of the Training Center in Gary but the building was delayed and she remained at the Academy of Our Lady until February 24 with Blanche Richardson and Caroline Meister. After her experience in New Mexico Marie Benes was anxious to have some practical training in nursing. She made arrangements for Blanche and herself to spend three days a week at a Catholic hospital in Chicago. For a short time they were allowed to bathe patients in the charity ward and to help in the free clinic where outpatients came for treatments. They asked that they be allowed to witness a birth. At this time Sisters were not permitted in the delivery room. The Catechists' request was granted but not without causing a bit of a shock.

On Friday evenings Blanche Richardson and Caroline Meister went to the home of Dr. Esther Quigley, a friend of John Sigstein's, a trip that necessitated changing street cars *four times*. The doctor instructed them in the treatment of children's diseases and in the care of infants. Blanche also attended the Berlitz School of Languages where she studied Spanish.

When the Catechists moved to Gary they had an opportunity to use their Spanish in their visits to the homes of the poor. Those who taught released time classes under the supervision of the Poor Handmaids of Jesus Christ had on-the-job training. Father Sigstein appreciated these advantages but he looked forward to the time when the Training Institute in Huntington would be completed and he could set up formal studies for the young women who were preparing to be Missionary Catechists.

Father Sigstein and the Catechists moved to Huntington December 7, 1924. At their first meal in their new home they had a guest who would be a frequent visitor at Victory Noll. She was Stella O'Brien, who headed the "Order of Veronica" at *Our Sunday Visitor*. That first evening Miss O'Brien brought with her the altar linens for the Mass that Father Sigstein would celebrate the next morning, the feast of the Immaculate Conception.

Stella O'Brien directed a department at the *Visitor* that was concerned with the making of altar linens for poor mission chapels. She recruited women for this work and gave them the names of missionaries who needed their help. An illustrated booklet was sent to each volunteer with explicit directives, measurements, and other information. John Sigstein gladly accepted Stella's offer to give sewing classes to the Catechists so that they in turn could instruct women and girls in the missions. He was very much aware of the poverty of the little chapels he had seen in New Mexico.

Miss O'Brien began her classes in January. There were other classes also. Dr. Edmund T. Dipple, a Huntington physician, had attended Mary Stickling in her last illness. When he learned about the work of the Catechists among the poor, he readily acceded to Father Sigstein's request to give regular lectures at Victory Noll. Later, Dr. Stanley Casey and Dr. Robert G. Johnston gave their services also. All of these classes were concerned mostly with illnesses of children and the prevention of diseases. An entry in the Victory Noll chronicles for November 9, 1925, notes that Dr. Casey lectured that day on bacteriology; and according to *The Missionary Catechist* for March 1928, Dr. Donald Bowers, also of Huntington, gave the Catechists a series of lectures on this subject. The doctors probably instructed the Catechists on communicable diseases and on the necessity of immunizations.

The doctors' classes were made still more practical by instructions in nursing. Beginning in March 1925, these were given at various times by Mary Jennings, Elizabeth Springer, and Elizabeth Sayle. Miss Jennings was a friend of John Sigstein's from Chicago. The other two women were public health nurses in Huntington County. When Aurelia McMahon entered the Society in 1928, she brought with her a wealth of knowledge and experience in health care. Father immediately asked her to direct this phase of training for the Catechists. Catechist McMahon worked closely with Dr. Johnston and Mrs. Sayle. Together, and with the cooperation of the pastors of the two parishes in Huntington, they set up a program so that the Catechists might take part in the health examinations of parochial school children. It would be to their advantage especially to be able to recognize abnormal conditions of the teeth and throat and to determine causes of underweight in children.

Aurelia McMahon taught what she called "home nursing" for ten years at Victory Noll, following techniques set up by the Red Cross. This practical training the young Catechists received proved invaluable when they cared for the sick in poor places where there was no doctor and where public health nurses were unheard of. In their classes they had achieved confidence in their ability by ministering to "Sarah," as they named their mannequin-patient. They were prepared to use their skills in caring for the sick poor in the missions.

In a letter to Julia Doyle written in January 1926, John Sigstein asked her to send him a list of illnesses that were most prevalent in the New Mexico missions. He said that Dr. Dipple had finished the first of a series of lectures and had covered diseases of the respiratory tract and various contagious diseases. Before beginning his second series of instructions he would like this information from the Catechists in New Mexico. In the same letter Father described other courses the Catechists were receiving. He mentioned in particular what he called "materia medica or pharmacy." A Miss Kessler and later, Eugene Huguenard, both registered pharmacists from Fort Wayne, taught the Catechists how to concoct simple preparations — salves, lotions, tonics, herbal teas, etc. — that would be helpful, inexpensive, and safe for them to use in their work. John told Julia that "we now have the fixtures for our pharmacy." For a number of years these simple "home remedies" were prepared at Victory Noll and sent out to the missions.

The summer of 1925 was a very busy one and yet there was no vacation from class work. Besides the usual classes, there was a six-week session covering courses in child psychology and pedagogy with emphasis on primary grades. The instructor was Estelle Bonner of Salina, Kansas, a public school teacher. She enjoyed her stay at Victory Noll so much that she returned during Christmas vacation and spent the holidays with the Catechists.

Until Father Sigstein found the right person to give the Catechists courses in social work, he was generously assisted by some of his friends who were employed by the National Catholic Welfare Council. Elizabeth Sweeney, Assistant Director of the Social Action Department of N.C.W.C., often came to Victory Noll to lecture. She had a special interest in the Society because she was particularly concerned with the plight of Spanish-speaking people. In an account of her first series of lectures, *The Missionary Catechist* for September 1925 reported:

> No one is better qualified than Miss Sweeney to guide us through the intricate mazes which confront and confuse the social worker among an alien race. She has made, at various times, surveys of social and economic conditions among the Spanish-speaking people of the Southwest, both for the Federal Government and for the National Catholic Welfare Council. A comprehensive outline of the result of a recent survey made by her at the commission of the latter body, was the subject of this first lecture.

Linna Bresette, National Secretary of the Catholic Conference on Industrial Relations, was another friend of Father Sigstein's who came several times to Victory Noll and talked to the Catechists. It was perhaps through Elizabeth Sweeney that John A. Lapp, Director of N.C.W.C.'s Social Action Department, came to Victory Noll in 1926.

John Sigstein appreciated the generosity of these professional people who came to Victory Noll at intervals, but he was eager to find someone who would come regularly and instruct the Catechists in social work. He found such a person in Marie Sheehan of Chicago. Miss Sheehan had been a social worker but at the time Father asked for her services, she was supervisor of the Home Study Department of Loyola University, Chicago. Like so many others who met Father Sigstein, Marie was totally won over to him and his Society, and without hesitation she offered to come to Huntington for one weekend a month. For the next eleven years Marie gave her services gratis, the Society paying only her railroad fare.

Marie Sheehan was the kind of teacher who would start out with a subject and before very long she would be telling her students about all kinds of interesting persons and events or she would use as an example an incident from her own childhood or family life with which most of the Catechists could identify. Many of her case histories were ones in which she herself had been involved. Though Marie's classes were often hilarious and though she sometimes got off course, the Catechists profited greatly from them. They looked forward to her weekends at Victory Noll and loved Marie not just as an instructor but as a friend.

In the summer of 1931 Father Sigstein arranged for Marie Sheehan to spend several weeks at Victory Mount in Las Vegas. He wanted her to give classes to the Catechists but most of all, he was anxious for her to see for herself the poor people in New Mexico. It was a revelation to her, as she wrote in *The Missionary Catechist* for April 1932.

> I had known quite intimately the work of the Catechists for the past seven years, but when I actually visited their missions among the poor Spanish-speaking people of the Southwest, I was astounded at its extent and excellence; for nothing I had heard or read had prepared me for the magnitude or necessity of their task. And I visited only a few of their missions!

Miss Sheehan used to say that she marveled that the people should settle in the little villages hidden deep in the mountains, but she marveled still more at Father Sigstein and the Catechists for discovering them there.

Another young woman who came from Chicago to share herself and her talents with the Catechists was Helen Hartke.[1] Beginning early in 1925 Mrs. Hartke traveled to Huntington every week to teach music. All afternoon Saturday and for two hours on Sunday morning she had singing lessons — chorus, choir, and individual Catechists. She would return to Chicago on the Sunday afternoon train. She refused any remuneration for her work. The Catechists did not ask for any remuneration from those they served, she told Father Sigstein, and this was her contribution to the poor missions.

When her family duties became more demanding, Mrs. Hartke came every other week. Then in 1929 she regretfully turned over the work of music instructor to Hilda App Hart of Fort Wayne. In 1932 she was succeeded by Frances Lock, also of Fort Wayne.

Because it was so important that the Catechists know the Spanish language, John Sigstein insisted that they have Spanish lessons every day. Marie Benes was their first instructor. When she was ill or away from Victory Noll, Evelyn Benton, the youngest person there, took her place. Evelyn was far better equipped to teach Spanish than anyone else in the community at that time and though she was very young and had just entered, she soon took over the classes.

Catechist Benton, or Sister Evelyn as she was known in later years, was from Pensacola, Florida. She began to correspond with Father Sigstein in the fall of 1924 when the Catechists were still in Gary. Though she would not be eighteen years old until March of the following year, she had already been graduated from high school. She had an excellent scholastic record, was proficient in French and Spanish, and had musical talent. Father Sigstein agreed to accept her and told her she might enter after the community was settled in Huntington.

It was a problem for her to convince her mother that the life of a Missionary Catechist was what she wanted. Her mother told her she should think of becoming a Sister of Mercy in Florida. "Besides," she added, "no one goes to Indiana in the middle of winter. The people from Indiana come to Florida then." This was early in January 1925. Her daughter was determined to have her way and finally her mother consented. But she herself would go to Huntington with Evelyn and find out what Victory Noll was like. When her daughter saw the place she probably would not want to stay. Or if she did, she would return home in a month or so. The daughter not only stayed, but her mother was so won over to Victory Noll and the Catechists that Evelyn used to say you would think it was all her mother's idea and not hers.

Sister Evelyn was gifted in languages. She knew both French and Spanish when she came to Victory Noll. She easily picked up Italian and Portuguese. She was the author of a bi-lingual book, *Bible Stories in the Language of Youth.* She edited also a number of Spanish leaflets and song books.[2]

Before they went to the missions, the young Catechists had opportunities for Spanish conversation not just from their own companions, but from Mexican priests who had come to the States in the wake of religious persecution in their country. Father Jose Lara and Father Angel Canamache resided at Victory Noll between 1926 and 1928. Father Lara, at least for some months, taught a course in advanced Spanish. Eventually Father Sigstein found work for these two priests among their own people. Jose Lara went to Indiana Harbor and Angel Canamache to California.

According to an entry in the chronicles for April 26, 1925, "Monsignor Noll conducted the first of his classes this afternoon at 3:30 o'clock." On May 30 the "monthly class of Monsignor Noll" is again noted. What the subject of these classes was is not known. The few Sisters who were at Victory Noll at that time have no recollection of them now. Evidently they were cut short when the Monsignor was made Bishop in June of that year and moved to Fort Wayne.

It is certain that the Monsignor's lectures were not on the spiritual life, for Father Sigstein himself had these classes. He also taught Christian doctrine, catechetics, and liturgy. Although at that time liturgy classes, even in seminaries, were concerned very much with externals — vestments, candles, rubrics, sacred books, etc. — Father Sigstein concentrated on the Mass, the heart of the liturgy. In 1929 he initiated the *Missa Recitata* at Victory Noll and urged the Catechists to encourage the same participation with the children in the missions wherever the pastor would permit it.[3]

Father Sigstein based his catechetical instructions principally on the works of Bishop Felix Antoine Dupanloup (1802-1878), brilliant nineteenth century Bishop of Orleans, France, whose writings are as timely today as they were more than a century ago. Nothing about them is theoretical. Dupanloup wrote from experience. As a young curate at the Church of the Madeleine in Paris, he taught religion to poor children. John Sigstein kept on his desk a well-worn copy of *The Ministry of Catechizing* that Dupanloup had written for the young priests of his diocese.[4] Nearly every page is marked; whole sentences are heavily underlined in pencil. On one of the first pages of the book Father Sigstein wrote what he called "An Act of Consecration." It reads:

> Most Dear and Blessed Mother! We, thy unworthy Catechists, offer you the first fruits of this catechism, with all the love and fervor of our hearts, and through you, to the Sacred Heart of your Divine Son. Deign, dearest Mother, to accept this offering, and grant that these children whom you have committed to our care, may be filled with true knowledge and love of our holy religion, and may persevere in its practice, so as to obtain through it the crown of everlasting happiness, through Jesus Christ, Our Lord. Amen.

Later, Father Sigstein modified this prayer of offering and incorporated it into the Catechists' morning prayer. Always, he emphasized the importance of imparting not just knowledge of the Christian religion, but love for the faith and perseverance in its practice. "Teach the practice of our holy religion; form habits of piety," he wrote on the flyleaf of Dupanloup's book.

Though money was always scarce, especially during the thirties, John Sigstein ordered excellent books for the library at Victory Noll and subscribed to the best periodicals available both at home and abroad. He rightly felt that this was very important for himself and for the Catechists. Besides mission magazines that were then being published — *The Field Afar* (now *Maryknoll*), *Jesuit Missions, Field at Home, Shield,* etc. — Father Sigstein also subscribed to *Ecclesiastical Review* (now *American Ecclesiastical Review), America, Commonweal,* and *New Mexico* magazine, among others. He was an initial subscriber to *Sponsa Regis* (now *Sisters Today), Orate Fratres (Worship),* and the short-lived newspaper, *The Catholic Daily Tribune.*

There were very few catechetical magazines in the English language in the twenties and thirties. *The Journal of Religious Instruction,* originally published by DePaul University of Chicago, was concerned more with Catholic schools than with the Confraternity of Christian Doctrine. It later changed its name to *The Catholic Educator.* Father's favorite publication, one he urged the Catechists to subscribe to and to read, was *The Sower,* published by Burns, Oates and Washbourne in London, and made famous by the perceptive writing of Father Francis H. Drinkwater, its founder and editor.[5] Bound copies of the magazine in the Victory Noll library date back to October 1925, though the little quarterly is older than that, having been founded in 1919.

When Father Sigstein learned through his reading or in some other way, of specialists in the catechetical field, he lost no time in contacting him or her. One such person whom Father was in touch with in the early twenties was Josephine Van Dyke Brownson. The February 1926 issue of *The Missionary Catechist* contained an advertisement for the text, *The Heart of the Child,* by Miss Brownson, published by Paulist Press. The author visited Victory Noll two months later and gave a few lectures to the Catechists. In the summer of 1930 she gave an extensive course at Victory Noll and a year later at Victory Mount in Las Vegas, New Mexico, for the Catechists in the missions.

Josephine Brownson (1880-1942) was the granddaughter of Orestes A. Brownson, the well-known nineteenth century journalist, editor, philosopher, and convert to the Catholic Faith. Miss Brownson organized the Catholic Instruction League in Detroit in 1916 and devoted all her spare time to teaching religion to public school children. In 1930 she resigned her teaching position in the Detroit public schools to concentrate on the work of the CIL. Nine years later the League was incorporated into the Archdiocesan Confraternity of Christian Doctrine.

Brownson was the author of several texts. *Stopping the Leak,* published in 1926, outlined her method of teaching and helped to recruit catechists. Her *Catholic Bible Stories,* published by Extension in 1923, was used widely. Best known was an eight-grade series *Learn of Me* which Our Sunday Vistor Inc. published in 1936. It became a standard for catechists during the next decade.

In recognition of her service to the Church, Josephine Brownson was awarded the papal medal *Pro Ecclesia et Pontifice* in 1933. That same year the University of Detroit conferred on her the honorary degree of Laws and Letters. Like her father before her, Miss Brownson was a recipient of the University of Notre Dame's Laetare Medal. Her father had received it in 1892; Josephine, in 1939. Her grandfather, Orestes A. Brownson, is buried in the crypt of Sacred Heart Church on the Notre Dame campus.

Through the magazine *Orate Fratres* John Sigstein was following the progress of the liturgical movement in the United States. Like the editor, Dom Virgil Michel, and his confreres at St. John's Abbey, Collegeville, Minnesota, Father Sigstein was convinced that the catechetical movement must complement the liturgical revival. He learned that the Grand Rapids Dominican Sisters were involved in writing a text to train children in the liturgy and he invited them to Victory Noll. Sister Estelle Hackett came in January 1930 and demonstrated *With Mother Church* which she and Sister Jane Marie Murray had developed under the direction of Dom Virgil.

In March 1929 Sisters Estelle and Jane Marie had visited Dom Virgil to consult him regarding training children in the liturgy. The priest suggested that the Sisters author a text; he would help them. In fact, he insisted that they begin that very night and outline the first lesson. They would discuss it in the morning. The eventual result was the *Christ Life Series,* textbooks for elementary grades. Sister Jane Marie visited Huntington in the summer of 1936 and gave the Catechists classes based on this series.[6]

Sisters of other religious communities also came to Victory Noll to teach the Catechists, among them two Franciscans from Milwaukee, Sister Lorettine and Sister Alana. Sister Lorettine had courses in child psychology and classroom management in July 1931. The following summer Sister Alana gave a four weeks' course in Christian pedagogy. During the thirties also, two seminary professors taught apologetics at Victory Noll and Victory Mount during the summer: Bernard Loeher of Sacred Heart Seminary, Detroit, and Gerard E. Picard, St. Mary of the Lake, Mundelein, Illinois.

A favorite teacher of the Catechists was Aloysius J. Heeg, S.J., assistant director of the Catholic Instruction League in Chicago and author of the First Communion text, *Jesus and I,* published by Loyola Press. Daniel A. Lord, S.J., lectured in 1937 on sodality organizational work. The recreational aspect of the Catechists' apostolate was not neglected. Father George Nell and his associates from Effingham, Illinois, demonstrated games and folk dances that the Catechists enjoyed learning and later, teaching their pupils.

These summer sessions for which Father Sigstein invited outside instructors were over and above the regular through-the-year classes conducted by the Catechists themselves. The same pattern continued after the elections of 1938. Gerald Ellard, S.J., William H. Russell of Catholic University, Johannes Hofinger, S.J., Timothy L. Bouscaren, S.J., and others came at various times. In 1955 Victory Noll Junior College was established and affiliated with the Catholic University of America. It continued until 1969 when Catholic University terminated its junior college affiliations. There were no regrets at Victory Noll, for by this time formation programs had changed radically and Victory Noll Junior College had served its purpose. By this time also, majors in religious studies were being offered in many colleges and universities.

Beginning in May 1929 Father Sigstein had gratefully entrusted the teaching of Christian doctrine to the Capuchin Fathers of St. Joseph Province who had just established themselves in Huntington. St. Felix Friary, the novitiate for the Midwest Province, was located only a little more than a mile from Victory Noll. The priests taught dogmatic and moral theology twice a week at Victory Noll until the junior college was discontinued. The Capuchins generously provided the Victory Noll Congregation with some of their best professors so that the Sisters might be well grounded in the doctrine they were preparing to teach.

In the late fifties more and more demands were being made on the Victory Noll Sisters to conduct teacher training courses. Though their own basic training and their years of experience in religious education equipped them for these classes, many of the Sisters had no academic degrees. And degrees were now necessary. It would not be easy to withdraw Sisters from mission work and let them go to school. Between 1950 and 1962 thirty-six convents were opened. The

Congregation staffed eighty centers, each of them involving a number of out-missions. No doubt it had been difficult for the administration to resist the pleas of bishops, but obviously the community was now spread too thin.

When Sister Florentine Lohr was elected Superior General in 1962, she immediately took steps to release Sisters for full-time studies. She notified the thirty-five bishops in whose dioceses the Congregation worked that the Sisters would not be available for religious vacation schools in the summer of 1964. Then she followed through by asking each diocese in which at least ten Sisters were stationed, to release ten percent during the coming year. Ten dioceses were involved. It became necessary to close a number of centers. For the most part bishops and priests were cooperative though they regretted the cutbacks. It was a courageous undertaking on the part of Sister Florentine at the beginning of her administration and the Sisters were grateful. The Congregation managed to meet the education expenses though very few dioceses contributed financial help.

This was the time that Juniorates were being established. Sisters in temporary profession were expected to complete their education before beginning mission work. Sister Francesca McGarry was released from her position at Catholic Social Services in Fort Wayne to become director of the Juniorate. With the cooperation of the Poor Handmaids of Jesus Christ, Sister Francesca and the Junior Sisters lived at what was then called the Villa, a diocesan institution for dependent children. They attended nearby St. Francis College conducted by the Franciscan Sisters of Mishawaka, Indiana.

As a result of the educational thrust throughout the entire Congregation, the gap was closed. The Sisters can now take part in summer courses for updating and enrichment. These are offered every year at Victory Noll and are enthusiastically attended by young and old alike.

Notes to Chapter XVII

1. Father Sigstein had known Mrs. Hartke since his years as curate at St. Pius Church in Chicago. See Chapter II.

2. Sister Evelyn Benton died at Victory Noll September 23, 1968.

3. In the *Missa Recitata* or Dialog Mass the congregation made the responses along with the servers. They also prayed in unison (but in Latin) the parts usually sung by the choir. This manner of participation in the Mass was at first looked upon with some suspicion. Pope Pius XI (elected February 11, 1922), however, seemed to favor it and so the Sacred Congregation of Rites did not forbid it but neither did it encourage it. After 1935 it was given wholehearted approval by Rome. An interesting account of the Dialog Mass is given by the late Gerard Ellard, S.J., in two of his books: *Christian Life and Worship* (1933) and *The Mass of the Future* (1948). Both books were published by Bruce, Milwaukee.

4. Felix A. Dupanloup, *The Ministry of Catechizing,* (Benziger, 1968). In the Victory Noll Library also is a copy of Dupanloup's *The Child* translated by Kate Anderson (Marlier Publishing Co., 1873).

5. Canon Drinkwater, now in his ninety-fourth year, though no longer editor of *The Sower,* is still active in the Catechetical apostolate. In 1978 he issued updated versions of several of his books. In answer to a letter we wrote him inquiring about the first issue of *The Sower,* he replied: "The names Victory Noll and Sigstein certainly ring a bell in the distant corridors of time, and I am happy to know that your holy founder's initiative has had such permanent and noble results in the handing on of the Faith, and that *The Sower* had some tiny part in helping it on." It would be a delight to quote at length from Father Drinkwater's long letter if it were not for the admonition: "If you ever feel wishful to print all this letter, please wait for 10 years or so until we are safely dead."

6. See Paul Marx, *Virgil Michel and the Liturgical Movement* (The Liturgical Press, Collegeville, Minnesota, 1957.)

18

Charism

ATHER SIGSTEIN'S MOTHER used to like to tell the Catechists that her son was born on a Sunday at the hour of the evening Angelus. The bells of the church dedicated to St. Vincent de Paul, apostle of the poor, were pealing out to remind all who heard them to pause and commemorate the mystery of the Incarnation.

The incarnational aspect of the mystery of Christ marked the spirituality of John Sigstein. He was attracted to the so-called French school of the eighteenth century exemplified by men like Cardinal de Berulle, Condren, Olier, St. John Eudes. The writings of these men centered on the Incarnation. Devotion to Mary naturally followed. Jean Gautier, in his *Some Schools of Catholic Spirituality,* writes:

> It is claimed that devotion to Mary leads to the cult of Jesus. The opposite is equally true. The French school, so devoted to the Word Incarnate, could not be unmindful of His Mother. It sees Mary in Jesus and goes to find Jesus in Mary. In this way Berulle's principles are given a new practical application. . . . It will also be remembered that M. Olier composed the well-known prayer, "O Jesus, living in Mary," to help us to find Jesus in Mary. It was Pere de Condren who supplied the basic elements of this prayer:
>
> > O Jesus, living in Mary,
> > come and live in your servants,
> > in the spirit of your holiness,
> > in the fullness of your power,
> > in the perfection of your ways,
> > in the truth of your virtues,

in the communication of your mysteries;
triumph over all our enemies,
in your Spirit,
for the glory of your Father.[1]

It was in the teaching of St. Louis Grignion de Montfort, however, that John Sigstein found the expression of the Incarnation that satisfied him most. Like St. Vincent de Paul, the Venerable Liebermann, and others, Montfort had been influenced by St. John Eudes. It was in 1910, a year after his ordination to the priesthood, that Father Sigstein consecrated himself to Jesus through Mary as St. Louis outlined in his *Treatise on True Devotion to the Blessed Virgin*.[2] Dedication to Jesus through Mary was to be the spirit of the Congregation of Our Lady of Victory Missionary Sisters. This is how the Founder expressed it in a conference given at Victory Noll March 2, 1936:

> Every religious community has its own particular spirit. Our dear Society then has its own particular spirit. It should be the "soul" or life-principle animating our dear Society. Our spirit is our True Devotion. We look to our Blessed Mother, not only as our patroness, but as our foundress. All our devotion, after God, is centered in her. We are ushered into membership in our dear Society by our solemn consecration to Jesus through Mary as a slave of their love forever. Properly considered, this slavery of love to our Blessed Mother is a slavery of love to our Divine Lord himself. It is our boast that our Divine Lord is our God, our Sovereign, our Master, that he has absolute dominion over us, and that we depend essentially and necessarily upon him.
>
> With the help of the almighty power of divine grace and the all-powerful help of Jesus and Mary, let us renew and persevere in this true spirit so that we and those who come after us will preserve our dear Society in its true spirit to the end.

Father Sigstein saw this spirit of dependence as the very essence of religious life. Following the teaching of St. Louis, he understood religious consecration as a deepening of one's baptismal commitment. The Fathers of the Second Vatican Council expressed it thus: "They [religious] have dedicated their entire lives to God's service. This constitutes a special consecration which is deeply rooted in that of baptism and expresses it more fully." (P.C. 5)

This legacy of devotion to Mary given to the Victory Noll Sisters by their Founder is spelled out in today's language in the dogmatic Constitution on the Church which describes Mary's role in the economy of salvation and the faithful's duties toward her. (L.G. 54) She is "full of grace" because she alone, of all the people of God, perfectly lived out God's plan for her. Article 68 speaks of her thus: "The Mother of Jesus shines forth on earth until the day of the Lord shall come, a sign of sure hope and solace to the wandering people of God." (L.G. 68)

Mary is the perfect Christian, an archetype of the Church. (L.G. 53 and 63) She is the fulfillment of the New Jerusalem. The Constitution on the Sacred

Liturgy expresses it in this way: "In celebrating this annual cycle of Christ's mysteries, holy Church honors with especial love the Blessed Mary, Mother of God, who is joined by an inseparable bond to the saving work of her Son. In her the Church holds up and admires the most excellent fruit of the redemption, and joyfully contemplates, as in a faultless image, that which she herself desires and hopes wholly to be." (S.C. 103)

A devotion which was such a source of grace in his own spiritual life, John Sigstein could not but bequeath to his spiritual daughters. It was his wish that authentic devotion to Mary should characterize the life of each member of the community. For Father Sigstein Mary was the way to Jesus and hence to the Father. His writings show that he clearly understood that "the maternal duty of Mary toward all people in no way impedes but rather fosters the immediate union of the faithful with Christ." (L.G. 60)

The motto of the community, "All for Jesus through Mary," sums up the devotion that was central in the spiritual life John Sigstein encouraged in his Catechists. They were to live in habitual dependence on Mary in order to reach a more intimate union with Jesus and through him with the Blessed Trinity dwelling within them. The doctrine of the Divine Indwelling was the subject of numerous conferences Father Sigstein gave the Catechists. He loved to quote from John's Gospel: "Anyone who loves me will be true to my word, and my Father will love him; we will come to him and make our dwelling place with him." (John 14, 23)

The core of devotion to Mary as taught by St. Louis consists in the making of an act of consecration which is a renewal of one's baptismal dedication to Christ and with him to the Father. It is made through Mary because she is the model of this covenantal baptismal commitment by reason of her preeminence as the perfect Christian, the woman of faith. Her faith-life is the norm of every Christian's faith-life, a life of complete openness, obedience, and active receptivity to the Word and to the Spirit of God. Mary's attitude of faith is reflected in her life of complete dependence on God as the source of all that she has and all that she is.

This life of dependence that the Catechists were to lead, John Sigstein wished to see reflected in them as a spirit of naturalness, joy, and simplicity. They were "to be themselves." Over and over he emphasized these characteristics. In his rules for superiors, he wrote: "Let each subject manifest at all times a simple, humble, natural, joyful disposition and spirit — one that indicates true peace and freedom of soul, evenness of mind, an entire absence of formalism, constraint, narrowness, or a cramped, unnatural, or institutional spirit." This spirit of naturalness, friendliness, of hospitality, and of informality was very important to Father Sigstein and nothing made him happier than to have visitors observe it and comment on it, as they often did.

The Jesuit, Daniel A. Lord, after a visit to Victory Noll in 1937, described the Catechists as a "happy and friendly crowd." In his syndicated column, "Along the Way," he wrote:

It's sometimes astonishing to feel, in the midst of an admittedly selfish world, the throb of that love and devotion which sends young men and women into religious and priestly life. . . . I felt that throb as I walked through the lovely, bright corridors of Victory Noll in Indiana where young women are training to be Missionary Catechists. They are a happy and friendly crowd. They look a little like Red Cross nurses, these Catechists, except that their professed habit is dark blue. . . . In about fifteen years their little group has grown from zero to close to two hundred members. And they all face a difficult life, working among children who cannot find nor afford a Catholic school, in districts where poverty is the rule and want, the ordinary mode of living. . . .[3]

Simplicity of life, a spirit of poverty, and love for God's poor — these John Sigstein linked together as the ideal for his Society. On July 29, 1923, he wrote Monsignor Noll:

I gave Mr. Steinbach [architect for Victory Noll] very explicit instructions regarding the character of the building. It is to be severely plain. Fortunately, the missionstyle of building lends itself to plainness and simplicity in every detail and construction. I informed the architect that our Catechists made profession of a life of poverty and detachment. The training we give them and shall ever give them tends to instill the spirit of poverty and a love for God's poor. In our preparatory training institute at Huntington it shall be our highest aim to cultivate this spirit so that the subjects may go forth from this institution which your generosity has made possible, like other Christs — loving and serving their charges.

Bishop Noll thought the training school need not be so large. September 15, 1923, he wrote Father Sigstein: "I really believe that we are building too big. ... We have not received a single application since I gave the darker side of the Catechists' sacrifice and work in our issue of September 9."

It is no secret that the Bishop and Father Sigstein did not always see eye to eye on everything. The Bishop thought too much money was being spent on the grounds of Victory Noll. Father Sigstein was convinced that beautiful surroundings were conducive to the Catechists' physical and spiritual well-being. He had them spend at least an hour a day working in the vegetable and flower gardens. It seemed that when there were not so many Catechists at Victory Noll, there was a common "garden hour" (everyone working outside at the same time), but it was frequently being changed. Now it was in the morning, again in the afternoon, and sometimes in the evening!

Father Sigstein and the Catechists were fortunate to have professional assistance from Adolph Jaenicke, superintendent of parks in Fort Wayne, Indiana. Mr. Jaenicke was only too glad to help and made no charge for his services. He came to Victory Noll almost every Saturday and pointed out what was to be done. He advised Father where he could buy evergreens, shrubs, and fruit trees at the lowest possible prices.

Adolph Jaenicke, a native of Germany, studied landscape architecture at the University of Berlin. After working for a time in his own country, he went to England for a few years and then came to the United States, settling in the West. Jaenicke was a seed expert and had prospects of a good position with the Burpee Seed Company. He was on his way to Philadelphia for an interview when, because of engine trouble, his train was delayed for two hours in Fort Wayne. He went to a hotel for dinner and there met Colonel David N. Foster, head of the Fort Wayne Park Board. The Colonel offered Jaenicke the position of superintendent of parks. He accepted immediately. The train went off without him, and Mr. and Mrs. Jaenicke and their family settled in the Summit City. Jaenicke Gardens in Fort Wayne are named in his memory. He is remembered at Victory Noll for his kindliness and his "Old World" courtesy. The Catechists who did the baking might remember best that they had to have a loaf or two of fresh bread on hand every Saturday afternoon to send home with their benefactor.

Though Adolph Jaenicke was responsible for the landscaping at Victory Noll, it was to the Society of the Divine Word at Techny, Illinois, that Father Sigstein had turned for help with his plan to erect outdoor stations of the cross in the ravine that he saw as a natural setting for them. Perhaps it was through his friend, Bruno Hagspiel, S.V.D., that he obtained the services of two Divine Word Brothers who were stonecutters. The stations begin at the foot of the hill near the highway and end with the grotto at the top of the hill, depicting the tomb of Jesus. A statue of the Risen Christ is set up high on the outside of the grotto, providing a kind of fifteenth station. Though the stations were completed in 1926, for one reason or another they were not formally erected until June 21, 1935, when the rite was performed by Alphonse Heckler, O.F.M. Cap., Guardian at St. Felix Friary at the time.

Victory Noll was always a busy place in late summer and fall when fruits and vegetables were preserved for the winter. The bountiful harvest was not the result of hard work only, but also, and especially of prayer. Whenever Father Sigstein was home, he had the procession on the rogation days preceding the feast of the Ascension. No time of year is so lovely at Victory Noll as May, and no time of day is so enchanting as early morning when the birds are singing and the grass and flowers are sparkling with fresh dew. This tradition of a procession to bless the grounds and pray for the fruits of the earth is still observed by the Sisters.

Processions have had a long history in the Church and though they were neglected for a time, they are again being recognized as hallowing space for worship. Their power in worship has been rediscovered. Processions have always been popular with the Missionary Sisters. Besides the usual processions prescribed by the Church for the feast of the Presentation of Jesus in the Temple, Palm Sunday, and other days, there is a special devotion, including a procession at Victory Noll, on the twenty-fifth of every month to commemorate the Incarnation of Our Lord. Father Sigstein introduced this "Twenty-fifth

Devotion" shortly after Victory Noll was erected. The intention was for an increase of vocations to the Society. In earlier times when the weather was favorable, the Sisters walked through the grounds, four novices carrying a statue of Our Lady of Victory on a litter. Today, when such a long walk would be difficult for some of the Sisters, though they want to take part in the devotion, the procession is confined to the chapel. Besides the special prayers for vocations, the Litany of Loretto is chanted and the rosary prayed.

Father Sigstein often reminded Julia and the other pioneer Sisters that even though, because of their work, they were not required to say so many prayers as other religious, they must be very careful to pray slowly, attentively, and devoutly. In keeping with his insistence on simplicity, Father Sigstein did not want the Catechists to pray in Latin. Rather than the Little Office of the Blessed Virgin which many communities prayed daily in Latin, the Catechists said the short Sodality Office of the Immaculate Conception. When they received their approval and new Constitutions in 1956, they began the recitation of the Short Breviary. This gave place later to the current breviary which the Sisters use for Morning and Evening Praise in common.

Besides devotion to the Blessed Sacrament, Our Blessed Mother, and St. Joseph, John Sigstein encouraged the veneration of saints who had a special love for Mary and of those who were catechists, missionaries, and lovers of the poor. On the windows of Our Lady of Victory chapel and in mosaic-like pictures high on the chapel walls are depicted Francis of Assisi, Vincent de Paul, Patrick, Boniface, Francis Xavier, Paul, Therese of Lisieux, Clare, Louis de Montfort, Bernard, Alphonsus Liguori, Cyril of Jerusalem, Augustine, and others.

Though morning and evening prayers, particular examen, rosary, and stations of the cross were prescribed for the Catechists, the celebration of the Eucharist had priority. John Sigstein had a pleasant singing voice, although his musical training was only what he received in the seminary. He liked to have sung Masses because it meant more participation. On October 7, 1929, the *Missa Recitata* or Dialog Mass was begun at Victory Noll.[4] Father Sigstein was encouraged in this by a visit from Michael Sheehan, a priest from Los Angeles. Father Sheehan spoke to the Catechists on the liturgy and the spiritually rewarding experience of greater participation in the Mass. From that time a Catechist read the epistle and gospel in English while the priest at the altar read them in Latin. They answered the prayers of the priest as acolytes were wont to do at that time.

Visitors, priests especially, liked it even though they seemed surprised when they were told that the Catechists would answer the Mass prayers together. As late as 1956 a priest visitor, editor of a Catholic paper, wrote:

> I had a wonderful experience this past week. I was celebrant of the Community Mass of the Sisters of Our Lady of Victory the day of Archbishop Noll's sister's funeral. It was a Dialogue Mass and if a priest ever needs any

assurance that he and his congregation are one, this will do it for him. A little surprise came along when the Sisters went to communion. No seniority was observed, with a postulant kneeling alongside a silver jubilarian and a novice alongside a finally professed. Final pleasantness of the morning was the singing of the Gregorian *Salve Regina* by the congregation.[5]

John Sigstein frowned on practices that were encouraged in some religious communities of his time. He would permit no public penances for external faults. There was to be no "chapter of faults." He discouraged prolonged fasting, lengthy periods of prayer, etc. He disliked even certain terms like refectory, habit, etc., preferring dining room, uniform. Because of this and other departures from accepted religious practices, it has been proposed that Father Sigstein would have had his Catechists be members of a secular institute rather than a religious community if secular institutes had been in existence in the twenties. The Sisters who knew their Founder best know that this is not true. For one thing, he put much value on *community*. This was all-important for him. He termed it, in the language of his day, religious union. He never stopped talking about "fraternal charity and religious union." "The religious life," he said in more than one conference, "is essentially a family life and the basis or foundation of this family life is fraternal charity and religious union. Without fraternal charity and religious union there can be no true family spirit in a religious community."

When Father Sigstein wrote to a priest whom he had engaged to give a retreat to the Catechists, he always asked him to stress "fraternal charity and religious union." "You know, of course," he wrote to Joseph Fagen, C.SS.R., on March 17, 1936, "how necessary it is for our Catechists to practice the virtue of fraternal charity and religious union with all possible religious perfection. Their work is a true work of charity and therefore to be charitable toward the poor under their care they must foremost show charity toward one another. May I suggest that you read to the Catechists our rules on this point, since they are very strong and explicit."

Did John Sigstein intend from the beginning to found a religious congregation? Some think he had no such intention. Even some of the first Sisters did not think they were entering a religious community like their friends who had become Franciscans, Dominicans, Sisters of Mercy, etc. Certainly the Catechists' life was different from these, but evidence shows that Father Sigstein indeed had a religious community in mind when he began his Society. In 1917 when letters were going back and forth between John Sigstein and Anthony Blaufuss, they used the term "new Sisterhood." During this time, too, John was writing to various congregations and asking for a copy of their constitutions. Only after he was released from the Archdiocese of Chicago and the Society was established, could he feel free to be more explicit in describing its purpose. In a letter to Julia written June 18, 1923, he expressed it thus: "We can soon emerge from the catacombs and assume the character of the work of a religious society done in a public manner."

Because of this ambiguity, some pastors were reluctant to have young women go to Victory Noll. Another objection on the part of a few parents and others, was that the Society was too young. It would be better to go to an older, well-established order. This new institute might not survive.

Four centuries earlier St. Francis Borgia had been faced with this same objection from the Emperor Charles V when Francis wanted to enter the newly formed Society of Jesus. The saint replied, "Gracious Majesty, there is no religious order, however ancient or approved, which was not once new and unknown."

When the Emperor asked, "But what answer would you make to those who object against your Company, that all its members are young and that there is not a gray head to be seen among them?" Borgia answered, "Sire, when the mother is young, how could your Majesty expect to find the children old? If this be a crime, it is one of which time will soon cure us. In twenty years from now, those who are young among us will have many a gray hair."[6]

As late as 1936, when the Society of Missionary Catechists had been established for fourteen years, Father Sigstein found it necessary to send an article to the Catholic press emphasizing that the Catechists were real religious. Many papers carried the story. *The New World,* as the Chicago archdiocesan paper was then called, headlined: "Catechists Are Truly Nuns Though Not Called 'Sister.'"

Though the Society might not have appeared to be a religious community in the beginning, it was inevitable that it should evolve as it did. Thomas E. Clarke, S.J., in *New Pentecost or New Passion?* calls attention to this fact: "The religious community," he says, "however charismatic its origin, must eventually institutionalize itself if it is to be rugged enough to withstand the erosions of time and cultural change. It needs its own formal structures and processes. And if it is to serve in the real, everyday Church, it must learn to reckon with (which is not the same as to capitulate to) the power structure and the sedentary element in official Church life."[7]

In the renewal called for by Vatican Council II, religious were asked to return to the source of all Christian life, the Gospel, and to the spirit of their founder. They were asked, moreover, to adapt to the changed conditions of their times. (P.C. 2) "The spirit of the founder is closely related to the purpose of the institute," writes Joseph Gallen, S.J., in a perceptive article in *Review for Religious* regarding the distinctive spirit of a congregation. He says:

> This spirit has not been too often analyzed accurately and completely by the founder's followers. It is not always easy to verbalize because the spirit consists to some degree at least of the intangibles of a person's life, of the impression he gave, the atmosphere he created in his approach to God, to men and women, and to things. It is more the way he acted than what he did; the things, the ways, the principles, truths, and works he emphasized in his

own spiritual, community, and apostolic life, his constitutions, writings, and conversations. It is therefore not necessarily the emphasis of a virtue such as poverty or obedience. Nor even in such an emphasis are we ever to forget, as we did at times in the past, that the moral virtues of obedience and those implied in poverty are a means to the theological virtues of faith, hope, and charity; that the latter are supreme and their summit attained in charity, the love of God and man that is not self-seeking.[8]

To organize a work to meet a pressing need; this was a special charism of John Joseph Sigstein. Throughout his long life he listened to the "signs of the times." And yet some of the works he began, the ideas he had, impelled as he was by his passionate love for the poor, were taken over by another person or agency or were given a different direction. Only his beloved Society, as he called the Congregation, came to fruition.

It might be inferred that Father Sigstein was an activist, but nothing could be further from the truth. He was first of all, a contemplative. Some, not understanding, called him a dreamer. He never took action until he had prayed long and fervently to the Holy Spirit and to our Blessed Mother. In Mary's hands he placed all his projects.

Many persons, both in the Congregation and outside it, found it difficult to understand Father Sigstein's penchant for going out in every direction, for attempting many different projects, most of which were thwarted. One Sister who knew him well confided that she sees all these things now as extravagant, often unreasonable manifestations of love trying to find new ways to express itself. "I saw Father Sigstein," she said, "as one frustrated by his very limited gifts and capabilities which doomed from the beginning his great dreams, desires, and ambitions. With his boundless love for Jesus and Mary, and with a nature sensitive to the sufferings of people, he would recklessly launch out into one new project after another, unable to restrain the desire of his own love and compassion. True love does not rest until all humankind is brought into the Kingdom of God."[9]

This love for the poor, this zeal for the spread of the Kingdom, Father Sigstein wished the Catechists to share with him. He gloried in telling them that the work they were called to do was the same mission that the Father had entrusted to Jesus, his Son. On the eve of each monthly retreat day, he had them say St. Alphonsus' prayer for zeal, part of which reads: ". . . How can I thank Thee enough for having called me to the same work that Thou didst Thyself on earth, that is, to labor for the salvation of souls? How have I deserved this honor, this reward . . .?" But such a great privilege entailed suffering. The Catechists not only worked among the poor, they also lived poorly. Moreover, they were deprived in a spiritual, as well as in a material way. In the early years in New Mexico they had Mass only once or twice a month.

Even when the Catechists lived in a mission where there was a "resident" priest, it did not mean daily or even weekly Mass. The Catechists wrote from

Chaperito, New Mexico, in the fall of 1927, rejoicing that they had had the Blessed Sacrament reserved in their home for five days the past month. During Advent and Lent the pastor was away the whole time, visiting his outmissions and stations in order to give his people the opportunity to assist at Mass and celebrate the other sacraments.

In a letter dated February 28, 1929, from Holman, New Mexico, where the missionary came for Mass only once a month, the Catechists tell of their disappointment the Sunday before when the priest on his arrival discovered that the wine had spilled on the trip. There could be no Mass. Even as late as 1938 conditions in Holman were very primitive. There was no electricity, no running water, no inside bathrooms. The Catechists had to carry water from a well the equivalent of almost a city block from their home.

During the first years in New Mexico opportunities to receive the sacrament of penance were few and far between. When a priest was available, it often happened that a confessional was non-existent. One missionary priest raised an umbrella between himself and the penitent. At least he was keeping to the letter of the law which then prescribed that confessions of women were not to be heard in the open! Some Catechists found the spiritual conditions more difficult than the material deprivations.

Even at Victory Noll during the first year or two there were many days when the community had what they called "spiritual Mass." They said the Mass prayers together and made a spiritual Communion, expressing the desire to receive sacramentally. Father Sigstein was away frequently. He was often ill and unable to celebrate. Bishop Noll came for Mass when he could. At other times either Father Kelly or his assistant, Father Dillon, came out to Victory Noll from St. Mary's parish in Huntington.

All this was changed in 1928. This was the year the Capuchin Franciscan Fathers and Brothers of St. Joseph Province broke ground for St. Felix Friary in Huntington. It is almost impossible to write adequately of the tremendous influence for good the Capuchins have been for the Victory Noll Sisters. Through the years they have given generously of their time and talents to Victory Noll as confessors, instructors, retreat masters, chaplains, and friends. It would be difficult to imagine Victory Noll without their spiritual ministrations. It was a happy day for the Huntington area and especially for the Missionary Sisters when the Capuchins accepted Bishop Noll's offer of land for the erection of the friary.

The story of how the Capuchins came to Huntington is told in *A Romance of Lady Poverty* by Celestine N. Bittle, O.F.M. Cap.[10] It is a history of the Province of St. Joseph in the United States. In 1926 the Provincial, Benno Aichinger, and his councilors decided to move their novitiate from Detroit to another location, preferably a place that would be more conducive to recollection. Father Benno wrote to Frank J. Jansen, a priest of the Fort Wayne Diocese whom he had known as a student at St. Lawrence College, the friars' preparatory seminary at Mt. Calvary, Wisconsin, to ask him whether he knew of a suitable location in northern Indiana. He intended only to "sound him out," meaning to write a more formal letter to Bishop Noll. Father Jansen, in his enthusiasm, immediately got in touch with the Bishop. Bishop Noll had made his studies at Mt. Calvary also and thought highly of the Capuchins. He wrote Father Jansen: ". . . You may assure Father Benno that my lifelong affection for the Capuchin Fathers disposes me very favorably toward his request, and I shall try to figure out where the best place would be to locate them. . . ."

A Michigan City priest offered the Capuchins a tract of land in that area. Bishop Noll proposed to give them thirty-seven acres of *Our Sunday Visitor* farm property a mile from Victory Noll. In November 1926 Benno Aichinger, Benedict Mueller, and Pacificus Raith, accompanied by Frank Jansen, visited Bishop Noll in Fort Wayne. The Bishop then drove them to Huntington. The Victory Noll chronicles for November 7, 1926, notes that the group visited the motherhouse that day.

When the Capuchin Provincial Chapter convened the following July, the delegates recommended that the offer of the Huntington property be accepted. In the elections that took place at this time, Benedict Mueller succeeded Benno Aichinger as Provincial, and Salesius Schneweis was one of the newly elected definitors or councilors. On April 16, 1928, Father Salesius arrived in Huntington to supervise the building of the friary. He took up residence at Victory Noll. On May 11 he began a long tradition when he had his first class in Christian doctrine for the Catechists. The cornerstone of the friary was laid May 18, 1928. According to Father Bittle, it was an informal ceremony. For the Catechists it must have been a red letter day. According to the records, "A number of Capuchins stayed overnight and we had six holy Masses."

Father Salesius endeared himself to all at Victory Noll during his stay of almost a year. On February 19, 1929, he moved to the friary and was soon joined by Father Benno, the newly appointed Guardian. Two weeks later Father Clement Neubauer and his fourteen novices and three candidates came from Detroit in a chartered bus. Father Salesius' account of the open house and the later dedication day is too interesting not to quote here. He wrote:

> Due to the large percentage of non-Catholics among the Huntington community, it had been considered best to open the doors of the monastery on one occasion to all comers. Easter Sunday, March 31, from 1 to 5 p.m., had been set aside for that purpose. This was, however, also done because it was felt that the small chapel could not accommodate even a small percentage of the Catholic affiliation on Dedication Day, April 2, much less the possible non-Catholic visitors. All were, however, encouraged to avail themselves of the opportunity to inspect the interior of the monastery about which they had heard so much.

> Since it happened to be Easter Sunday, we did not expect much of a crowd.

We were confirmed in this view all the more when at 11 a.m., it began to drizzle. Father Guardian, therefore, could not help smiling when some of the local Knights of Columbus offered their services as "traffic cops" for the afternoon. They succeeded at last in having him accept their proffered services, perhaps more out of a spirit of accommodation than of conviction. . . .

It had been planned that each Father should head a group of visitors and lead them through the building, explaining things as they moved through the various apartments. But this idea had to be abandoned at once. The eager crowds pressed in at all doors, and within a few minutes every room and corridor was filled....Since guidance of the jamming crowd was found impossible, the Fathers restricted their attendance to the larger apartments such as the main chapel, the refectory, the choir, infirmary, etc., where they could give explanations to a larger number. The people were encouraged to ask questions in regard to things that they did not understand or that seemed strange to them. Quite a few availed themselves of the invitation...[They asked] how we could obtain our livelihood, whether we also accepted non-Catholics into the Order, how much tuition we charged, whether our splendid infirmary was also open to outsiders. One asked why we had so many shields in the Latin tongue above the doors of the various rooms. When he was told that we understand the Latin very well, he objected, "But we don't." The answer that the shields were there, not for them but for our benefit, did not seem to satisfy him entirely. . . .

One of the Fathers, noticing a gentleman with a somewhat forlorn expression on his face, had pity on him and offered to show him through the building, but was told to his surprise, "Why, I put up this building!" He was the senior partner of the contracting firm.

The ladies were interested mainly in the kitchen, which had been "cracked up" to the skies by some of the workingmen. One lady asked at every room, "Is this the kitchen? I am only interested in the kitchen." It is impossible even to summarize the remarks made in reference to the kitchen and its equipment....All kinds of questions were put to the Brother Cook. They wanted to have his personal assurance that a man, i.e., he himself, really did the cooking. Others pitied him because he had to cook for so many. One gentlemen was determined to get a loaf of bread and asked continuously to whom he would have to apply. We know that he did not buy any, but that does not imply that he did not get a loaf.

. . . It will be a very conservative estimate to place the number of visitors at 10,000. Many others were discouraged from attempting the approach when they met the congestion of cars stretching away from the monastery for more than half a mile in every direction. What would the crowd have been, if it had been fair weather!

There was a heavy downpour in the course of the afternoon, but it did not deter the crowds. Some of the cars near the monastery had been parked on refilled ground. The wrecking car had to be called, and it pulled out forty-eight cars. The owner of the outfit did the service free of charge.

The dedication day, a week later, must have been, in a sense an anti-climax. Besides Bishop Noll who presided, and Bishop Rohlman of Davenport who was present, there were eighty priests, thirty Catechists (everyone at Victory Noll), and only thirty or so lay people. Through a misunderstanding, the local people thought the dedication ceremony was for clergy only.

One of the highlights of the day was the presentation of a Resolution of Appreciation from the Huntington Chamber of Commerce. A lengthy, beautifully worded document, it extolled the Capuchin Franciscan Order, expressed the gratitude of the City of Huntington at the founding of the monastery, and welcomed the friars, asking that "the Divine Benediction may rest upon the Order and upon the Provincial Superior, the Very Reverend Benedict Mueller, O.M. Cap., Father Salesius, O.M. Cap., Provincial Secretary, and the Very Reverend Benno Aichinger, O.M. Cap., Superior of the Monastery, and upon all those who labor so worthily with them."

The blessings on the Huntington community that the Chamber of Commerce anticipated with the coming of the Capuchins, have indeed been abundant. In the half-century that followed their foundation, the "brown-robed, bearded friars," as they were usually referred to, became well known and loved throughout northeastern Indiana. They established a number of Third Order fraternities and made themselves available to parish priests for help on weekends. In 1954 Archbishop Noll presided at the silver jubilee of the founding of the friary. At that time St. Felix was the clericate of the Province; in 1952 the novitiate had been transferred again to Michigan. This was necessary because of the increase of personnel. St. Joseph Province, having become too large, was divided, and the Province of St. Mary created, with headquarters in the East. Clement Neubauer, who had been master of novices for a number of years, served as Provincial in 1942, and subsequently as Minister General of the whole Capuchin Order.

Though St. Felix became again a novitiate after other provisions were made for the education of the young students, it became evident at the end of the friary's second twenty-five years that it was no longer needed. Fewer men were entering the Order and such a building as the friary was too large. Besides, and most important, the building was constantly in need of repairs that would be too expensive to continue. After much deliberation on the part of the provincial administrators and in consultation with all the friars, it was decided to sell the friary or dismantle it and sell the land. However, after having been such a part of the area for so many years, the friars did not want to leave it altogether. Nor did the diocese want them to leave. More importantly for the Victory Noll Sisters, the Capuchins wished to continue their ministry to the Congregation and to the people of the Huntington area. They proposed forming an evangelization team that would involve, at least in the beginning, two of their priests and two Victory Noll Sisters. They would continue acting as chaplains at Victory Noll.

Such an arrangement would have pleased Father Sigstein, for he was greatly devoted to the Capuchins. Father Clement had served as his spiritual director when he was stationed in Huntington, and Father had kept in touch with him throughout his life. One of the last letters he received before his death March 13, 1963, was from Father Clement. It was written from the Capuchin Generalate in Rome and dated ten days before Father died. Father Clement wrote:

Dear Father Sigstein

Sincere thanks for your very kind letter of January 24. It awakened happy memories of the "early" days at Victory Noll. We Capuchins also recall your kindness and that of the Sister Catechists in our pioneer days at St. Felix. It is a great consolation to know that the cordial relation between our institutions has remained unbroken throughout the years. I pray that it may ever continue so.

It gives me a thrill of satisfaction to know that you, Reverend Father, can serenely watch your Society grow "in wisdom and age and grace before God and man." I know that the bishops in whose dioceses you carry out your apostolate, are more than pleased. May Our Lady of Victory continue to guide and direct your wonderful foundation.

With regards to the Sisters I may know, and with very best wishes to yourself, I am

Gratefully yours,
fr. Clement, o.f.m. cap.

Notes to Chapter XVIII

1. Jean Gautier, *Some Schools of Catholic Spirituality* (Desclee, Paris, 1919) p. 336.

2. St. Louis Mary DeMontfort, *True Devotion to the Blessed Virgin Mary,* tr. Frederick William Faber, revised edition, (Montfort Fathers' Publications, Bay Shore, N.Y., 1950).

3. *The New World,* Chicago, May 30, 1937.

4. See Note 3, Chapter XVII for explanation of Dialog Mass or *Missa Recitata.*

5. James Quinn, Lafayette Edition of *Our Sunday Visitor,* June 24, 1956. Used with permission.

6. See Margaret Yeo, *The Greatest of the Borgias,* (The Bruce Publishing Co., Milwaukee, 1936) p. 253 adapted.

7. Thomas E. Clarke, S.J., *New Pentecost or New Passion?* (Paulist Press, 1973) p. 80. Used with permission.

8. Joseph F. Gallen, S.J., "Revision of the Constitutions," *Review for Religious,* 1974, Vol. 33, p. 380. Used with permission.

9. Sister Regina Torzewski, O.L.V.M.

10. Celestine N. Bittle, O.M.Cap., *A Romance of Lady Poverty,* (The Bruce Publishing Co., Milwaukee, 1933). The information given here is taken from Chapter IV of Part II: "New Clericate and Novitiate," pp.472 ff. The direct quotations are used with permission. It is interesting that the copy in the Victory Noll Library is inscribed: "Jan. 16, 1934. To Dorothy Radler: In appreciation of your generous help in typing the manuscript of this book, and with the compliments of the Author, C.N. Bittle, O.M.Cap." Three years later Dorothy Radler of St. Boniface parish, Milwaukee, and a personal friend of the late Father Celestine, entered Victory Noll. She is known now as Sister John Francis.

19

Today

A WHOLE NEW WORLD IS COMING into existence. God grant that we are a part of it."

It was in the early fifties that Pope Pius XII made this prediction and offered this prayer. A few years later this new world was here. It came so fast that it almost seemed to have appeared over night. Economical, sociological, technological, cultural, and theological changes affected world and Church. These changes had a profound effect on religious life, especially in the United States.

Significantly, it was Pius XII himself who was, in many ways, responsible for the changes in the Church. We sometimes remember only John XXIII as the Pope who brought about renewal principally through the Second Vatican Council. We forget that if Pius XII had not paved the way, the renewal would not have been successful. Three of his encyclicals were especially effective in "opening the windows," to use the expression of Pope John. In June 1943 Pius issued *Mystici Corporis,* the encyclical on the doctrine of the Mystical Body, a doctrine as old as the Church but which had been neglected for centuries. That same year in September, the Pope gave the green light to Scripture scholars, as it were, when he wrote *Divino Afflante Spiritu.* Four years later he gave the Church his encyclical on the liturgy, *Mediator Dei,* which, some scholars maintain, if it had been heeded, would have spared some of the confusion that followed the modern liturgical renewal.

It was Pius XII also who urged religious women to be more professional in their apostolic work. A result of this in the United States was the Sister Formation Movement of the late fifties. For the most part, religious communities had been too much isolated from one another. Now they were beginning to come together for common goals. In 1956 major superiors of women religious began to meet annually. The association, originally known as the Conference of Major Superiors of Women, is now called the Leadership Conference of Women Religious.

It is not our intention here to point out in detail the conditions that brought about the changes in the Church and especially in religious life. Nowhere are they so well enumerated as in the Constitution on the Church in the Modern World, *Gaudium et Spes.* If we were to mention one trend or current of thought that has been especially significant in shaping religious life today, it is personalism or, to put it another way, recognition of the uniqueness of the human person. The spirit of personalism permeates the pastoral Constitution on the Church. The first chapter affirms that "all things on earth should be related to man as their center and crown." (G.S. 12) Man and woman are unique, made in the image and likeness of their Creator.

Emphasis on the uniqueness of the human person has enhanced the dignity of *woman,* and this has been highly significant in relation to women religious. For too long a time Sisters had been treated as minors. Uniformity had been imposed on their institutes despite the differences in their charisms. They were expected to conform to laws that deprived them of initiative and their own self-determination.

The first winds of change began to blow by the mid-twentieth century. In Rome during the Holy Year of 1950, Pius XII convoked the First International Congress of Religious. In his Allocution he spoke of "the efforts of religious institutes to adapt themselves to our changed times, and to join the new and the old in harmonious union."[1] When Vatican Council II summoned the Church to renewal, it was the religious communities of women who responded immediately and enthusiastically to the call.

In the sixth chapter of the dogmatic Constitution on the Church, *Lumen Gentium,* the Council asserted that the rightful place of religious life is within the Church. It belongs to the very life and holiness of the Church. ". . . this sacred council gives its support and praise to men and women, brothers and sisters, who in monasteries or in schools and hospitals or in missions adorn the Bride of Christ by the steadfast and generous service of the most varied kinds to all manner of men." (L.G. 46)

It was the Decree on the Appropriate Renewal of Religious Life, *Perfectae Caritatis,* that gave direction to change in religious communities. The Decree gave congregations general principles for renewal and adaptation while leaving each one's special character intact. This differed radically from the traditional manner of imposing precise and uniform laws on every institute. *Perfectae Caritatis* mandated change from within the communities themselves, a welcome departure from earlier tradition. Religious were directed to review everything in the light of the Gospel, the source of all Christian life. They were to return to the original spirit of their founder and be guided by the changed conditions of Church and world. Everything was to be subject to scrutiny: constitutions, directories, customs, prayers, ceremonies — anything that concerned the manner of life, of work, of prayer. What was obsolete, irrelevant in the modern world, was to be suppressed.

Like all the documents of the Council, *Perfectae Caritatis* set forth principles; norms for implementation were given later. On August 6, 1966, Pope Paul VI issued a *Motu proprio, Ecclesiae sanctae,* to implement decrees concerning bishops, priests, and religious. The section dealing with religious communities called for each institute to convoke a special General Chapter. The purpose would be to set in motion the renewal and adaptation called for by conciliar documents.

How did Our Lady of Victory Missionary Sisters respond to the call for renewal? Like other religious institutes the Victory Noll community had developed a structured, canonical form of living. To others this might not have seemed so, for the Sisters were looked upon by some as "freewheelers." It was not unusual to hear a priest or bishop say of them, "They are like other Sisters but not so strict." In a way this was true. They drove cars, went into the homes of lay people, wore a very simple habit, lived in small groups. But these things were necessary because of the type of apostolate that was theirs. Yet they were subject to the same restrictions that had been imposed on other religious institutes of women.

"Community" had unfortunately come to mean, in religious life, doing everything together, being together at the same time, in the same place. It was forgotten that members differed in personality, background, temperament, desires, ideals. Each person is unique but all come together to share common values and grow together in love. The common interest around which religious are united is a *Person,* the Person of Jesus Christ. Faith in Christ is the basis for their coming together. United to Christ, they are united to one another.

The basic idea of community is mutual exchange, a group bound together for common service — sharing, loving, giving. This real meaning of community makes it easier to see the difference between the old idea understood simply as doing things in common: eating together, praying together, studying together, doing everything *together;* and the true concept: being of one heart and one soul, even though not always doing the same things at the same time in the same way.

This true concept of community is summed up in a passage taken from the Acts of Documents of the General Congress of the States of Perfection held in Rome under Pope John in 1960. The Pope said:

Common life consists not so much in always doing everything together; for example, prayer, work, study, walks, etc., as in mutual love that is sincere, profound, supernatural; and in a deeply genuine attachment to the spiritual-apostolic family of which one is a part . . . There is no need of confining oneself to a material concept of the common life, but one should look more to creating a communion of persons who live the same ideal, sharing with one another their individual experiences; who pray, work, study, suffer, and rejoice together and discuss together the better means for apostolic success.

The first timid changes at Victory Noll came about in recognition of this proper concept of community. In the late fifties the Sunday schedule was relaxed so that the Sisters were free to perform some of their community exercises privately. The regular General Chapter of 1962, however, was the turning point for change. It was held in August before the opening of Vatican II. Sister Florentine Lohr, former novice mistress, was elected Superior General. Her four Councilors were new, none having been in office before. Even before the Chapter took place there had been some consultation with the members of the Congregation concerning the election of delegates. At the Chapter minor changes were approved regarding clothing. Small as they were, they seemed momentous at the time, for such changes had to be sanctioned by the Holy See before they could be put into effect.

The Chapter was typical of those held at that time in the Church. The most important business was that of elections. Other matters were taken care of in a rather perfunctory way. The meetings lasted only a few days and were closed to everyone except the delegates. Secrecy was the order of the time.

The newly elected Superior General and her Councilors saw a need for better communication in the Congregation which, though small, was scattered throughout the United States. The first issue of *Views and News,* a congregational newsletter begun in the fall of 1962, explained that its purpose was not only to disseminate pertinent community information, but also to offer a forum for an exchange of ideas. The publication continued for five years. By 1967 it had been replaced by other types of communication. Two years before, Sister Florentine had initiated a personal monthly letter that also was informative and designed to help raise awareness of what was happening in the Church, especially as it affected religious women. Material from the Victory Noll Archives was assembled during this time and sent out to each convent so that the Sisters might be more conscious of their heritage and traditions.

By the end of 1965 the Second Vatican Council had closed, and Sister Florentine urged the Sisters to reflect on its message, singling out for special study the dogmatic Constitution on the Church, *Lumen Gentium.* Beginning in January 1966 the Congregation sponsored workshops conducted by the Sisters themselves. These became known as Contemporary Theology Institutes and were held in six different locations: Tucson, Arizona; San Antonio, Texas; Redlands and Monterey in California; Salt Lake City, Utah; and Denver, Colorado. Most of the discussions centered around Church renewal based on *Lumen Gentium.* Toward the end of the year the CTIs, as they came to be known, were held at Victory Noll; New Brunswick, New Jersey; and six different places in the West. The Superior General and one of her Councilors attended each workshop. The subject this time was Christian morals.

During these years a number of changes were made in disciplinary matters. The Victory Noll Sisters had never taken all their meals in complete silence. At the beginning of breakfast they had a very brief reading from the life of the saint whose feast was being commemorated, and at the end of the meal, a short passage from the *Imitation of Christ*. During Lent and on Fridays throughout the year, they had reading during the noon and evening meals, but never at breakfast. In 1965 reading at meals, including the brief breakfast reading, was discontinued.

Like other women religious, the Victory Noll Sisters were required to have a companion with them when they went out. The Constitutions they had received from Rome in 1956 specified that a Sister be accompanied by a "pious woman" if no other Sister were available. Often the "pious woman" was a little girl from religion class. At least the spirit of the prescription was being kept. In 1965 the rule was abrogated. Another welcome change was the discontinuance of the custom of restricting correspondence to specified times. Also, the Sisters could once again take meals with their guests, something that had been permitted during the first eight years of the Society.

During these years there was some experimentation with dress. Limited at first to certain convents, it was later opened to everyone. As the Sisters grew in a spirit of loving trust and acceptance of one another, they tended to be less affected by exterior differences. From the beginning of the community the Sisters have worn a distinctive medal of Our Lady of Victory. Today this is, more than ever before, the symbol that identifies a Victory Noll Sister.

The subject of religious habits continues to provoke discussion, however, both inside and outside of convents. Bishop Leonard Crowley, Auxiliary Bishop of Montreal, reflects on a symbol of identity in an article in *Review for Religious*. He writes:

> For many communities today the habit stands as a symbol of the past. And the search for a clear, contemporary sign of identification whereby new members might feel a sense of oneness with the community has been a very frustrating one. Yet, in the beginning, it was not the habit that gave identity; it was the spirit and zeal of the Founder, as these drives inspired the community, giving a clear sense of purpose and single-mindedness to all who embraced the Holy Rule. It is that spirit which must be renewed in religious communities today if the symbols of religious life are to have any role to fulfill within the Church.[2]

As "research for renewal" continued in the Victory Noll Congregation, a changed climate was becoming evident; a climate of flexibility, of mutual trust in which Sisters could assume more and more responsibilities for their own lives. So that renewal might be guided in the proper direction, more than meetings were called for. For renewal to be authentic, the guidance of the Holy Spirit was needed. A more intensive prayer life was a necessity. At the beginning of

1966 Sister Florentine asked the community to have a weekly holy hour and/or a day of fast. The intentions were for peace and unity in the Church, for interior renewal, for love and understanding among the Sisters, and for an increase of vocations. At Victory Noll and in many of the missions, though not all, this weekly program has been continued.

The summer of 1968 was decided on for the renewal Chapter called for by Pope Paul VI to implement the decrees of the Vatican Council. Plans for this special Chapter began in 1965. When, in 1967, religious communities of women were invited to take part in a survey sponsored by the Conference of Major Superiors of Women and directed by Sister Maria Augusta Neal, a Sister of Notre Dame de Namur and a well-known sociologist, Our Lady of Victory Missionary Sisters accepted the offer. It required hours of work answering questions that covered sheet after sheet, but the Sisters doggedly attacked the tedious job, knowing it would be helpful in their *aggiornamento*. It was a way to assess their strengths and weaknesses. It was revealed that one of their strengths, their "highs," was in theology, though at the same time, they were below average in graduate degrees. This was at the time that education efforts were being intensified.

In the spring of 1968 "Little Chapters" were held in seven different locations: two at Victory Noll and two in Redlands, California; one each in New Jersey; Denver; Ogden, Utah; Las Cruces, New Mexico; and San Antonio in Texas. The purpose of these meetings was to discuss goals and proposals. It was evident that the intense research, the meetings, and the expense involved in travel were all worthwhile, resulting in deep interest and open sharing. Everyone was ready and enthusiastic when the renewal Chapter opened July 1, 1968.

Though it was a representative Chapter, that is, the total Congregation being represented by forty elected delegates, indirectly all Sisters were involved and could attend as observers if they wished. There was to be no more secrecy. Each Sister was free to follow the discussions. And the elections, too; for Sister Florentine's term of office and that of her Council had ended. The community recognized their Superior General's dedicated leadership and re-elected her for a second term. This time it would not be for six years, however. The delegates voted to change the term for general officers from six to three years, with eligibility for re-election for one more term only. The Chapter of Affairs would be held also every three years.

Since it was apparent that another general meeting would be necessary to evaluate and refine what had been accomplished, the delegates voted to adjourn temporarily and reconvene the following summer. New guidelines were drawn up and some of the articles of the Constitutions amended. Where it was a question of Canon Law, the changes required permission from the Sacred Congregation of Religious. In 1969 the delegates discussed the possibility of making the *next* General Chapter an assembly of the total Congregation. At first it seemed almost preposterous. For one thing, Victory Noll could not provide space for the more than three hundred Sisters who would attend. And yet the more the delegates talked about a "Collegial Assembly," as they began to call it, the more attractive the idea became. It was decided to give everyone an opportunity to vote on whether or not to hold such a gathering in 1971. Its purpose would be not simply to allow all the Sisters to take part in a Chapter and elect officers, but especially to provide for a renewal of community spirit and friendship. When the votes were counted, eighty-one percent were in favor of the Collegial Assembly, seventeen percent opposed to it, and two percent turned in blank ballots. By the time the assembly convened, it had won more adherents. All but fifteen Sisters came to Victory Noll for two weeks in August 1971.

The Sisters who worked on details for the assembly were surprised to learn that Father Sigstein had planned such a gathering for the summer of 1938. His purpose was also to renew community spirit. Besides, he hoped to have Father Lord, Father Heeg, Father Picard and others share their insights with the Catechists. Because of the financial situation, the plan did not materialize. Even with some railroad passes and reduced rates, it was not possible to meet transportation costs. But remembering that there was a precedent for a "Collegial Assembly" made the Sisters happy.

Without the generosity and good will of the people of Huntington, the gathering could not have taken place. Roberta Meitzler (Mrs. Eldon) coordinated "operation hospitality" and found fifty-one homes for the Sisters among Catholics and those not of the Catholic faith. The majority of the Sisters were housed at Victory Noll including a few who lived in a camper and a tent on the edge of the orchard.

The general sessions were held in the Archbishop Noll Memorial Chapel, the only place large enough. Although in retrospect the Sisters realize that they attemped too much legislation in such a short space of time, on the whole they agreed that the assembly accomplished its purpose.

A more objective appraisal of the experience was given by Emma Lou Benignus from Harvard University whose role was that of resource person. She wrote in part:

> To me what seemed so fine about the assembly was that there were so many growth areas and growing edges. It wasn't just a time to get business done. It was a time when people and community came into more fullness of being. I like to think that where love and caring are, a relationship, a community, is built, in which the truth can be let come to light, where truth can be known, faced, responded to, incorporated into the next round of living. That kind of dynamic or movement seemed to happen again, and again, and again. . . . The centrality of the liturgy for the work and life of the assembly becomes increasingly clear to me. As I think back in recall it

is the worship services that remain most vivid of all we did. Whoever the people were who steered us through the sequence of impressive and expressive services certainly deserve our thanks. . . .[3]

The final Eucharist of the assembly, Sunday, August 29, marked the solemn opening of the golden jubilee year of the Congregation. It was to culminate August 5, 1972, fifty years after Julia Doyle and Marie Benes began their apostolate in New Mexico.

Gertrude Sullivan was elected President by the entire Congregation in 1971, succeeding Florentine Lohr who had been in office two terms. Sister Gertrude had been Sister Florentine's first assistant for three years and like her, was a woman of deep faith and of dedicated leadership.

Sister Gertrude and her Councilors aimed to make the best possible use of their Council meetings. Like all religious women they wished to take seriously the responsibility of examining, reflecting, verbalizing, and actualizing the strength and depth of personal convictions. "We meet," Sister Gertrude could report to the Congregation, "in a prayerful reflective way which puts us at ease in the presence of one another and in the presence of the Lord."[4] This reflective process that the Councilors employ has been carried over into all the meetings of the Congregation, and with the same effectiveness.

It had become more and more clear to all the Sisters that a Chapter was not simply an event involving elections and decisions. They saw it as an ongoing process of growth, of renewal in community and in ministry. It was an integrated event in the life of a religious Congregation. In this a Chapter might be likened to Vatican II which gave the Church documents of vision rather than of legislation. In Chapter the Sisters reflect together on basic issues in the light of the Gospel, their charism, and the signs of the times. So that the Tenth General Chapter might be all of this, so that it might be the unifying force it should be, it was decided that the Chapter of Elections would be held apart from the Chapter of Affairs. Sister Gertrude was not eligible for re-election; by 1977 she would have been in office two terms. By holding elections a year before the opening of the Chapter of Affairs, the new President would be in a better position than she would be if she were to begin her term of office at the Chapter.

The entire Congregation took part in the Chapter of Elections, the Sisters coming together in their respective areas. All had been encouraged to engage in a prayerful reflective process prior to and at the time of elections. Because of the preparation that preceded the meetings, the elections were accomplished in two days. By an overwhelming vote, the Congregation chose Jeanette Halbach for their leader. Four Councilors were re-elected, the fifth one being new. Sister Jeanette had served on the Council six years, three of them as Vice President. For two years previous to her taking office as President, she was director of the Justice and Peace Office in the Archdiocese of Denver.

On the feast of Our Lady of the Snow, August 5, 1977, Sister Jeanette and her assistants were solemnly installed in office. The President's first official act was the missioning of all the Victory Noll Sisters present. Describing the ceremony in the semi-annual newsletter to relatives, friends, and benefactors of the community, Sister Regina Torzewski wrote:

The apostolate of our Congregation involves a wide variety of ministries to the people of God in the United States and in Bolivia. At Victory Noll many of us are called to minister within our own community, and some have lovingly accepted the ministry of prayer and redemptive suffering. The ceremony of missioning reminds us that whatever our ministries, we all share in one MISSION, the mission of Jesus; that is, we are called to proclaim the Good News of the Kingdom of God, to witness by our lives to our belief that the Word of God can be lived, and to make real, God's caring presence to all people through loving service.[5]

By the time the Tenth General Chapter of Affairs opened in the summer of 1978, every Sister in the Congregation knew that she was a part of the Chapter even though she was not an elected delegate, even if she were not at Victory Noll taking part as one of the various types of observers. The real work of the Chapter would come as each Sister tried to live out the theme, *The Victory Noll Expression of Religious Life: A Life of Justice for the Sake of the Kingdom.*

The tone was set the day before the first session of Chapter when all participated in a Charism Day. At the Eucharistic Celebration offered in the morning, Martin Pable, O.F.M.Cap., Guardian and Master of Novices at St. Felix Friary, referred to Father Sigstein's "holy boldness" and urged the Sisters to keep his spirit alive in the Congregation. Slides, talks, nostalgic stories and anecdotes culminated after Evening Praise in a candle light procession to the cemetery where a litany was sung, two chanters invoking Father Sigstein, Archbishop Noll, and the deceased Sisters. The ceremony ended with the singing of the Sisters' special song to Our Lady of Victory. At no time do the Sisters seem so united as when they sing this hymn which they refer to by its first line, "We Have a Holy Mother." It was not written by a Victory Noll Sister but by a member of the Society of the Atonement who long ago gave the Catechists permission to use it. The melody is that of an old hymn tune, "O Savior, Precious Savior."

That the Chapter proved to be a unifying force was no accident. Besides plans and preparations, there was much prayer both before the Chapter and during it. June 24 to July 24 was a period described as Thirty Days of Intercessory Prayer. Sister Margaret Ann Harrison who organized the event asked that those who participated be open to the use of the prophetic and prayer gifts of the Holy Spirit as these are operative in the Charismatic Renewal.

Besides the core group who lived together at the House of Prayer the whole time, other Sisters joined them for a week, two weeks, or for a few days. Altogether, more than fifty Sisters participated. On each morning of the week a different area was prayed for. In the afternoon Sisters were prayed for individually by name, so many each day. The schedule was sent out to members of the Congregation so that they could join in spirit with their Sisters at Victory Noll. During the time the Chapter was in session, several Sisters, especially those who are retired or semi-retired, were always in chapel praying before the Blessed Sacrament.

When Sister Germaine Stadler, General Secretary of the Congregation, gave her report to the Chapter assembly, she began with this statement: "We grow older, more beautiful, and fewer." It was probably the "beautiful" part of Sister Germaine's remark that evoked spontaneous applause. That the Sisters are growing older and fewer is something that must be acknowledged. When the Sisters are asked about vocations, someone often says, "But you should not have trouble finding young women who want to join you. You are doing all the things that appeal to women today." It might be true of the Sisters' ministry, and yet women are not entering the Congregation.

During the late sixties and early seventies a number of women left the Congregation to seek new life-time commitments. And in the last fifteen years, thirty Sisters died. These two factors contributed to a depletion in numbers. Another reason so few are entering is that criteria for admission have changed. Formerly very little contact was expected or asked for before entrance. The young woman had to be a high school graduate and was required to have psychological testing, a physical examination, etc. Now she must have at least two years of working experience and/or two years of college. She must take part in an affiliate program and be directed by vocation personnel in reading and reflection. She is asked to live in one of the convents of the Victory Noll Sisters for a time before being accepted as a postulant in the community.

Whether these criteria have direct relationship to the dearth of vocations, it is not easy to assess. The Sisters refuse to be discouraged at their dwindling numbers. They agree with their President, Sister Jeanette, when she told them, shortly after her election:

> . . . We can look upon our median age and frown. Or we can look upon it and rejoice in the number of elderly Sisters we have, Sisters who possess wisdom and grace and contribute a dimension to our Congregation that is invaluable and that no one else can contribute. We look upon the small number of women entering our Congregation and ask "Why?" The question remains and we must live with that question. The important thing, I believe, is that we face the fact squarely and accept it as just that, i.e., a fact of our time. We are doing all we can to live our lives as we ought; the Vocation/Formation team are faith-filled, prayerful, dedicated women, doing their best. God asks no more of us. We must continue to do our best in the midst of dwindling numbers of Sisters. Perhaps this is an important piece in the mysterious mosaic of God's plan. Let us look upon it as that, live our lives to the fullest and rejoice, confident in the words of the Lord to the Prophet Jeremiah: "I know well the plans I have in mind for you, says the

Lord, plans for your welfare, not for woe! Plans to give you a future full of hope." (Jer. 20, 11-13)[6]

It might seem that after 1960 the only happenings in the Victory Noll community were Chapters, meetings, workshops, and conferences, but that was not the case. Much attention was being given to the Sisters who were no longer able to keep up with the fast pace of mission life. Some preferred to stay in the missions and do a limited amount of work; others returned to Victory Noll. Recognizing that the whole Congregation should be involved in retirement plans, a Life Planning and Development Commission was formed with Sister Lucy Marie Vega as director. This has helped to make easier the transition from an active to a less active life, and to help the Sisters plan for a "second career" where that is desired.

In the summer of 1974 a number of Sisters took part in a House of Prayer Experience (HOPE Program) held under the direction of Sister Rita Musante in what had been the former rectory on the Victory Noll grounds. The residence had been built in the early sixties for Father James P. Conroy and Father Joseph R. Crowley. Father Conroy had been chaplain for the Sisters since 1946.[7] He worked in the editorial department of *Our Sunday Visitor,* later becoming editor of the diocesan weekly, *The Harmonizer.* After the death of Archbishop Noll, Joseph Crowley was asked to become editor of *Our Sunday Visitor.* At the same time he was given the still more difficult task of supervising the building of the new plant for *OSV.* When the Diocese of Fort Wayne became the Diocese of Fort Wayne-South Bend, Monsignor Crowley was named Auxiliary to Bishop Leo A. Pursley. At almost the same time, Monsignor Conroy left Huntington to become pastor in Bluffton, Indiana. For a while the new rectory was used by Vincent Yzermans and later by Albert J. Nevins, M.M., editor-in-chief at *Our Sunday Visitor.*

By the year 1974 the still new rectory was unoccupied. What could be done with it? It was designed to be lived in by more than one person. How could it best be utilized? The prayer experience of the summer of 1974 seemed to be the answer. And so the Victory Noll House of Prayer began. A core group of Sisters live at the House and direct activities. Sister Rita and the Sisters with her (who sometimes differ from year to year) are trained to give directed retreats. The House of Prayer is primarily for the Victory Noll Sisters, but religious of other communities, priests, and lay persons take advantage of the opportunity to spend time there in closer union with the Lord. Some come for a day, a weekend, a week, or still longer. All leave refreshed in body and spirit. Bernard Haring, C.SS.R., was greatly responsible for the House of Prayer Movement in the United States. His description of a House of Prayer is applicable to the Victory Noll House. He says:

> The House of Prayer has as goal to create an oasis where we can listen together to the Word of God, but not only the Word of God written in the Bible — surely the Bible has a preeminent place — but also to listen to the

voice of God in the signs of the times, in the present opportunities, the present needs of people. One of the fundamental ideals and longings of the House of Prayer is that God-experience that makes us apostles. It is our deepest conviction that evangelization of the world is possible only by people who have experienced God's holiness and God's mercy, as the Prophet Isaiah, as all the great preachers of the Gospel.[8]

One of the theological constants is the centrality of prayer. The centrality of prayer in religious life is a sign of the presence of the King in his Kingdom. The House of Prayer is one of the means, and an important one, of making the Victory Noll Sisters a praying community, to help them live a more intense Gospel-oriented prayer life.

In 1970 Victory Noll opened its doors to mothers of Sisters, mothers who were no longer able to care completely for themselves. Rather than have the Sisters go home to care for their aged parents, the mothers were invited to make Victory Noll their home. There have always been at least two in Holy Family Building, sometimes more. Through the years God has called a number of them home.

Of all the happenings during the years after 1960, the most important event, *the* event, was the return of Father Sigstein to Victory Noll. For years the Sisters hoped for this and prayed for it. Father knew well that he would be given an affectionate and heartfelt welcome. Mother Cecilia Schmitt, the Superior General, many times had personally invited Father to make Victory Noll his home. Finally, in May 1960, he made his own decision to come back to Huntington. His return was a moving, touching occasion for all, but especially for the Sisters who had personally known and loved their Founder. From the day of his arrival, it was as if he had not been gone. He wrote to his friends:

From the very beginning I felt right at home. Everything seems to serve as a happy reminder of the many years I spent here at Victory Noll in my old apartment. It is a great consolation for me to live so close to our dear Eucharistic Lord. Only a few steps bring me to the altar. Now I have the blessed opportunity and privilege of visiting Him often during the day and night. You may be sure that I do not forget you in my prayers. I hope that at some time you may be able to visit me and enjoy the scenic beauty of this country "on the banks of the Wabash."

Many of his friends did visit him and again he enjoyed the role of gracious host. His health seemed to improve and he was able to celebrate Mass at the altar of Our Lady of Victory a few times, but usually he joined the community at the Eucharist.

In March 1963 Father Sigstein suffered a weak spell and requested the Sacrament of the Sick from Monsignor Conroy. The doctor was not alarmed but the nurses who looked after his needs thought it well to stay in an adjoining room during the night so that he might call them if necessary. About two o'clock in the morning of March 13 one of the Sisters went to his room though he had not called her. While she was observing him from the doorway, he stopped breathing. He was in his eighty-eighth year.

Shortly before Father Sigstein died, one of the Sisters asked him whether he thought the community had kept its original spirit. His answer was a wholehearted *yes*. He rejoiced that Our Lady of Victory Missionary Sisters continued to answer the call to serve the poor and neglected in a spirit of complete dependence on Jesus through Mary and to live in faith and love with others who share this same vision.

Is there a future for his vision? The Victory Noll Sisters believe firmly that there is. They share the optimism of Sister Jeanette Halbach when she became their President in 1977. She expressed her belief in the future of religious life and in particular as it is lived by Our Lady of Victory Missionary Sisters when she said:

I accept the call to serve as President of the Victory Noll Sisters because I believe in us! I believe that religious life has value and meaning in today's world. I believe that women and women religious have an essential contribution to make to the Church and to society.

Our contribution as religious women is not so much in the service we render as in the stance from which we render that service. In other words our unique contribution is not so much in that we are catechists or nurses or social workers or pastoral ministers or community organizers or directors of clinics or directors of diocesan religious education offices or in the service of our own Sisters — although all of these apostolates and the many more our Sisters are engaged in are important, fruitful, and effective ministries. Our unique contribution comes from the stance of women of faith who have freely chosen to live and minister and pray as celibate women in community for the sake of the Kingdom.

Notes to Chapter XIX

1. See *Chicago Studies,* Fall 1976, Vol. 15, No. 3, p.318.

2. Leonard Crowley, "Reflections of a Bishop on Religious Communities," *Review for Religious,* January 1979, Vol. 38, No. 1, p. 24. Used with permission.

3. Letter to Sister Florentine Lohr September 29, 1971.

4. Sister Gertrude Sullivan's Report to the Congregation April 1975.

5. Fall Newsletter 1977.

6. At the beginning of 1980 the number of professed Victory Noll Sisters was 312.

7. Other chaplains were Francis P. Faust (1939-43) and Frank Gartland, C.S.C. (1943-46).

8. Reprinted from "The House of Prayer Movement" with permission from CRUX Cassettes, a division of CRUX Publications (publishers of the weekly newsletter for priests, deacons and religious, CRUX of the News, $29.75; and the monthly Crux of PRAYER, $15.75), 800 N. Pearl St., Albany, N.Y. 12204. Cost, 60-min cassette: $7.95. Material is copyrighted. No additional written or audio reproduction allowed without authorization from the publishers.

Index